The Passchendaele Campaign 1917

Andrew Rawson

Pen & Sword
MILITARY

First published in Great Britain in 2017 by
PEN AND SWORD MILITARY
an imprint of
Pen and Sword Books Ltd
47 Church Street
Barnsley
South Yorkshire S70 2AS

ISBN 978 1 52670 400 9

Printed and bound in England by
CPI Group (UK) Ltd, Croydon, CR0 4YY

Typeset in Times by CHIC GRAPHICS

Pen & Sword Books Ltd incorporates the imprints of
Pen & Sword Books Ltd incorporates the imprints of Pen & Sword
Archaeology, Atlas, Aviation, Battleground, Discovery,
Family History, History, Maritime, Military, Naval, Politics,
Railways, Select, Social History, Transport, True Crime,
Claymore Press, Frontline Books, Leo Cooper, Praetorian Press,
Remember When, Seaforth Publishing and Wharncliffe.

For a complete list of Pen and Sword titles please contact
Pen and Sword Books Limited
47 Church Street, Barnsley, South Yorkshire, S70 2AS, England
E-mail: enquiries@pen-and-sword.co.uk
Website: www.pen-and-sword.co.uk

Contents

Regimental Abbreviations

Regiments in Alphabetical Order	Abbreviations Used
Argyll & Sutherland Highlanders Regiment	Argylls
Bedfordshire Regiment	Bedfords
Black Watch Regiment	Black Watch
Border Regiment	Borders
Buffs (East Kent) Regiment	Buffs
Cambridgeshire Regiment	Cambridge or Cambridgeshires
Cameron Highlanders Regiment	Camerons
Cameronians (Scottish Rifles) Regiment	Scottish Rifles
Cheshire Regiment	Cheshires
Coldstream Guards	Coldstreamers
Connaught Rangers	Connaughts
Devonshire Regiment	Devons
Dorsetshire Regiment	Dorsets
Duke of Cornwall's Light Infantry	DCLI
Duke of Wellington's (West Riding) Regiment	Duke's
Durham Light Infantry	Durhams
East Lancashire Regiment	East Lancashires
East Surrey Regiment	East Surreys
East Yorkshire Regiment	East Yorkshires
Essex Regiment	Essex
Green Howards (Yorkshire) Regiment	Green Howards
Gloucestershire Regiment	Gloucesters
Gordon Highlanders	Gordons
Grenadier Guards	Grenadiers
Hampshire Regiment	Hampshires
Herefordshire Regiment	Herefords
Hertfordshire Regiment	Hertfords
Highland Light Infantry	HLI
Honourable Artillery Company	HAC
Irish Guards	Irish Guards
King's (Liverpool) Regiment	King's
King's Own (Royal Lancaster) Regiment	King's Own

King's Own Scottish Borderers	KOSBs
King's (Shropshire Light Infantry) Regiment	KSLIs
King's Own (Yorkshire Light Infantry) Regiment	KOYLIs
King's Royal Rifle Corps	KRRC
Lancashire Fusiliers	Lancashire Fusiliers
Leicestershire Regiment	Leicesters
Leinster Regiment	Leinsters
Lincolnshire Regiment	Lincolns
London Regiment	Londoners
Loyal North Lancashire Regiment	Loyals
Manchester Regiment	Manchesters
Middlesex Regiment	Middlesex
Monmouthshire Regiment	Monmouths
Norfolk Regiment	Norfolks
Northamptonshire Regiment	Northants
North Staffordshire Regiment	North Staffords
Northumberland Fusiliers	Northumberland Fusiliers
Oxford and Buckinghamshire Light Infantry	Ox and Bucks
Queen's (Royal West Surrey) Regiment	Queen's
Queen's Own (Royal West Kent) Regiment	Queen's Own
Rifle Brigade	Rifle Brigade
Royal Berkshire Regiment	Berkshires
Royal Dublin Fusiliers	Dublin Fusiliers
Royal Fusiliers	Royal Fusiliers
Royal Inniskilling Fusiliers	Inniskilling Fusiliers
Royal Irish Fusiliers	Irish Fusiliers
Royal Irish Regiment	Irish Regiment
Royal Irish Rifles	Irish Rifles
Royal Munster Fusiliers	Munster Fusiliers
Royal Newfoundland Regiment	Newfoundlanders
Royal Scots Regiment	Royal Scots
Royal Scots Fusiliers	Scots Fusiliers
Royal Sussex Regiment	Sussex
Royal Warwickshire Regiment	Warwicks
Royal Welsh Fusiliers	Welsh Fusiliers
Scots Guards	Scots Guards
Seaforth Highlanders	Seaforths
Sherwood Foresters (Notts and Derbyshire)	Sherwoods
Somerset Light Infantry	Somersets
South Lancashire Regiment	South Lancashires

South Staffordshire Regiment	South Staffords
South Wales Borderers	Borderers
Suffolk Regiment	Suffolks
Welsh Guards	Welsh Guards
Welsh Regiment	Welsh
West Yorkshire Regiment	West Yorkshires
Wiltshire Regiment	Wiltshires
Worcestershire Regiment	Worcesters
York and Lancaster Regiment	York and Lancasters

Introduction

All eyes on the Western Front were focused on the British-held Ypres Salient during the summer and autumn of 1917. But it was not the first time the area had been the site of a big battle involving the British Expeditionary Force (BEF). The British soldiers had fought against overwhelming numbers around Polygon Wood, Gheluvelt and Nonne Bosschen in the autumn of 1914. The four-week battle would help earn the men of the regular army the name the Old Contemptibles. The following April, the Germans used chlorine gas for the first time, creating a large breach in the Allied line. Tough battles followed around Langemarck, 's Gravenstafel and Frezenberg but again the BEF held its line as territorial soldiers and men of the Indian Army stood shoulder to shoulder with the surviving Old Contemptibles. The same place names would resurface during the three-and-a-half-month-long Passchendaele campaign. Only this time regular soldiers, territorials and men of Kitchener's New Armys fought side by side.

General Sir Douglas Haig had wanted to attack in Flanders in the summer of 1916, however the French Army had suffered badly in the spring around Verdun. General Joseph Joffre wanted a combined attack in the Somme region, where the British and the French could attack together. The British agreed and the Flanders scheme was shelved. But after five and a half months of bitter fighting, there had been no breakthrough on the Somme, only heavy casualties.

French plans again proposed Allied strategy in the spring of 1917. Joffre's replacement, General Robert Nivelle, wanted the British to make a preliminary assault at Arras while the French made the main attack later along the Aisne. However the Germans had their own plans, retiring slowly across the Somme before making a rapid withdrawal to the Hindenburg Line in March. The move shortened the front line, creating reserves for both armies, and it left the Allies needing to re-plan their offensives.

Both the British and French spring attacks started well and lessons learned about combined arms warfare on the Somme were applied while new lessons were learnt. But they soon ground to a halt and there were heavy casualties on all sides; too heavy in the case of the French. Their armies were left in a mutinous state and short of replacements. They also had a new commander. General Nivelle had been replaced by General Phillipe Pétain and he had to sort out their troubles.

The Nivelle offensive had left the French incapable of offensive action but strategic events were changing fast. An unrestricted submarine campaign against merchant shipping and a diplomatic indiscretion had brought the United States of America into the war on the Allied side. The politicians discussed and then rejected the idea of shifting men and guns to the Italian front. An idea to delay the next campaign until the Americans could deploy an army to France was also shelved. But the continuing revolution in Russia and a stalemate in Italy meant it would be down to the British to continue the fight against the Germans during the second half of 1917.

This book concentrates on the British Army's experience between June and December 1917. It does not dwell on the politics nor the German view and there are few references to the personal experiences of the men. It starts with the British plans for Flanders and the reasoning behind the year-long delay to the offensive. It continues with the capture of the Messines ridge, to the south of Ypres, and the huge mining operation which made it a unique attack. After discussing the planning for the Passchendaele campaign, each stage of the battle between 31 July and 2 December is given equal attention no matter how large or small.

The information for the book comes from many sources but the backbone of the narrative comes from the single *Military Operations in France and Belgium* volume on the campaign. It is one of the twenty-eight Official Histories on the Great War and it was a controversial one. Cyril Falls had been appointed to write it in 1939 but he resigned and was replaced by Captain Graeme Wynne. General Gough objected to the first draft and parts had been rewritten by the time it was finished in 1946. The series editor, Brigadier General Sir James Edmonds, spent another two years changing so many parts that Wynne refused to have his name put to the volume.

The content of the volume has been discussed by historians for many years. The conclusion is that the various drafts shifted blame from Gough to Haig and back again. Questions over Haig's conduct have been a controversial point while the casualty figures quoted in the volume have been disputed. The level of tactical detail in the book is limited compared with other volumes. My own studies have shown that some actions have been omitted from the narrative.

A lot of information comes from the many divisional histories and regimental histories which were published before the Official History came out. The quality of information in these published histories varies and while some are virtually a copy of the daily unit War Diary, others only give the bare details. They all provide more information than the Official History.

They always explain the successes and disasters although they tend to blame the actions of others rather than their own. Most of these histories are very good at describing the heroic exploits of individuals.

Most of the divisional and regimental histories can be accessed for a small fee at the www.militaryarchive.co.uk. You can also access medal rolls, army orders and army lists, and get assistance with the location of biographical information, awards and photographs of individuals. Joining the archive gave me prolonged access to all these resources for the same cost of a day visiting the London archives. If you are interesting in printed histories and medal rolls this is the website for you.

There is little information from the war diaries in the National Archives held at Kew, London. In my experience they sometimes say little about a battalion's battle experiences because the diarist is fully occupied, both physically and emotionally. Also material you would expect to find has occasionally been removed or lost.

I had to judge at what level of detail to pitch the information. There is nothing new to learn if it is too shallow but it can become overwhelming if there is too much detail. While this is not an exhaustive account of the Passchendaele campaign, it is a comprehensive account of the British Expeditionary Force's experience in the summer and autumn of 1917.

A comprehensive study of the campaign would be twice the length of this book, so what has been left out? There is little talk of the relationship between the War Cabinet, the Chief of the Imperial General Staff and the BEF's General Headquarters. But there are brief explanations about the meetings between the British and the French politicians and generals. There is also little information on the German units involved in the battles, but there is information on their defensive arrangements and their tactics. There are few details of casualties unless they were disproportionately high or low because records are incomplete. Casualties were always high and both sides suffered. You will not find narratives from the personal diaries which usually follow a depressing theme of mud and blood. The quotes used have been because they demonstrate the men's pride in their spirit and achievements; sometimes their dark humour illustrates a point perfectly.

So what will you find? There is the planning behind each attack and the objectives. There is information about the bombardments, the tactics, the weather and the terrain. There are the reasons behind the successes and failures of each attack. When possible, the men who led the attacks or who stopped the counter-attacks are mentioned; so are all the men who were awarded the Victoria Cross.

The British Army faced many tactical problems, some caused by the terrain and some by enemy activity. They tried different methods and we see how they learned from their successes and failures.

The problem was that trying new tactics against a resourceful enemy and sometimes in difficult conditions cost many casualties. But the cadre of survivors kept fighting, teaching those who replaced the casualties.

Many military books rely on a few small-scale maps which do little to help the reader understand the events described in the text. They say 'a picture is worth a thousand words' and I believe the same applies to maps. Over sixty tactical maps have been included to help the reader understand the different stages of the campaign. Typically there is one for each corps on each day it was engaged. Plenty of detailed maps has been a feature of all the books in this series.

My inspiration was Noah Trudeau's *A Testing of Courage*, a book about Gettysburg in the American Civil War. I was still confused after reading several books on this epic three-day battle but Trudeau's book explained it clearly. He uses large-scale maps every few pages, each illustrating the developments on part of the battlefield, sometimes hour by hour. It helped me understand the unfolding battle when I visited Gettysburg. I wanted to do the same for the events around Ypres during the second half of 1917.

The Official History maps are sometimes cited as good examples but the level of detail and clarity on the Passchendaele campaign maps is poor. Some cover large areas while most are devoid of all but the main terrain features. This book uses trench map extracts, which are well known to anyone with an interest in the First World War, for the topographical background. Their grid system is 1,000 yards (914 metres) for each large square and 100 yards (91 metres) for each minor graduation. In many cases the main terrain features have changed little since the battle. Contours, roads, watercourses and woods have rarely altered while villages have changed little; only the trenches and the shell holes have gone. It means these maps can be used to help locate places on the battlefield.

The symbols have been kept as simple as possible. Front lines before the battle commenced are marked by solid lines while the ground captured and held is marked by a line of dots. Temporary positions are marked with a dashed line while corps boundaries are marked by a line of dashes and dots. Arrows are often used to indicate the direction of the advance. Each division and brigade is marked with its number, either at zero hour or at the end of an advance. Battalions leapfrogged each other every few hundred yards and it would be impossible to chart their progress on maps of this scale without obscuring too much topographical information. But it is quite easy to estimate a battalion's movements by checking the text and the maps together.

I have also bucked the Army trend of describing events from right to left. We read text and look at maps from left to right, so I have written the narrative the same way unless the sequence of events dictated otherwise.

This is the fifth book in a series on the British Expeditionary Forces campaigns on the Western Front in the Great War. I first visited the Ypres area in detail in January 1994. I cycled around the cemeteries and memorials trying to work out what happened across the muddy fields. A concentrated study of the events during the summer and autumn of 1917 has increased my understanding of the campaign. I have enjoyed writing about the Messines ridge and the Passchendaele campaign and I hope you enjoy reading about them.

I would like to thank Professor John Bourne for his help with details on the British generals. I am also grateful to Dr Michael LoCicero for bringing the final attack of the year around Passchendaele to my attention. His doctorate thesis, titled 'A Moonlight Massacre', is an important study of all aspects of a small-scale action and illustrates how easily a planning oversight can cost many lives.

I stayed at two places during my visit to the Ypres Salient. Before and after my 2015 visit I stayed at No 56 Bed and Breakfast in La Boisselle. David and Julie Thomson have looked after me many times at their 'Oasis on the Somme' during my battlefield research trips. I also stayed at the Regina Hotel in Ypres where the view across the Grote Markt to the Cloth Hall is inspiring.

Andrew Rawson 2017

Chapter 1

A Growing Danger

The Plan for Flanders

Following the war of movement during the early months of the First World War, the front line settled down in October 1914. The British Expeditionary Force was transferred from the Aisne to Flanders, to shorten its logistics route, and it spent six weeks fighting against overwhelming numbers in the First Battle of Ypres. While some things could be acquired in France, soldiers, weapons and ammunition had to be shipped from England across the English Channel. The wounded had to be shipped back. First Lord of the Admiralty Winston Churchill was concerned that the German Navy would use the Flanders ports of Ostend and Zeebrugge as bases from which to attack the British convoys.

Churchill wanted the BEF to attack east of Ypres while the Royal Navy landed an invasion force on the Flanders coast. He suggested the idea to Field Marshal Sir John French, the commander of the British Expeditionary Force, in December 1914. The commander of the French armies, General Joseph Joffre, was more concerned about defending Paris.

A German gas attack in April 1915, the first time chlorine gas was used, threatened to capture Ypres for a time but instead it just reduced the Salient to a much smaller area and the Flanders strategic situation did not change. The threat from the German Navy remained and the Admiralty announced it was 'a growing danger' in November 1915. The War Office's General Staff, the Admiralty's War Staff and the Dover Patrol's staff (who tried to stop German shipping and submarines) studied how to get artillery in range of Ostend, either by advancing from Ypres or by landing on the coast.

The front available around Nieuport, on the coast, was too narrow, while draining the flooded River Yser either side of Dixmude would alert the Germans. General Sir Douglas Haig had just taken command of the BEF and he had a bigger scheme in mind, one which involved advancing north-east from Ypres, to clear the Germans from the whole Flanders coast.

First Army's commander, General Sir Henry Rawlinson, was given the task of working out the details and he presented them on 13 January 1916.

He suggested taking the plateau between Hooge and Gheluvelt first, before advancing north-east along the Passchendaele ridge. General Herbert Plumer, whose Second Army held the Ypres area, said they needed to capture Messines ridge, to the south of Ypres, first, to cover the flank of such an advance. His tunnellers had started digging three mines the previous August and another twenty tunnels had been started over the New Year period.

General Joffre soon agreed that the main British effort would be made in Flanders in the summer of 1916.

Rawlinson expanded his plan into six phases and it was issued on 5 March:

1) Capture Pilckem ridge, Gheluvelt plateau, Hill 60 and Messines ridge
2) Make a subsidiary attack around Neuve Chapelle, to draw attention from Flanders
3) Advance a mile east of Ypres
4) Advance across the Gheluvelt plateau and beyond Messines ridge
5) Clear the Passchendaele ridge, some 7 to 10 miles from Ypres
6) Advance towards Roulers and make a coastal attack at Nieuport

A month later General Plumer was asked to plan Second Army's attack on Pilckem and Messines ridges, with a July date in mind.

But there were problems on the French front. The Germans had attacked on a 10-mile-wide front at Verdun on 21 February, advancing 3 miles towards the city in just three days. Two weeks later they extended their offensive to the west bank of the River Meuse. The advance had been stalled by the end of March but the huge number of casualties was wearing down the French army. On 27 March Joffre told Haig that he wanted the British to switch their main attack to the Somme where their two armies could fight side-by-side.

The BEF's General Headquarters (GHQ) was still working on the Flanders scheme as plans for a battle on the Somme were pushed forward. On 16 May the Chief of the General Staff, Lieutenant General Lancelot Kiggell, confirmed General Rawlinson's new Fourth Army would attack north of the River Somme while the French attacked south of the river.

The date was set for the end of June but General Plumer was still to plan an attack in Flanders in case the French could not fight on the Somme or if the attack failed. In either case, he planned to send Lieutenant General Sir Hubert Gough's new Reserve Army north to Ypres. The Somme battle began on 1 July and while the French captured most of their objectives, the British only took a few, suffering 57,000 casualties on the first day. Despite the huge setback, Haig decided to continue Fourth Army's attack while Gough's Reserve Army took over part of its front. Second Army's plans and its tunnels would have to wait until the following summer.

A Difficult Winter
The Somme campaign was coming to a close in October when Colonel Renouard of the French Operations Bureau and Brigadier General Davidson, head of GHQ's Operations Branch, discussed plans for 1917. General Joffre was considering an attack between the Rivers Somme and Oise and he wanted Haig to do the same between Vimy and Bapaume. In mid-November, the two armies' staffs met at the French general headquarters (Grand Quartier Général) in Chantilly. Joffre explained that the French Army was exhausted but the BEF was still growing, despite its huge losses on the Somme. It would soon have sixty-eight divisions supported by 1,500 heavy artillery pieces and British industry was able to provide enough ordnance and ammunition for them all. But the big unanswered question was, how much had the 1916 battles reduced German morale?

Haig, Field Marshal Sir William Robertson, Chief of the Imperial General Staff (CIGS), and his Director of Military Operations, Major General Frederick Maurice, agreed they had to make attacks of a 'decisive character' on all fronts to divide the German reserves. General Sir Herbert Plumer was instructed to revise his plan for a Flanders offensive and prepare to capture the Messines ridge at only a month's notice. He would submit one on 12 December and it had not changed.

The War Cabinet confirmed its interest in a Flanders operation on 23 November, stating there was no 'greater importance than the expulsion of the enemy from the Belgian coast'. Robertson explained the consequences of leaving the coast in German hands to Joffre while the War Office wrote to the French asking for a Flanders offensive to be included in the plans for 1917. A meeting on 6 December confirmed there would be coordinated offensives on all fronts. However Russia was suffering political, military and economic problems and while the French wanted to increase their commitment in Macedonia, Robertson refused because of the difficult logistics.

December 1916 was a busy time on the political front. David Lloyd George replaced Herbert Asquith as Prime Minister of the United Kingdom on the 5th. Lloyd George was a critic of Haig but he had to go along with the Unionists and the press, approving his promotion to Field Marshal at the end of the month. French Prime Minister, Aristide Briand, reformed his government in December, creating a War Committee with President

Raymond Poincaré at its head. Joffre resigned at the same time and his replacement, General Robert Nivelle, was famous for his defence of Verdun in the spring and summer of 1916. He immediately made optimistic promises for a huge attack in the spring.

Haig and Joffre agreed to a combined offensive on the Western Front at the end of February 1917 with the British attacking on the Somme and the French on the Aisne. Joffre also agreed there could then be a combined British and Belgian advance in Flanders followed by a landing by five divisions on the Flanders coast. Haig argued they should only land if the Ypres attack succeeded and that the BEF could only put two divisions ashore.

Lessons Learned

Many lessons had been learned during the Somme campaign. The artillery knew how to fire bogus barrages, to make the enemy gunners reveal their positions, and they used practice barrages to keep the enemy infantry on the alert. They also knew how different combinations of shrapnel and high-explosives worked while a new graze fuse, which exploded on contact rather than according to a timer, increased the effectiveness of their barrages.

The field artillery had been reorganised with many batteries formed into army field artillery brigades, so they could stay in action longer. It left each division with two mixed brigades, armed with 18-pounder and 4.5-inch howitzer batteries. The gunners had developed ways of firing an accurate creeping barrage which advanced at the optimum speed to suit the ground conditions. The infantry knew that staying close to (known as hugging) the exploding shells was the best way to survive. Communications had also been improved so defensive barrages, known as SOS barrages, could deal with counter-attacks.

Weather stations across France had been forwarding regular reports to GHQ for some time. Experiments had also shown that air temperature, wind speed and barometric pressure affected the artillery. GHQ issued weather corrections to the artillery on a daily basis, starting in January 1917. It was particularly helpful for making the creeping barrage more accurate.

Good infantry tactics had also been developed, with companies advancing in two waves. Each wave deployed its platoons in two lines and men were trained in specific tasks. The Lewis gunners and rifle bombers were trained to put down suppressive fire while the riflemen and bombers manoeuvred against the enemy position. Moppers up were detailed to deal with pockets of resistance and round up prisoners from dugouts. Other groups would carry equipment and ammunition forward to consolidate captured positions.

The Royal Flying Corps had thirty-six squadrons on the Western Front and there were another twelve squadrons fighting the Zeppelin menace over England. The Dover Patrol also had many planes patrolling the English Channel. Cooperation between the artillery and the Royal Flying Corps was always improving. There were increasing numbers of spotter planes equipped with wirelesses and crews were becoming more proficient at finding targets. Each corps had staff checking aerial photographs for targets and assessing damage, so they could keep the artillery busy.

Peace Proposals

By the end of 1916, the Chief of the German General Staff, General Paul von Hindenburg, and his Quartermaster General, General Erich Ludendorff, knew they had a problem. The Verdun and Somme campaigns had left the German armies short of men but the defeat of a Romanian attack in the autumn of 1916 had left them in a confident mood.

The main problem was that the Allied naval blockade was reducing the supplies reaching Germany to dangerous levels increasing the rationing which had been in place since the beginning of 1915. Meanwhile the Hindenburg Programme had been introduced in August 1916 to make every able-bodied man work for the war effort.

They considered a campaign of unrestricted submarine warfare against the Allied merchant ships. It could bring Great Britain to the brink of starvation and force it to the peace table. But there was a danger it could also bring the United States of America into the war, if one of its ships was sunk. But Hindenburg and Ludendorff concluded that Great Britain could be forced to the peace table before an American army could be put into the field and it was a gamble they were prepared to take.

On 5 December 1916, Germany proposed peace discussions with the United States and the Holy See in Rome. The ambiguous offer was rejected and Germany used the refusal as an excuse to launch their submarine campaign. Two weeks later, President of the United States of America Woodrow Wilson suggested peace talks but the Allied governments refused to meet the Central Powers. Kaiser Wilhelm II issued the order to begin unrestricted submarine attacks on 9 January 1917 and the German Ambassador to the United States was handed his passport.

The Germany's *Unterseeboots*, or U-Boats, went on the offensive on 1 February and their attacks were immediately successful. They sank nearly 500,000 tons of shipping in February and March while over 850,000 tons went to the bottom of the sea in April. It appeared the German plan could work.

But it was another unrelated development which caused the United

States to declare war. The German Foreign Office had sent a telegram to their ambassador in Mexico suggesting an alliance between the two countries if America joined the Allied cause. British intelligence intercepted the telegram and it was published under the name of the German Foreign Secretary, Arthur Zimmermann. The Zimmermann telegram enraged public opinion across the United States, forcing President Wilson to declare war on 6 April.

Around the same time, France received a peace proposal from the Austro-Hungarian Empire. Charles had become Emperor when his father Franz Joseph died in November 1916. He was also the Supreme Commander-in-Chief of the armed forces and believed they would be unable to fight much longer. Charles dismissed his Chief of the General Staff, Field Marshal Conrad von Hötzendorf, and gave his brother-in-law Prince Sixte de Bourbon-Parma (an officer in the Belgian Army) a letter suggesting a separate peace deal. It reached President Raymond Poincaré in March 1917 but the secret negotiations failed. The letter would drive a wedge between Germany and Austria when it became public knowledge in April 1918.

Nivelle's Spring Plan
On 20 December, General Nivelle met General Haig, knowing that he was about to replace Joffre. He wanted the BEF to take control of twenty miles of the Somme front, to release reserves so the French armies could break the German line on the Aisne. The British could attack after the French had broken through and their converging attacks would force the Germans to abandon around seventy miles of front either side of Compiègne.

Haig only wanted to take control of ten miles of trenches from the French, so the BEF could keep probing the German line. He also wanted to hand the sector back if the French offensive failed, so he had reserves for the Flanders offensive. Nivelle was annoyed by Haig's suggestion and the British proposal was withdrawn during Nivelle's visit on New Year's Eve.

At the Inter-Allied Conference in Rome Lloyd George suggested sending 500 British and French heavy guns to Italy but everyone unanimously rejected the idea. Haig and Nivelle agreed at the next meeting in London on 15 January that the BEF would take control of twenty miles of front so the French would attack around 1 April. The politicians met again in Calais at the end of February and Robertson threatened to resign when Lloyd George suggested Nivelle should have authority over Haig. Instead the Calais Agreement stated that the British would give the French their full support during their offensive.

Haig was worried the Flanders plan would be shelved now the French

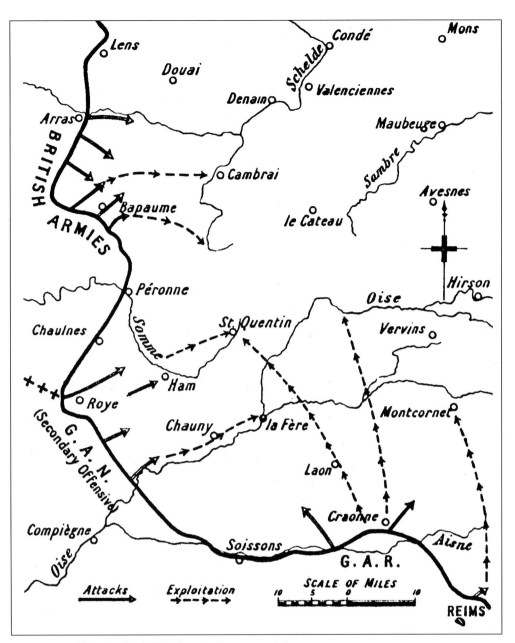

Nivelle's plan for 1917 before the Germans withdrew.

were in charge while Nivelle was concerned about the British commitment to his plans. So both Haig and Nivelle were called to London on 13 March to sign an agreement pledging their support for the plans for 1917. Haig then told the War Cabinet how the BEF would make a spring offensive at Arras and a summer offensive in Flanders.

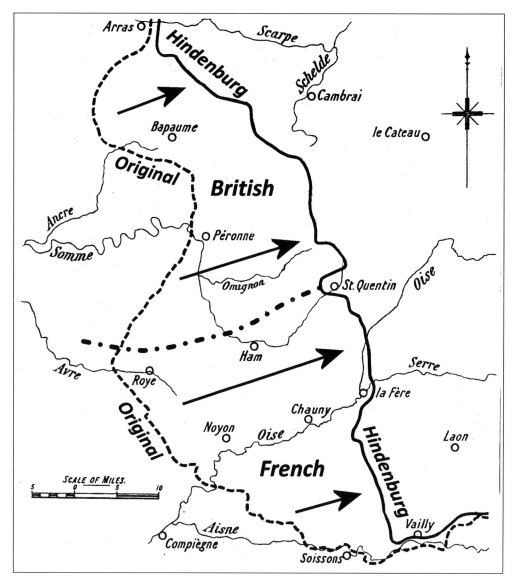

The German withdrawal to the Hindenburg Line in March.

Meanwhile, back in France the Germans were carrying out their own plan, Operation *Alberich*. A rapid withdrawal from the Somme region to the Hindenburg Line would leave the Allies facing a pre-prepared, fortified line while releasing divisions to increase their reserve. But it released British divisions, allowing Haig to extend his Arras offensive as far north as Vimy Ridge. The withdrawal had also affected the French front, leaving Nivelle having to reconsider his plans for the Aisne.

There was trouble in Paris when Prime Minister Aristide Briand resigned over Nivelle's plans on 20 March. His replacement, Prime Minister Alexandre Ribot, chose Paul Painlevé as his Minister of War. Although Painlevé disagreed with Nivelle's plans, he had to approve them because it was too late to cancel them.

The Battle of Arras

A massive bombardment of over 2.5 million shells devastated the German defences around Arras. On 9 April, First Army's Canadian Corps drove the Germans off Vimy Ridge while Third Army advanced three miles east of the town. They had created an 8-mile gap which was increased over the next few days, including a major withdrawal towards Lens. But the advance stalled due to logistics problems and bad weather while casualties rose at an alarming rate. Meanwhile, Fifth Army's attack at Bullecourt, to the south-east, was a failure.

The French Minister of Munitions, Albert Thomas, told Prime Minister David Lloyd George what the French government was thinking while the British battle was ongoing. They hoped that Russia would recover from the recent revolution and continue the fight on the Eastern Front (they would not). They also wanted the United States to deploy an army in France (they would). Lloyd George informed the War Cabinet on 16 April, the day the Nivelle Offensive began and the War Office's Director of Military Operations, Major General Frederick Maurice, reported the news to GHQ.

Haig's Chief of the General Staff, Lieutenant General Kiggell, told Generals Allenby and Horne to keep their First and Third Armies pushing, to divert German attention from the French attacks. Haig's despatch said the offensive would be continued 'until such time as the results of the French offensive should have declared themselves'. It left GHQ having to keep some divisions in Flanders while attacking at Arras with half-trained replacements, worn out guns and few tanks.

Haig told Nivelle he wanted to save some of his reserves for Flanders on 24 April but he planned to keep attacking in support of the French. The French offensive had not lived up to Nivelle's optimistic forecast (French casualties had topped 100,000) and Haig realised the offensive would be stopped after meeting Minister of War Painlevé on 26 April. He told Generals Horne and Allenby to make one last attack, to secure a good defensive line around Arras.

First and Third Armies' attack on 3 May failed while the prolonged fight for Bullecourt was inconclusive. General Gough was told his Fifth Army headquarters would move to Flanders to take control of the Ypres Salient from Second Army. But the new French Chief of the General Staff, General

Phillipe Pétain, still refused to take control of any more of the front from the British. Haig and Robertson concluded the French were exhausted after discussing the situation with Nivelle and Pétain, leaving the BEF to continue the fight on the Western Front on its own. On 7 May Haig told his army commanders that his plan was for General Plumer's Second Army to capture Messines ridge first. General Gough's Fifth Army would then attack east of Ypres.

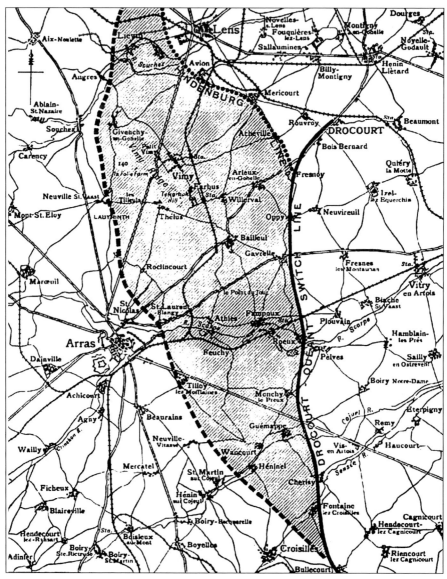

The ground captured by the BEF during the Arras campaign.

Chapter 2

Hell Itself Burst Forth

Tunnelling under the Ridge

The Germans had driven the BEF off Messines ridge on 31 October 1914, following an epic battle. Their observers had been able to see deep into the British rear, making it an uncomfortable area to serve in. Second Army knew it was pointless trying to advance up the slopes unless the plan included seizing the crest, an advance of 2,000 to 3,000 yards. By the spring of 1917 General Herbert Plumer had been working on such a plan for eighteen months.

The idea began when Second Army's engineer-in-chief, Brigadier General George Fowke, proposed digging a number of deep mines in September 1915. They would be detonated simultaneously, disrupting the German defences so badly that an advance to the summit would be possible. John Norton Griffiths had been a civil engineer before the war but he was a major in the Royal Engineers when he formed the first tunnelling companies on the Western Front.

Fowke's men sank six deep shafts around 350 yards behind the British front line even though there were no formal orders. They were signposted 'deep wells', to keep them a secret, and they were far deeper than anything tried before. They dug below the saturated sand into blue clay, which was safer to tunnel through. The tunnellers used a technique known as 'clay-kicking', a technique which was suitable for quietly digging small-diameter tunnels. The tunnels usually ended up around 100 feet deep under the German strongpoints. Two types of mechanical diggers used on the London Underground where tried but they were noisy and prone to break down. It was soon clear that relays of miners could dig faster and quieter than any machine.

Over time, the Royal Engineers provided 171st, 175th and 250th Tunnelling Companies, the Canadian Royal Engineers supplied 1st and 3rd Tunnelling Companies and the Australian Royal Engineers deployed their 1st Tunnelling Company. The tunnelling was kept secret with the help of quiet air pumps which removed the water. The deep tunnels were hard to detect and the Germans thought the British had given up tunnelling because they could not hear any activity. Secrecy was maintained by carefully hiding the excavated clay in woods or burying it under parapets.

The appointment of General Sir Douglas Haig as the BEF's commander-in-chief resulted in the formal approval of the Messines tunnelling scheme in January 1916. GHQ's original plan was to attack in Flanders in the summer but the BEF's efforts were soon switched to the Somme, so they could attack alongside the French. The long-drawn-out campaign in that area resulted in the Flanders plan being shelved.

Originally it was thought it would take around six months to dig each mine but most took longer. The postponement gave the tunnellers time to extend the existing tunnels and add new ones. But it also gave the Germans time to dig deeper and a couple of tunnels were damaged when they detonated small mines, known as camouflets, nearby.

The miners were helped by new surveying instruments and tested listening devices. They were often saved by tried and tested shoring techniques and good quality rescue equipment. Each mine had an average of twenty-one tons of explosives, all of it placed underground by hand. Ammonal was used while gun-cotton and gelatine, which were more dangerous, would be used to detonate the mine.

Eventually, after months of nail-biting work, Second Army completed twenty-six mines, with the last one being set only just before zero hour. Only twenty would be used because the Petit Douve mine was discovered by the Germans and abandoned, a second mine under Peckham Farm was abandoned after it flooded, and four at the Birdcage south-east of Ploegsteert Wood turned out to be outside the attack area.

X Corps
Hill 60 and the Caterpillar, two mines   St Eloi, one mine

IX Corps
Hollandscheschuur Farm, three mines   Petit Bois, two mines
Maedelstede Farm, one mine   Peckham, one mine
Spanbroekmolen, one mine   Kruisstraat, four mines

II Anzac Corps
Ontario Farm, one mine   Trench 127, two mines
Trench 122, two mines

Second Army's chief engineer, Major General Frederic Glubb, organised many other underground projects with the 183rd British, the 2nd Canadian and the 2nd Australian Tunnelling Companies. They excavated huge

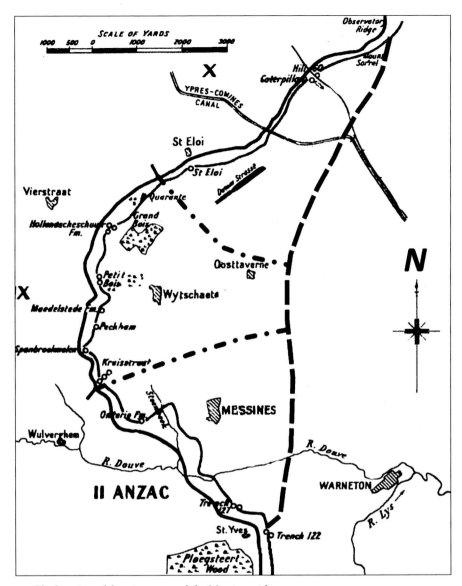

The location of the mines around the Messines ridge.

chambers for headquarters, communications, medical facilities and billets. They also dug 5,000 yards of tunnels, created sleeping places for 6,000 men and made shelters for another 10,000.

General Plumer had to wait until the Arras campaign was drawing to a close before work could start in earnest above ground. Thousands of men started moving into Second Army's area and nearly 35,000 men were soon labouring on many tasks, ranging from roads and railways to battery positions and stores.

Second Army's staff had had nearly a year to make its plans and its preparations were very thorough. For example, twenty railheads were built alongside the two rail lines from Hazebrouck. Each one was dedicated to a specific type of stores, to make it easier to organise deliveries to the front. They were connected by 115 miles of broad gauge which could cope with 180 trains a day. Another 58 miles of narrow gauge railways allowed large-calibre shells to be delivered to the heavy batteries.

The Bombardment

First Army and Third Army sent one in three of their guns to Flanders when the Arras campaign ended at the beginning of May. The end of the battle of Bullecourt a week later meant that Fifth Army could send half of its guns north. The ammunition began to arrive while the fighting was still going on around Arras but the bulk of the shells were delivered to Second Army as soon as the battle finished. A total of 144,000 tons were delivered in a short space of time.

Eventually over 1,500 field guns and howitzers were assembled in sixty-four brigades. Over half the artillery pieces were heavy and medium guns or howitzers as follows:

186 60-pounders	110 9.2-inch guns and howitzers
336 6-inch guns and howitzers	13 12-inch guns and howitzers
108 8-inch howitzers	3 15-inch howitzers

Major General George Franks prepared Second Army's artillery plan, using lessons learned during the Arras campaign. His instructions were passed to the three corps commanders on 20 May, so they could organise their heavy artillery groups and the divisions' field artillery. They were concentrated into forty groups, with some dedicated to counter-battery work and others focused on hitting trenches, roads, billets and strongpoints. The three corps would only fire so many guns at a time, so it was difficult to locate them all. Some stayed silent to keep their location a secret.

Second Army's guns started registering targets and hitting fortifications the following day. Observers could see the front slope of the Messines ridge and the high water table meant that the Germans had built bunkers rather than excavate dugouts. They camouflaged them but exploding shells soon exposed them, so the garrison troops were instructed to take cover in shell holes over 100 yards away during daylight hours.

The bombardment intensified on 31 May and the occasional thunderstorm did little to interfere with the gunners' work. Observers' reports were compiled on daily charts which were issued to the artillery and machine-gun batteries. Targets were often confirmed by captured documents and prisoners' statements.

Some of the field artillery batteries targeted the wire entanglements while the rest of the field artillery and machine guns targeted the bunkers, to wear down the men inside. Plans to fire flaming oil drums were cancelled due to the unfavourable wind but the medium howitzers hit Wytschaete with high explosive and gas shells on 3 June and then hit Messines the following day. The heavy howitzers shelled distant targets including bridges, villages, road junctions and railways, while the Royal Flying Corps bombers aimed for the rail junctions in Menin, Wervicq and Comines.

The big question was, would the Germans evacuate the ridge? They could easily leave outposts on the ridge and withdraw the rest of their troops to the Warneton Line, around two miles east of the summit. Haig met Plumer and his corps commanders on 30 May to discuss what they would do if they did pull back. The mines would be useless, a liability if anything. There was talk of detonating them early and making a short advance to occupy the German front-line trench system. It would also get the German artillery to open fire and reveal their positions.

General Plumer and his corps commanders wanted to stick to the plan and they agreed to fire a full barrage programme on 3 June instead, to draw fire from the German guns. The plan worked and dozens of hidden batteries gave away their location as they responded to the infantry's SOS signals from the front line. The fact the guns were behind the ridge meant it was some time before they knew there was no infantry attack. A second fake barrage on 5 June proved that the Germans had deployed many of their guns north and south of the ridge. In all the aerial observers spotted over 200 German batteries and the 3.5 million shells fired had neutralised many by dusk on 6 June.

Second Army's artillery plan was similar to the one used by Third Army at Arras. It had been successful on 9 April and it was hoped it would have the same result on 7 June. One in three field guns fired at targets as far as the first objective while the rest created the creeping barrage.

Second Army had over 450 machine guns and each one would fire around 20,000 rounds ahead of the bursting shrapnel. They could also switch to firing SOS barrages, to protect the infantry if the Germans counter-attacked. The field guns and machine guns together created a 700-yard-deep band of shrapnel and bullets. There was also a plan to fire gas during the advance to the first objective, to disrupt the German gunners while the infantry crossed no man's land. Many howitzers fired at the German batteries while the rest hit strongpoints during the advance, switching to roads when aerial observers spotted troops on the move.

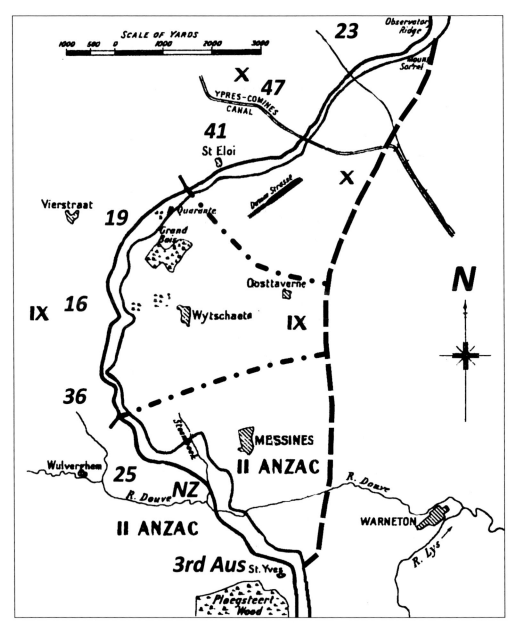

Second Army's deployment of divisions around the Messines ridge.

Infantry Planning

Second Army based their training on four General Staff pamphlets covering infantry, artillery, engineering and communications. They were based on lessons drawn from the Somme and Arras campaigns. One innovation improved the reporting made by the infantry. It was difficult to explain a situation at the front line in a written message and even more difficult to draw a map. It was nigh on impossible to locate a position using map references without a map, but it would have been foolish to issue a lot of marked-up maps in case they fell into enemy hands. Instead every officer and NCO was issued with a postcard sized 'message map'. It had a map of the company's sector on one side which could easily be annotated. The other side of the card had 'a skeleton message with code signs to indicate every important fact bearing on a situation'. Runners would carry the cards back to the battalion headquarters where the staff would plot the information onto one large map. They in turn could inform brigade and divisional headquarters so they could deploy reserves quickly and direct artillery barrages accurately.

The Royal Flying Corps

Most of the German artillery batteries were out of sight behind the ridge, so the Royal Flying Corps had plenty to do, locating them and tracking damage. II Brigade's squadrons had around 300 planes operating and they had an advantage of two-to-one machines over the German *Luftstreitkräfte*. They were backed up by 2nd Kite Balloon Wing which had six balloons deployed around six miles behind the front line. Two more were sent up on the day of the battle.

The battlefront was divided into two sectors, and four or six planes flew high-altitude observation patrols during the bombardments. An additional six or eight machines flew low-altitude missions, taking a close look at targets on the ridge. Battery positions were photographed every second day so the damage could be assessed while other targets were checked every day.

During the battle, the infantry would light flares when they had reached their objectives, often in trenches where they could not be seen by the enemy ground observers. Aerial observers marked the line of flares on trench maps and then flew to the report centre at Locre Château, five miles behind the lines. The maps and notes would be put into a weighted bag and the pilot would swoop low as his observer dropped it onto a target in the grounds. The report centre assessed the information and forwarded copies to the relevant corps headquarters. They in turn distributed the information to the artillery batteries so appropriate action could be taken.

The Tanks

Tanks had been on the Western Front for nine months by June 1917 and were a regular feature in all actions. Numbers had increased, tactics had been developed and mechanical improvements had been made. GHQ wondered why the Germans had not introduced a version of their own to the battlefield. Ten tank-like armoured vehicles had been ordered at the beginning of 1917 but another ninety had been ordered to be used as transporters to carry ammunition across rough terrain. The first German tank, the A7V (taken from its parent unit's name), would not appear on the battlefield until March 1918. The Germans never relied on tanks to spearhead their attacks.

Instead the Germans developed defensive tactics and weapons to stop tanks ruling the battlefield. The infantry dug some trenches wider and deeper, to act as tank traps. They also dug ditches or felled trees across roads. Armour-piercing bullets were distributed but they could burst a rifle's chamber. Field guns were also supplied with armour-piercing shells and mounted on small wheels so they had a lower profile. They were often deployed along roads, the most likely route tanks followed.

The Heavy Branch of the Machine Gun Corps had expanded to three brigades of three battalions. It had also expanded its maintenance facilities and had better logistics. Infantry training included lessons on how to coordinate their tactics and improve their communications with the tanks. But GHQ still considered them an experimental weapon which supported the attack rather than led it.

The Mark I had appeared during the battle of the Somme. Early problems had been ironed out and the Mark II had contributed to Third Army's success at Arras. The Mark III was an experimental model but it was a new model that was about to make its appearance at Messines.

The Mark IV travelled across the battlefield at the same slow speed as the earlier marks but the engine was more reliable so there would be fewer breakdowns. It also had a larger petrol tank so it could travel over longer distances. It had improved steering and the cumbersome trailing wheels had been ditched. Wooden beams reinforced with sheet metal were stowed on the roof ready to be chained to the tracks. They would produce extra grip if they became bogged down.

Improvements had also been made to make life easier for the crew including hatches which were easier to climb through. But it still had a crew of eight crammed inside a noisy interior filled with engine fumes. It had been impossible to thicken the armour because it would increase the weight, but it had been upgraded to hardened steel.

The Male tank still had two 6-pounder guns but it was now armed with three Lewis machine guns. They were less reliable than the Hotchkiss but they used flexible ammunition belts which held many more bullets. The Female tank had five Lewis guns and one Hotchkiss gun.

So, for the first time, there were enough tanks, they were an improved model, and the ground was good. The infantry also knew how to work with them. Messines was going to be a chance for the men of the Heavy Branch to show what they could do.

The German Defensive Plans

As stated earlier, Haig's biggest fear was that the Germans would discover the mines and abandon the ridge. Crown Prince Field Marshal Rupprecht's chief of staff, Lieutenant General Hermann von Kuhl, had considered such a move but the local commanders did not want to withdraw to the Oosttaverne Line because the ridge would look over it. Kuhl also considered withdrawing behind the River Lys before dismissing the idea.

Documents captured at Arras gave an insight into German thoughts on fortified zones. They wanted a large reinforced concrete pillbox every 200 yards. They would protect thirty men from all shells up to 6-inch while an 8-inch howitzer needed a direct hit to destroy one. They also built small shelters every fifty yards where men could wait until a bombardment was over. They were called MEBUs – *Mannschafts Eisen Beton Understands* or Iron and Concrete Crew Shelters. They had three walls and a roof and the men would deploy into nearby shell holes or slit trenches the moment the artillery moved on. Thick belts of barbed wire protected them all.

The garrison troops wore white armbands and they had to delay the assault troops until their comrades were ready to fight back. Counter-attack divisions were held in reserve, ready to strike if any British troops broke through the fortified zone. Efforts were made to relieve the garrison troops every two days but Second Army's bombardment often cut the front-line troops off from their supplies. Two of the four front divisions had already been exhausted by the shelling by 31 May.

The amount of preparations made it obvious that an attack was imminent and a prisoner gave away the date of the attack on 29 May; all that remained was to identify zero hour. The German miners had heard little activity under their trenches and they assumed the British tunnellers had given up. They were wrong; the British, Canadian and Australian tunnellers made their final checks to their charges as zero hour approached and 'at 3.10 am hell itself burst forth'.

Chapter 3

Each a Volcano in Itself

Zero Hour

On 4 June General Plumer set the day of the offensive for the 7th. On 6 June he set zero hour for 3.10 am; ninety minutes before sunrise. The troops would be able to see 100 yards, light enough to advance in an organised manner but dark enough to blind the machine-gun teams and artillery observers.

The forecast was for dry weather and while the early morning mist would be clearing by zero hour, a post-dawn haze could limit observation. An evening thunderstorm did little to dampen the men's spirits as they filed into the trenches and the weather cleared while the guns fired at their usual rate throughout the night, so as not to alert the Germans. Royal Flying Corps planes flew low over the German rear during the early hours, drowning out the sound of tanks crawling into position. The Messines ridge grew quiet for the final thirty minutes before zero as the gunners prepared and some said they heard the nightingales singing their early morning chorus.

The first mine erupted seconds before 3.10 am. Nineteen mines detonated over the next nineteen seconds and their explosions echoed around the countryside. The blasts caused panic in Lille 15 miles away and they were heard 170 miles away in London. The British troops watched in awe as 'great leaping streams of orange flame shot upwards, each a volcano in itself… followed by terrific explosions and dense masses of smoke and dust, which stood like great pillars towering into the sky, all illuminated by the fires below.'

One observer watched as 'nineteen giant roses with crimson petals, or as enormous mushrooms, rose up slowly and majestically out of the ground and then split into pieces with a mighty roar, sending up multi-coloured columns of flame mixed with a mass of earth and splinters high in the sky.' Many Germans who survived the blasts were either dazed by shockwaves or stunned by the spectacle.

Almost simultaneously, hundreds of shells started pounding the German trenches before creeping up the slope. The smoke screen and dust thrown up by the explosions reduced visibility to as little as fifty yards, hiding the SOS flares calling for artillery support. The German gunners would have been able to do little if they had seen them because they were being hammered by high explosive and gas shells. Those who did reply hit the British trenches long after the assault troops had left.

Second Army's thorough training paid off as officers and NCOs led their platoons through the smoke and dust, following compass bearings towards their objectives. A lot of Germans had been killed by concussion near the mines and many bodies were found without a mark on them around the craters. Others were too dazed and shocked to fight while those who ran up the slope had to pass through the British barrage. There was virtually no resistance in the front line and the leading battalions reached their objectives on time. The support battalions then climbed the slope to the crest of Messines Ridge.

Colonel Courage had assembled forty-eight tanks of II Tank Brigade for the attack. Twelve had been allocated to X Corps' advance astride the Comines canal, sixteen joined join IX Corps' attack on Wytschaete and twenty helped II Anzac Corps clear the Messines area. However, few were able to keep up with the infantry who were 'hugging' the creeping barrage. Instead they dealt with a few pockets of resistance crawling to the top of the ridge.

X Corps
The German front line ran between Mount Sorrel, Hill 60, the Bluff and St Eloi as it crossed the Comines canal. There were only low hillocks opposite X Corps front but the German observers could see right across the south half of the Ypres Salient. Consequently they were fortified and the garrison was double the strength it was elsewhere. Lieutenant General Thomas Morland's corps had to advance 700 yards to clear these high points and then push east another 600 yards so they could see the Flanders I Line, around 4 miles to the east.

No man's land was narrow and Morland's men were in the enemy trenches while the garrison were still reeling from the 'overpowering and crushing' explosions. The German batteries around Zandvoorde were smothered with counter-battery fire, so it was some time before they responded to the SOS flares.

23rd Division, Mount Sorrel
Major General James Babington's line faced Mount Sorrel on the left and Hill 60 on the right. There had been mining around Hill 60 since the front line had settled down in October 1914 and the spoil heap was pitted with

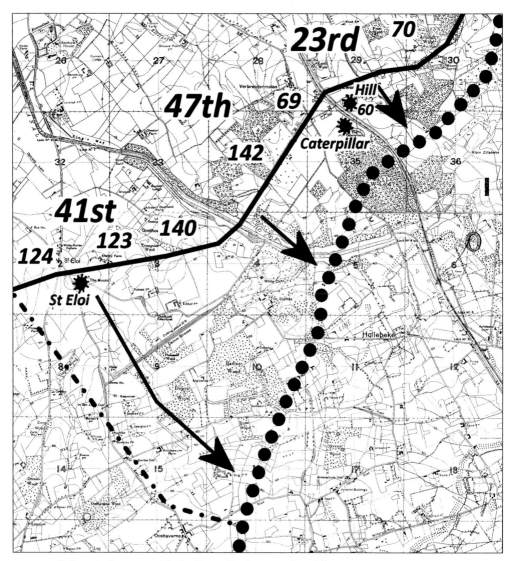

X Corps' advance astride the Ypres–Comines canal on 7 June.

craters. Digging began in August 1915 and it had taken twelve months to complete the 'Berlin Tunnel' and set a mine because work had been delayed by underground fighting. A branch was also dug under another spoil heap called the Caterpillar, across the Comines railway. The tunnellers fired a camouflet to destroy a nearby German gallery in October 1916 and then filled their own chamber with explosives.

Three mines totalling fifty-six tons exploded at 3.10 am and the Germans were stunned as 'the ground trembled as in a natural earthquake. Heavy concrete shelters rocked, a hurricane of hot air from the explosions swept back for many kilometres, dropping fragments of wood, iron and earth and black clouds of smoke and dust spread over the country.' The sky was 'then lit up by flashes of guns and bursting shells' as the artillery opened fire all along X Corps front.

On 70 Brigade's front, Brigadier General Gordon's men reached the crest before the ground stopped shaking from the mines. The 11th Sherwoods were delayed by wire which had lain hidden in a hollow but Major Hudson led them forward. The Sherwoods and 9th York and Lancasters advanced either side of a valley, west of Mount Sorrel, and a barrage of rifle grenades silenced the only pocket of resistance at the far end. The 8th KOYLIs wheeled to form the defensive flank beyond Mount Sorrel but Captain Barlow had to reorganise the 8th York and Lancasters, so they could clear the wood south of the hill.

On 69 Brigade's front, the 11th West Yorkshires advanced across Hill 60 while Captains Pearson and Lambert were hit leading the 8th Green Howards astride the railway; the 10th Duke's advanced into Battle Wood. The 12th Durhams continued the advance along the railway while a company of the 8th Green Howards mopped up the dugouts along the cutting. But the 9th Green Howards were disorganised by machine-gun fire in Battle Wood and they could not get to the far side of the trees. Brigadier General Lambert had to report that his men could not clear their objective until 47th London Division captured the spoil along the canal bank.

47th Division, Comines Canal

Major General Sir George Gorringe's division held the centre of X Corps' position, astride the Ypres-Comines Canal. The 1/22nd and 1/24th London Regiments led 142 Brigade along the north bank of the Comines canal, finding the Germans dazed and wanting to surrender or running away. On the left, the 1/21st London Regiment came under enfilade fire from Battle Wood and was then pinned down in front of the Spoil Bank. Meanwhile, Lieutenant Kemble was mortally wounded as the 1/23rd London Regiment crossed the canal to contact 140 Brigade east of the White Château. It then gave covering fire as the 1/21st London Regiment tried to silence the machine guns hidden under the mound of spoil. The Londoners eventually withdrew while Brigadier General Bailey organised another bombardment.

In 140 Brigade's sector, the 1/7th and 1/8th London Regiments advanced south of the Comines canal until they ran into resistance. The smoke screen was clearing. One tank ditched north of the White Château and it was four hours before Lieutenant Preston's men cleared it, taking sixty prisoners. The 1/15th London Regiment continued to move along the canal bank as the 1/6th London Regiment saw two tanks ditch near the stables. Lieutenant

Colonel Mildien had to shepherd his men past a stream before they could advance towards Hollebeke.

41st Division, Damm Strasse

Major General Sydney Lawford's division was opposite the German line either side of St Eloi and it faced the longest advance in X Corps. His men had to clear the blockhouses along the Damm Strasse, the long driveway which connected the White Château to the St Eloi road. They then had to clear a number of woods before they reached the Oosttaverne Line.

St Eloi sat astride the Ypres–Wytschaete road, on a small rise at the north end of the Messines ridge. It was possible to see into Ypres from the village and tunnellers had dug under it since the beginning of 1915. The mine in question was started in August 1915 and it survived the detonations made when Second Army tried to capture the salient in the spring of 1916. The mine was set by June 1916 and it was the deepest of the Messines mines at 120 feet deep. It was also the largest charge at nearly 42.7 tons of ammonal and the explosion made a crater 90 yards across the top of the Mound, demolishing blockhouses and obliterating trenches around St Eloi.

When the mine exploded, 'the ground trembled with these vast explosions and the debris hurled high into the air could be seen against the grey dawn of the morning sky.' The Canadian engineers were disappointed by the size of the crater but the infantry were more than impressed with the effect the explosion had on the enemy. General Morland later wrote that everything went like clockwork and the various objectives were taken according to programme. The Germans only put up a fight in a few places and surrendered freely.

On the left the 11th Queen's, 10th Queen's Own, 23rd Middlesex and 20th Durhams of 123 Brigade encountered little resistance around Ruined Farm and Eikhof Farm. But Brigadier General Gordon's men then faced a tough fight to clear the dugouts along the shallow cutting formed by Damm Strasse. On the right, the 10th Queen's, 26th Royal Fusiliers, 32nd Royal Fusiliers and 21st KRRC of 124 Brigade found that most of the Germans had fled as they climbed the slope south of St Eloi. Brigadier General Clemson's men also took time to clear the dugouts at the west end of Damm Strasse, particularly Lieutenant Brockworth's men of the 26th Royal Fusiliers.

Brigadier General Towsey's 122 Brigade took over the advance from Damm Strasse, plunging into a series of woods. The 18th KRRC and the 15th Hampshires advanced towards Ravine Wood and Deny's Wood. Regimental Sergeant Major Greenwood captured Englebrien Farm and Second Lieutenant Whaley then led his platoon through the barrage to capture another group of prisoners. The 12th East Surreys continued the advance through Ravine Wood and cleared the Oblong trenches while the 11th Queen's Own worked their way through Deny's Wood and Rose Wood.

IX Corps

The bulk of Second Army's mines exploded opposite IX Corps front and Ludendorff said, 'the aural effect of the explosions was simply staggering.'

19th Division, Bois Quarante and Grand Bois

Major General Cameron Shute's men faced Bois Quarante and Hollandscheschuur Farm to the north of Wytschaete. The combined effects of the recent bombardment and mine explosions were too much for many.

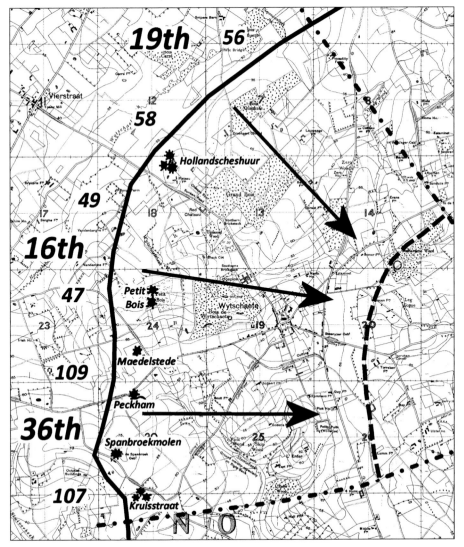

IX Corps' advance onto the ridge around Wytschaete on 7 June.

The advancing soldiers encountered 'little resistance from the Germans, who either ran forward to surrender or, if they could do so, ran away; very few put up a fight.' It was difficult to maintain direction in the swirling smoke and dust but the second wave filled any gaps in the first line.

On 56 Brigade's front, the 7th Loyals crossed Orbit Trench and Captain Maule was wounded as forty prisoners were rounded up around Piccadilly Farm. The 7th King's Own cleared the Object Trench system around Bois Quarante before they advanced to Obstruction Trench. The 7th East Lancashires and 7th South Lancashires then continued to Obstruction Support, clearing Oaten Wood and Zero Wood en route.

Three small mines totalling thirty tons of explosives obliterated the trenches around a low spur called the Nag's Nose salient on 58 Brigade's right. The 9th Welsh Fusiliers and 6th Wiltshires overran Oblige Trench before taking Croonaert Chapel and Hollandscheschuur Farm. They then cleared Oblige Trench before entering Grand Bois, which had been torched by hundreds of flaming oil drums and high explosive shells on the night of 3/4 June. The 5th SWBs and the 9th Cheshires took over the advance beyond Obstruction Trench and they continued up the slope to Obstruction Support and Onraet Wood. Both Brigadier Generals Craig-Brown and Glasgow were able to report their men had reached the Red Line on time.

Brigadier General Cubitt's 57 Brigade made the final advance across the St Eloi road and captured October Support on the crest north of Wytschaete. The 10th Warwicks, 8th Gloucesters, 10th Worcesters and 8th North Staffords cleared Oosttaverne Trench and then sent men into Oosttaverne Wood, meeting little opposition.

16th Division, Wytschaete

Digging towards Petit Bois started in December 1915 and the men had to resume work when the tunnelling machine failed. A camouflet mine demolished eighty yards of the gallery in June 1916, trapping twelve men underground. It took nearly a week to clear it out and Sapper Bedson was the only survivor. The mines were completed soon afterwards but they had to be left underground until the following summer. Another huge mine had been dug under Maedelstede Farm on the division's right.

At zero hour the explosions sent plumes of earth and dust into the sky west of Wytschaete. The Petit Bois mines exploded twelve seconds late and they were the last to blow. The first wave of Irishmen were already in no man's land and the explosion knocked some off their feet while others were hit by falling debris. But the men were filled with 'keenness and eagerness' and 'the difficulty was in restraining them'.

The 7th Inniskillings cleared the Nail system of trenches, the Red

Château and the Northern Brickstack along the Vierstraat road on 49 Brigade's front. Meanwhile, the 7/8th Irish Fusiliers worked their way through the Name system of trenches to Unnamed wood. The 2nd Irish Regiment followed Obvious Avenue and cleared the Southern Brickstack before moving past the north side of Wytschaete. Tanks helped the 8th Inniskillings silence the few pockets of resistance in Brigadier General Leveson-Gower's sector, rounding up fifty prisoners at the Hospice.

Brigadier General Pereira reported that the advance across the 'awful country' was 'a sight never to be forgotten' while a captured German officer said 47 Brigade 'moved as if on parade'. The 7th Leinsters cleared Nancy Trench then plunged into Petit Bois on the left while the 6th Irish Regiment mopped up the Nap trenches around Maedelstede Farm. Lieutenant Colonel Monck Mason's 1st Munsters then advanced through Bois de Wytschaete, which had also been hit by 1,000 drums of blazing oil and hundreds of high explosive shells on the night of 3/4 June.

The Munsters then followed a tank into Wytschaete, leaving the 6th Connaughts to mop up the wood. The village perimeter was protected by Obvious Trench and backed up by machine-gun teams hiding inside the cellars along the west side. More were stationed in the houses around the square while the church had been turned into a fortress. However, many buildings had been demolished by high explosive bombardment on 3 June while a deluge of gas shells made the cellars uninhabitable.

Major William Redmond MP and his brother John had called on Irish men to join Irish regiments on the outbreak of war. While they hoped their contribution to the war effort would improve their chances of getting Home Rule for Ireland, it had split the Nationalist movement. William had been one of the first to enlist and he spoke at many recruitment events. Before the battle he had insisted on joining his old battalion, only to be mortally wounded as the 6th Royal Irish moved on Wytschaete.

The final advance down the slope was made by Brigadier General Ramsey's 48 Brigade. Captain Cowley and Second Lieutenant Hughes led the 8th Dublin Fusiliers as they cleared the only two obstacles, Sonen Farm and Leg Wood.

36th Division, Messines Ridge

A mine had been driven under Peckham House, on the division's left, but it had been dangerous work. The clay swelled, squeezing the timbers until they cracked, so it was re-dug and re-timbered. The tunnel then flooded in January 1917 so it had been lined with steel segments to keep the water away from the 39½-ton charge.

A tunnel was completed under Spanbroekmolen, a high point jutting towards the centre of the division, in June 1916. A branch to Rag Point was damaged by camouflet mines in February 1917 and another small mine damaged the main tunnel on 3 March. The men of 171st Tunnelling Company dug around the damage to get to the 41-ton charge but the primer was only replaced a few hours before zero. Major Hudspeth said that he was 'almost certain' it would explode so Major General Oliver Nugent made it clear the infantry would only to wait for fifteen seconds before advancing into no man's land.

Three tunnels were dug under the Kruisstraat Cabaret, on the division's right. A camouflet flooded one tunnel in February 1917, so the tunnellers dug a new chamber and reset the charge. Four mines were set (two sharing one tunnel) totalling a massive 49½ tons. It brought the total amount of explosives which detonated in front of 36th Division to 130 tons.

The combined effect of the explosions either killed or stunned all the Germans in front of the Ulstermen. Only two German machine guns opened fire along the whole division's front in the minutes after zero hour.

The 11th Inniskillings and 14th Irish Rifles cleared the Naples trenches on 109 Brigade's front. The 9th Inniskillings then climbed the slope past Scott Farm and took 150 prisoners at Bogaert Farm en route to the Wytschaete–Messines road on the summit. Orange flags marked which pillboxes had been taken and they took fifty prisoners in the buildings at the south end of Wytschaete.

The 10th Inniskillings moved through Skip Wood only to be pinned down en route to Pick House. A sergeant ran up to a passing tank, climbed on top and banged on the hatch with a Mills bomb. He directed the tank until it silenced the weapon and his comrades then continued to the road on the crest. The 11th Irish Rifles (attached from 108 Brigade) were left to mop up the few centres of resistance on the slopes.

The Ulster barrage was a complicated affair because it had to curve around the Spanbroekmolen salient but the mine had done its job. The 9th Irish Rifles faced little resistance in the Narrow trench system before clearing Rag and Hag Points. The 14th Irish Rifles helped them silence two machine guns and take 150 prisoners around Skip Farm. The 8th Irish Rifles also had no trouble in the Nathan trenches around Kruisstraat Cabaret and they went on to capture Bone Point. L'Enfer Wood and the adjacent Farm were taken by the 10th and 15th Irish Rifles and they reached the hill-top road, near Four Huns Farm, as the 12th Irish Rifles (attached from 108 Brigade) mopped up behind. Brigadier Generals Ricardo and Withycombe were pleased to report that both 109 and 107 Brigades had reached their objectives.

The 15th Irish Rifles had a tough task clearing Lumm Farm and Captain Miller called it 'a very warm spot, as our barrage was dropping around there'. Lewis gunners gave covering fire as Lieutenant Falkiner charged and then cleared the complex. But two tanks helped clear the trenches along the summit, taking the staff of a battalion headquarters prisoner in one house.

Two contact planes had been circling overhead; they sounded a Klaxon horn and fired a Very light at set times. The infantry fired green flares, lit in bunches of three, to notify the observers of their position. They also used Watson fans, a pleated canvas disc marked black on one side and white on the other, to report their position to ground observers.

II Anzac Corps
25th Division, North of Messines
The first attempt to tunnel under Ontario Farm, on 25th Division's right, failed because the ground was too waterlogged, so 171st Tunnelling Company went deeper into the clay. Captain Thornton stopped the digging short of the objective on the day before the attack and the twenty-seven-ton charge was completed only hours before it was detonated.

Major General Guy Bainbridge's men started from the trenches east of Wulverghem, 600 yards behind the New Zealand Division to their right. Three mines, totalling thirty-six tons, demolished Kruisstraat Cabaret on the division's left flank while Ontario Farm disappeared in a cloud of dust and flames on the right. The Ontario Farm crater immediately filled with wet sand but the explosions left the Germans in Nutmeg trenches 'dazed and terrified and the survivors surrendered at once'.

Captain Hadley and Lieutenant Andrews led the 8th Loyals past the smoking Kruisstraat craters on 7 Brigade's front before Captain Tindal and Lieutenant Tollett advanced to the Steenbeek. Meanwhile, Lieutenant Hudson and Captain Mason took the 3rd Worcesters to Bell Farm before Captains Birch Jones and MacDonald continued the advance to the dried-up stream. Lieutenant Colonel Howell's 10th Cheshires then climbed the slopes and Captain Fry and Lieutenants Owen and Cheetham worked together to capture fifty prisoners around L'Enfer Wood. Meanwhile, Captain Morgan's company captured Hell Farm on the right.

Sergeant Conway silenced a machine-gun post as Lieutenant Colonel Williams's 1st Wiltshires moved over the summit. There was little resistance from Four Huns Farm on the Wytschaete road but Major Ogilvie and Sergeant Cook needed help from the 11th Lancashire Fusiliers to make the forty men holding Lumms Farm surrender. Brigadier General Onslow's men were then able to dig along the crest.

Lieutenant Pigot and Captain Thomas led the 13th Cheshires past Mortar Farm and then Lieutenant Gilderall and Captain Moir continued the advance

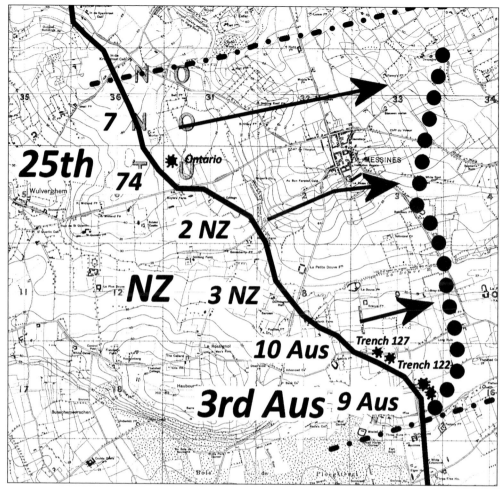

II Anzac Corps' capture of Messines on 7 June.

to the Steenbeek stream in 74 Brigade's sector. Meanwhile, Lieutenant Colonel Goodman's 2nd Irish Rifles moved past the site of Ontario Farm on 74 Brigade's right.

Major Munday and Lieutenant Sharp took forty prisoners in Occur Trench as Lieutenant Colonel Martin's 11th Lancashire Fusiliers climbed the slope. Captain Ward and Lieutenant Hadfield then cleared October Trench, near the Wytschaete road, while Second Lieutenant Skelton helped the Wiltshires capture Four Huns Farm to the north. Major Munday and Captain Ward encountered resistance at Middle Farm until Captain Thompson of the Irish Rifles outflanked the forty-strong garrison. Munday would help the New Zealanders clear Swayne's Farm on the Wytschaete road so Brigadier General Bethell's men could dig in. However Captains

Robinson and Laurie were hit as they led Lieutenant Colonel Craigie-Halkett's 9th Loyals past Sloping Roof Farm.

<u>New Zealand Division, Messines</u>
The New Zealanders deployed astride the Petit Douve stream without difficulty well before zero hour. The left flank was hidden by the dust thrown up by the Ontario Farm mine and everyone marvelled how the 'huge bubble was swelling, mushroom shaped, from the earth, and then burst to cast a molten rosy glow on the under surface of some dense cloud low above it.' The New Zealanders were in awe at the spectacle but 'as its brilliance faded, two more bubbles burst beside it'; they were the mines at Kruisstraat, 1,000 yards to the north-west. The mine planned for Petit Douve Farm on the New Zealanders right had been lost when a German camouflet destroyed the miners' work.

The New Zealanders moved into no man's land in awe at the 'astonishingly beautiful display of fireworks stretching away north as far as the eye could see'. As the debris from the Ontario mine settled, smoke kicked up by the barrage covered the rest of Major General Sir Andrew Russell's front.

The 2 New Zealand Brigade crossed the Steenbeek stream bed and began the long trek across no man's land, confident that the Germans around Ontario Farm on their flank had been silenced. Brigadier General Braithwaite's men overran the Oyster and Uhlan network of trenches around Sniper's House and then moved astride the Messines road towards the village. The 1st Otagos captured Moulin de l'Hospice while a large shell exploded next to Birthday Farm, convincing thirty men to surrender their two field guns. A tank silenced a machine gun at Swayne's Farm, north of the village, before crashing into the building, forcing thirty men to surrender. Major Stitt's 1st Canterbury Regiment cleared Au Bon Fermier Cabaret, on the south-west side of the village but Lance Corporal Hewitt and Private Garlick were wounded when they went forward to take prisoners; they shot six and the rest surrendered for a second time.

An injured Major Digby-Smith led the 3rd New Zealand Rifle Brigade through the Uhlan and Ulcer trenches and past the south edge of Messines. Lance Corporal Sam Frickleton ran through the New Zealand barrage to kill two machine-gun crews on the south side of the village while Rifleman Maubon silenced another machine gun near the large institution building. Major Roache's 1st New Zealand Rifle Brigade captured Petit Douve Farm on the right and Corporal Jeffrey captured one pillbox armed only with a pistol and a few grenades. Over one hundred prisoners were taken en route to Ulcer Reserve.

Brigadier General Fulton's men dug in east of Messines, alongside the smashed remnants of six anti-tank guns which had been knocked out by the artillery. They had not had any targets because the tanks supporting the New Zealanders were still climbing the ridge.

The Germans had dug a perimeter trench around Messines and built five strongpoints covering the streets. A sector based defence plan made sure that each block would continue fighting even if others had fallen. Men waited in cellars and they each had a map to help them find their way to their defensive position as soon as the barrage had passed over. It was a formidable task but the Germans were in the process of relieving the village garrison as the New Zealanders approached.

The 2nd Otago Regiment cleared October Support north-west of the village, so the 2nd Canterbury Regiment could cross the Wytschaete road to attack Oxonian Trench. They were then able to enter the north side of the village and take the rest of the perimeter trench in the rear. The 2nd Canterbury Regiment and the 4th New Zealand Rifle Battalion entered the village as the creeping barrage slowed down to a crawl. Machine guns and anti-tank guns had been placed to cover the streets, so most of the New Zealanders moved through the ruined buildings when possible.

Lance Corporal Samuel Frickleton ran ahead of the 3rd New Zealand Rifles and bombed two machine-gun teams at the edge of the village; he was awarded the Victoria Cross. Private White captured one machine-gun team who had placed their weapon next to a dressing station and he then killed another crew with his bayonet. One by one the enemy posts were located, outflanked and silenced while other men were smoked out of the cellars. There was sniping, bombing and fighting with butt and bayonet and five machine-gun teams were silenced before they had deployed their weapons. Another five were outflanked and captured while rifle grenades knocked out two more covering the square. Around twenty machine guns and three anti-tank guns were taken in total.

The 4th New Zealand Rifles covered Oxonian Trench on the south side of the village as German snipers fired and bombers threw grenades from windows and doors. The New Zealanders used Stokes mortars to supress targets while smoke bombs concealed the infantry as they moved in for the kill. They would eventually find the village commander and his staff hiding in concrete bunkers beneath the Institution Royale.

3rd Australian Division, North of Ploegsteert Wood

Gas shells sprayed 10 Australian Brigade with clouds of phosgene, chlorine and tear gas as it marched to the front. Over 500 of Brigadier General McNicoll's men were incapacitated and the rest struggled to find their way to the front line with their gas masks on. Meanwhile, 9 Australian Brigade was delayed moving through Ploegsteert Wood but officers shepherded their companies to their jumping off positions just before the mines detonated. Everyone was optimistic and one observer noted that 'things must be right now, one feels as if it were a won battle' as zero hour approached.

Two mines detonated at Trench 127, opposite Major General John Monash's centre, while two more exploded on his right, at Trench 122. An accurate barrage crashed down in no man's land and the Australian troops followed as close as they dared, sometimes too close and there were more casualties from the exploding shells than from enemy fire.

Only 120 men of the 40th Australian Battalion advanced on time but Lieutenant Crosby's men overpowered the single machine-gunner firing at them. The rest of the Germans around La Douve Farm and Avenue Farm were just wanting to surrender; '…they made many fruitless attempts to embrace us, I have never seen men so demoralised.' A similar small number of men were ready to advance from the trenches north of Anton's Farm but Captain Paterson reorganised 39th Australian Battalion and led them along Ash Avenue.

There were anxious moments as Major White ushered his company of 33rd Australian Battalion into position moments before zero hour on 9 Australian Brigade's front. The two Trench 127 mines lit up the sky as they moved into no man's land and there was the usual struggle to keep in line as they moved through the dust and smoke around the craters. On the left, the 34th Battalion moved past Broken Tree House while 33rd Battalion rounded up dazed prisoners around Factory Farm. Private John Carroll rescued a captured comrade and silenced a machine-gun team as Lieutenant Colonel Morshead's men consolidated their position; he would be awarded the Victoria Cross. Brigadier General Jobson's troops then waited for an hour while the New Zealanders caught up.

Captain Trebilcock led 38th Australian Battalion across Ungodly Trench on 10 Australian Brigade's front and captured two field guns around Betlheem Farm. Captain Fairweather's men mopped up as their officer used a captured machine gun to shoot down the running Germans. The 39th Australian Battalion was keeping up but only one hundred men completed the advance along the south side of the Douve stream.

Captain Paterson silenced two machine guns during 34th Australian Battalion's advance to Grey Farm. Captain Stewart took over the area around the farm and some men built strongpoints along 9 Australian Brigade's front, using tools and wire taken from German stores. Others went 'prospecting', the term used for hunting down anyone shooting at the consolidation work.

The Black Line

The smoke and dust had cleared by the time the sun rose on the bright June day. The troops waited two hours on the Black Line, or observation line, while the reserve brigades deployed. Corps cavalry patrols and eight tanks joined them; they would soon be joined by another twenty-five tanks. The guns of the standing barrages waited for SOS calls while the guns of the creeping barrage crept back and forth over the east slope of the ridge. It caught many Germans hiding in shell holes and they were confused because they had been told they were in reserve, ready to reinforce the front-line troops. The mines had either killed or shaken them so badly that they had either surrendered or run. Low-flying RFC planes looked for targets to strafe and add to the confusion.

Chapter 4

More Like a Picnic than a Battle

The Counter Attack

The British, Irish, New Zealanders and Australians were established all along the observation line, around 1,000 yards east of the Wytschaete–Messines road by 9 am. They could see across the German rear areas around Hollebeke, Wambeke and Warneton, reversing the situation of only a few hours before.

Second Army's planners had estimated casualties could be anything up to fifty per cent; there had been far fewer because the mines had shattered German morale. But a lack of discipline led to overcrowding on the east slope of the ridge, giving the German artillery and machine guns many targets. One observer noted that 'crowds of British infantry were seen to take off their coats on this warm summer morning and begin to dig in along the skyline of the ridge, working in their lighter coloured shirt sleeves, they made admirable targets for our machine guns.'

General Plumer's staff had expected a counter-attack around mid-morning and they had made preparations to meet it. The guns of Second Army's three reserve divisions opened fire for the first time, adding to the curtain of fire covering the troops as they dug in. Aerial observers circling overhead watched the likely approach routes but they saw no one for some time. The mines had completely disrupted the German plan to hold the forward slope until the counter-attack divisions were in place. The German commanders were anxious to establish how far Second Army had advanced before they moved their troops forward. Meanwhile, the consolidation was progressing at a steady rate. Men were digging in while observers looked across the green fields towards the woods and villages of the Lys valley. It was a pleasant change to the usual depressing sight of shell holes, barbed wire and rubble.

The aerial spotters saw the first signs of movement just before midday and the ground observers saw the infantry approaching soon afterwards.

Around 3,000 troops were spotted heading out of Houthem along the Wytschaete road towards IX Corps' sector. Another 1,000 troops were spotted crossing the canal at Warneton and they were marching towards I Anzac Corps' sector east of Messines. Two hours later two more columns were seen approaching X Corps, one heading down the Zandvoorde road and the other along the canal past Kortewilde.

In each case the news was delivered to Second Army report centre at Locre Château so the heavy artillery batteries could shell the roads. The largest column was scattered and the survivors reinforced the front line facing IX Corps. Part of the group heading towards I Anzac Corps advanced towards 25th Division while the rest attacked the New Zealand Division. In both cases the artillery disorganised the waves of advancing infantry before machine-gun fire pinned them down. None of the Germans reached Second Army's outpost line.

The Advance Continues

Each of Second Army's three corps had a division in reserve. Plumer's had also left the time for the advance to the final objective open until he knew the ridge was secure. He chose 3.10 pm, which gave time for his reserve of twenty-four tanks to reach the front line while around forty batteries moved closer to the new front. Some deployed next to pre-stocked ammunition dumps while others lined out in the original no man's land. Around 200 machine-gun teams deployed near the crest where they could provide an overhead barrage in support of the new advance. Meanwhile men and mules carried ammunition and water to them so the guns could keep firing.

X Corps

47th Division, Comines Canal

The Spoil Bank was a problem in X Corps' centre and Major General Gorringe ordered his artillery to shell the position for four hours. A German barrage disorganised the 1/20th London Regiment as it prepared to attack astride the canal at 6.55 pm. The left and right companies were then pinned down so the centre company were unable to advance across the embankment. German infantry moved into tunnels under the mound, before driving the Londoners back.

24th Division, White Château Park and Ravine Wood

Major General Louis Bols' men were ready along Damm Strasse before 1 pm but Brigadier General Dugan held his left back because 47th Division had not captured the Spoil Bank on the Comines canal. Tanks joined 73 Brigade's advance from the château area but they found no one in Ravine

Wood and few Germans around Verhaest Farm because many had withdrawn. The tanks eventually helped Dugan's men round up nearly 300 prisoners and six field guns in the Oosttaverne Line pillboxes.

Brigadier General Stone's men encountered little resistance as they moved from Deny's Wood through Rose Wood and Bug Wood on 17 Brigade's front. Second Lieutenant Compton was killed taking Odyssey Trench for the 1st Royal Fusiliers; he was one of only six casualties. The brigade took 130 prisoners and two field guns.

IX Corps
Lieutenant General Alexander Hamilton Gordon instructed 11th and 19th Divisions to deploy reserves to clear the Oosttaverne Line but a late change in the orders caused problems for them both.

19th Division, East of Oosttaverne
Major General Shute heard of the change when he was in Grand Bois but his request to delay the advance by twenty minutes was denied. The runners did not reach the battalions until around 3 pm and 57 Brigade's company and platoon officers had no idea what their objectives were when they

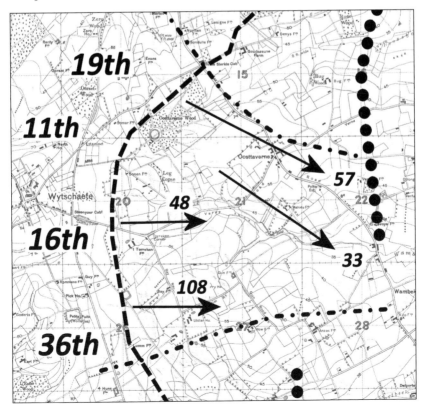

IX Corps faced problems approaching the Oosttaverne Line on 7 June.

advanced. All they could do was to follow a compass bearing as close to the barrage as they dare. Fortunately the German bombardment was weak and haphazard and there were few men holding the Oosttaverne Line bunkers. Brigadier General Cubitt's men found the Australians on the right at Polka Estaminet and men from 33 Brigade contacted their left an hour later.

11th Division, South-East of Oosttaverne

Brigadier General Daly received Major General Henry Davies' instruction to advance at the last minute and the 6th Lincolns and 7th South Staffords faced a rushed march to reach the front. Only one company of Lincolns reached Vandamme Farm on time but Lieutenant Colonel Gator told the commander to advance anyway. A few of the 6th Borders and the rest of the 7th Staffords followed forty minutes later. Captain Howis led the rest of the Lincolns to join them and four tanks helped them clear Van Hove Farm and Joye Farm, beyond the objective.

II Anzac Corps

The slope west of Messines was crawling with columns of men on the march, tanks rumbling forward and horse teams hauling their guns forward. One observer said the area looked 'more like a picnic than a battle'.

New Zealand Division, East of Messines

Brigadier General Brown's men had moved past Messines in small columns during the pause on the second objective. The 1 New Zealand Brigade then made the final advance down the slope astride the Huns Walk. Private Lee silenced two machine guns firing on the 1st Wellington Regiment's left company while a tank crashed into Fanny's Farm, helping the centre company to capture one hundred men. Second Lieutenant Blennerhassett's company had veered right to maintain contact with the 1st Auckland Regiment and they captured thirty men in an artillery headquarters at Blauwen Molen. The 1st Auckland Regiment crossed an abandoned Ungodly Trench and then shot or captured the German artillery men before they could haul two guns away.

Lieutenant General Godley had sent the II Anzac Mounted Regiment forward to check the German reaction around Gapaard. Their patrols came under fire as they approached the front line and the troopers had lost most of their horses before they found shelter. The artillery 'crumpled up' the only German counter-attack, allowing the New Zealanders to dig in undisturbed. The one piece of bad news later in the morning was the death of Brigadier General Brown. He had been killed when a shell exploded as he spoke to General Russell outside the Moulin de l'Hospice on the west side of Messines village.

4th Australian Division, Oosttaverne Line

The order to advance to the final objective reached Major General William Holmes late, causing some confusion. Brigadier General Robertson did not hear about the change in time and 12 Australian Brigade was moving forward when a German spotter plane reported the fact to their artillery. Both 45th and 47th Australian Battalions had to run the gauntlet of exploding shells to reach the New Zealand line and then learnt they had to wait two hours before they could advance. There was no room in the shallow trenches, so the Diggers found shelter in nearby shell holes and, in many cases, caught up on their sleep. Lieutenant Hallam decided to go exploring during the wait and he found four field guns and a howitzer around Despagne Farm.

Brigadier General Glasgow heard about the delay in time and he chose to keep 13 Australian Brigade behind the ridge for a time. The 52nd and 49th Australian Battalions eventually moved forward at 1.40 pm but they too had to pass through the German barrage to reach their jumping off line between Lumm Farm and Blauwen Molen. The delay had given 4th Australian Division time to deploy properly but it had also given the Germans time to reorganise. Many who had withdrawn after their counter-attacks had failed had reoccupied the Oosttaverne Line bunkers, where they were joined by reinforcements.

The order to 'fix bayonets' was given at 3.10 pm but the tanks detailed to support 13 Australian Brigade were late, so Brigadier General Glasgow's men advanced alone. Captain Stubbings had replaced an injured Lieutenant Colonel Pope and he noticed there were no troops on 52nd Australian Battalion's left. Captain Maxwell was instructed to lead his men towards Lumm Farm, to try to contact 33 Brigade, but they rounded up eighty Germans in shelters around Wambeke instead. His men ended up occupying a long length of the Oosttaverne Line the Germans had abandoned. Maxwell was holding an isolated position half a mile north of where he should have been and there was still no sign of 33 Brigade.

The rest of the 52nd Australian Battalion and part of the 49th Australian Battalion also veered north as they tried to keep in touch with Captain Stubbings. Meanwhile the 49th Australian Battalion had reached its objective north of the Blauwepoortbeek stream but all four of its company commanders had been hit. The advance had left 13 Australian Brigade in a vulnerable position, with large gaps on its left and in its centre.

The arrival of the 8th Gloucesters and a few men of the 10th Worcesters on Maxwell's flank helped the situation. Then three tanks led the 6th Borders down the Wytschaete road, where they reinforced Captain Stubbings' Australians and cleared Van Hove Farm. Two tanks would ditch near Despagne Farm while the third was knocked out as it headed home.

Three more tanks led 12 Australian Brigade along Huns' Walk, firing their guns at Oxygen Trench and Uncanny Trench. The 45th and 47th Australian Battalions advanced alongside but some men got ahead of the tanks and many were hit as they approached the Oosttaverne Line bunkers.

The 45th Australian Battalion was pinned down in front of Delporte Farm until Captain Allen found a gap in the barbed wire and Lieutenant Muir tossed his bombs inside the pillbox. The rest of Lieutenant Colonel Herrin's men cut through the wire and captured the field guns emplaced around the farm. The 47th Australian Battalion then faced a hand-to-hand fight because the Germans dared not run through the creeping barrage. Captain Williams led the final advance, taking thirty prisoners north of Huns' House, allowing Brigadier General Robertson to report that his objective had been taken.

3rd Australian Division, South of the Douve

The men of 37th Australian Battalion dodged from hedge to hedge as they cleared the bunkers south of the Douve stream. Captain Grieve's company was pinned down by Hun House, near the Warneton road, so he moved up its blind side and pushed two grenades through the firing slit. The wounded survivors came out as he stood on top of the bunker and waved his men forward. Grieve was later wounded by a sniper but he survived to be awarded the Victoria Cross. Lieutenant Stubbs' men rounded up eighty prisoners while Private McCarthy silenced another pillbox, allowing Captains Symons and Giblin to secure the objective.

Temporary Withdrawals

General von Lambert had spent the afternoon considering whether to withdraw the *Group Wytschaete* behind the Comines canal and the River Lys. However he abandoned the idea when it became clear that Second Army was going no further than the Oosttaverne Line. Instead he withdrew his artillery to safer positions and gave the infantry instructions to locate the British and Anzac positions. Meanwhile, Second Army was struggling to hold onto what it had taken.

11th Division, Oosttaverne

A group of Germans were seen assembling opposite Oosttaverne during the evening but the British SOS barrage nearly ended in disaster. The machine-

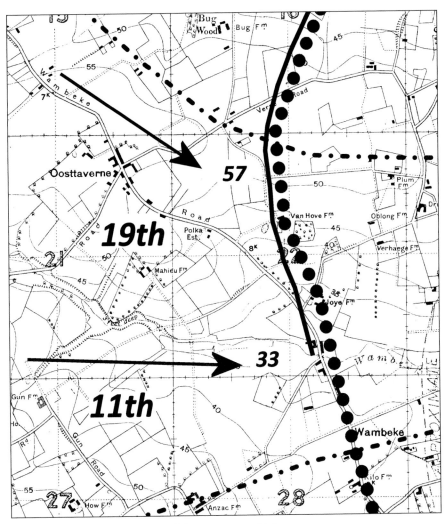

IX Corps' reduced sector around Oosttaverne on 14 June.

gunners had got the range right but the field batteries fired short, hitting IX Corps' front line. Rumours of a German breakthrough were telephoned to the rear as a mixed group of British and Australian companies fell back. Units were stood to and the artillery shortened its range even more, forcing the rest of IX Corps' front-line units to withdraw. Fortunately the Germans were unaware of the confusion in the dark and Major General Davies was relieved to hear that the Oosttaverne Line had been reoccupied before dawn.

4th Australian Division, Warneton Road
The men of 12 Australian Brigade also called for an SOS barrage to deal with a counter-attack along the Warneton road late in the afternoon. The Germans were stopped but the Diggers discovered that they were in front

of their objective because they were being shelled by their own artillery. A junior officer instructed his company to withdraw to safety and others followed; only they kept going back. They were half towards Messines by the time senior officers turned them back.

The Australian withdrawal left the New Zealanders feeling exposed, so they called down artillery fire onto the abandoned area astride Hun's Walk. But the barrage hit the Australians who had stayed behind and they too fell back, taking the 37th Australian Battalion around Hun's Farm with them. It meant virtually all of the Oosttaverne Line east and south-east of Messines had been abandoned. Again the Germans had no idea of the Anzacs' confusion in the dark.

Lieutenant General Godley instructed Major Generals Holmes and Monash to reoccupy the abandoned line, unaware that 52nd Australian Battalion was holding part of IX Corps front while German troops held the pillboxes astride the Blauwepoortbeek stream.

Godley's order was to advance between Hun's Walk and the Douve, east of Messines, at 3 am. Both 4th and 3rd Australian Divisions retook their parts of the Oosttaverne Line. Brigadier General Glasgow reinforced 49th Australian Battalion's position in Owl Trench, so it could not be outflanked from the Blauwepoortbeek area. Lieutenant General Godley had also arranged for 11th Division to relieve 52nd Australian Battalion that evening, so it could help 49th Australian Battalion clear the Blauwepoortbeek area.

Summary
Second Army's advance had been a complete success except for one thing. General Plumer had wanted to capture 120 artillery pieces and had told his corps commanders that 'risks may and should be taken in order to secure that line'. However the German horse teams had hauled most of their guns to safety and only forty-eight had been captured, the majority of them damaged. The new Mark IV tanks had proved to be a success and 16 out of 24 had reached the objective. The Germans had deployed a large number of field guns in an anti-tank role but most had deployed in the open and had been knocked out by the British artillery.

Later Moves
The day after the attack was quiet and then the reliefs started at dusk. British observers thought 33 Brigade's relief of 52nd Australian Battalion was the start of another German attack while German observers thought it was the start of a British attack. Guns from both sides hammered the Wambeke area for several hours, causing many casualties. The problem was caused by a lack of coordination between the divisions holding the front line and those

in support on the ridge. The confusion meant the planned attack along the Blauwepoortbeek had to be postponed until the following evening.

The 19th and 11th Divisions relieved the 16th and 36th Divisions east of Wytschaete over the next forty-eight hours. The 4th Australian Division also took over from the New Zealand Division east of Messines.

The German Withdrawal, 10 and 11 June
General Plumer wanted to advance a little further, to clear areas not taken in the main attack or improve the line. On the left, X Corps had to clear Battle Wood and Spoil Bank, next to the Comines canal. In the centre, IX Corps was to take Joye Farm and Wambeke hamlet. Meanwhile, II Anzac Corps was to push 1,000 yards east, astride the Douve towards Warneton.

Late on 10 June, the 4th Australian Division advanced astride the Blauwepoortbeek while the 3rd Australian Division advanced astride the Douve. Prisoners complained they had wanted to withdraw from their poorly sited trenches but the Anzac bombardment had stopped them moving. Early the following morning, 4th Australian Division reported the Germans were withdrawing from the Blauwepoortbeek area, allowing them to finally close the gap in their line.

25th Division, Gapaard, 13 June
Lieutenant Colonel Allsopp's 8th South Lancashires and Lieutenant Colonel Evans's 11th Cheshires advanced north-east of Messines. Four field guns were captured near Oculist Trench while Major Drummonds' Lewis guns shot down two horse teams before they escaped with their guns. Some men went ahead of the barrage to clear Despagne Farm and then took shelter in nearby shell holes. Lieutenant Colonel Birt's 8th Border Regiment came under fire from an artillery battery so Corporal Carter and Private Brown hailed a passing tank and directed the crew towards it, capturing two of the guns as the rest fled.

The whole of 75 Brigade's front, east of Messines, was poorly sited, so Brigadier General Baird sent two battalions forward, a few men at a time. The 7.30 pm creeping barrage took the Germans by surprise and the 8th Border Regiment and 2nd South Lancashires cleared Gapaard, Les Quatre Rois Cabaret and Ferme de la Croix. Private William Ratcliffe was working as a stretcher bearer with the South Lancashires when he decided to stop a machine-gun team inflicting casualties on his comrades. Ratcliffe later used the weapon against its former owners; he was awarded the Victoria Cross.

The only counter-attack from the Oosttaverne Line had been easily stopped and while Major General Bainbridge's men had taken all their objectives, it had cost them dearly. The 25th Division had suffered over

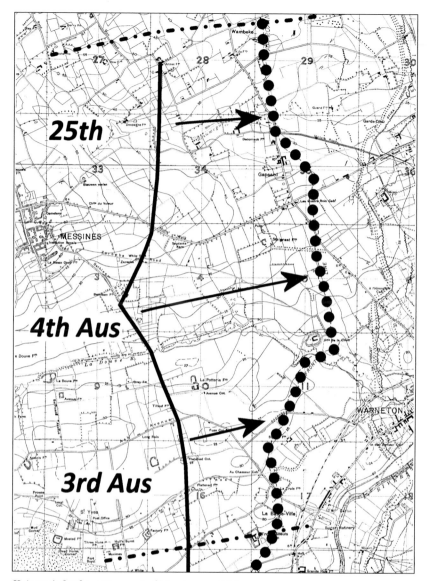

II Anzac's final position east of Messines on 14 June.

3,000 casualties, most from artillery fire during the final stages of the advance.

24th Division, Battle Wood, 14 June

Lieutenant Colonel Studd's 8th Buffs took over Battle Wood on the north side of the Comines canal. All the officers were hit as Captain Hall's left company advanced astride the railway at 7.30 pm but an injured Second Lieutenant Wilkinson stayed to consolidate the position while Sergeant

Shute cleared nearby dugouts. The Buffs' right company rushed Spoil Bank next to the canal but Second Lieutenant Paige was killed chasing Germans across the canal. The 1st Royal Fusiliers' left company cleared a ravine while the right rounded up many hiding in dugouts.

Summary

The rest of Second Army's plans to advance were shelved because the Germans withdrew, basing their main line of resistance on the Warneton Line. The ground was occupied by 14 June and the four mines around the Birdcage, east of Ploegsteert Wood, had to be abandoned. One would be detonated by a lightning strike in 1955; the rest are still there.

Second Army's attack had been a complete success. Over 7,350 prisoners and nearly 50 artillery pieces had been taken. But Second Army suffered over 24,500 casualties, half of them in the II Anzac Corps; most

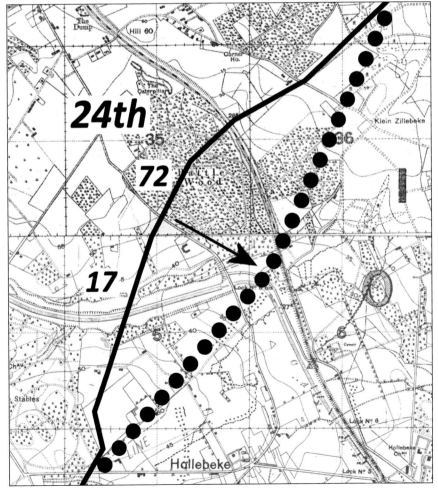

X Corps' final line astride the Ypres–Comines canal on 14 June.

came about because of the crowding on the ridge during the late morning and afternoon of the first day.

GHQ's original plan had been for Second Army to clear part of the Gheluvelt plateau once the Messines Ridge had been captured. Haig had reminded General Plumer of the plan on 24 May and he in turn asked Lieutenant Generals Hunter-Weston and Jacob to prepare to make an advance of 1,200 yards. Haig also told Gough, 'we may be able to exploit the [Messines] success quickly and reach a position which would materially help your operations.' But Gough either wanted to organise an attack with VIII and II Corps or incorporate it into Fifth Army's advance across the Pilckem ridge.

The problem was, the Germans had reinforced the Gheluvelt plateau after the loss of the Messines ridge, so Second Army had to redeploy its troops and guns. Haig lost patience when Plumer asked for seventy-two hours to relocate his artillery and he handed control of VIII and II Corps to Fifth Army, with orders to attack at once. But at an army commanders' conference on 14 June Gough said it was unsafe to advance across the Gheluvelt plateau because it would create 'a very exposed and difficult salient'. His suggestion to combine the Pilckem ridge and Gheluvelt plateau attacks into one, all controlled by Fifth Army, was accepted.

Chapter 5

A Change from Going Over the Top

Operation Hush

The front line had run close to Nieuport since the Belgian army flooded the River Yser in October 1914. The coastal town stood on the west bank of the canalised river and while the ruins were riddled with tunnels, the surrounding area was just 'one vast sea of mud'. No man's land was on the east bank and troops had to brave sniper fire as they crossed the water by the locks or plank-and-barrel bridges. Once on the far side, they had to rely on sandbags to protect them because it was impossible to dig trenches in the sand. Shell bursts repeatedly demolished the breastworks while wind blew the sand from the pillboxes, exposing them to the enemy observers.

The Admiralty was concerned how easy it was for the German ships and submarines to attack British shipping. But the German coastal guns outranged the Royal Navy's monitors, so they could not shell the ships anchored in Bruges docks or Zeebrugge harbour.

In January 1917, Lieutenant Colonel Macmullen suggested landing troops on the Flanders coast, on the proviso that the BEF could advance east of Ypres and threaten the railway centre of Roulers. Admiral Sir Reginald Bacon, Commander of the Dover Patrol, planned three landings while a feint was made east of Ostend. Two British divisions would capture the German trenches east of Nieuport, diverting attention from a landing further up the coast a few hours later.

The plan was to land three brigades between Westende Bains and Middelkirke Bains. They would clear the German reserve trenches and then advance inland with the 'greatest boldness and resolution' to link up with the Belgian Army advancing from Dixmude. They would also silence the heavy coastal batteries at Raveshyde, two miles west of Ostend. The final objective was to deploy heavy howitzers in range of Zeebrugge, forcing the German ships to abandon the harbours.

A cover plan called Operation Hush was put together to keep the landing plans a secret. GHQ declared 'an acute attack of cerebra-spinal meningitis', a contagious condition which required all the men of 1st Division to be put into quarantine. They were confined to 'Hush Camp' at Le Clipon, seven miles west of Dunkirk, and began training at the beginning of July.

The Belgian architect who designed the Flanders sea wall helped build an accurate test panel and the men became proficient at climbing it loaded with weapons and equipment. Training on the 'Obstacle Course' was pleasant compared to living in muddy trenches and 'everyone was keen on it for its novelty... it was at least a change from going over the top.'

The men also practised loading and unloading rafts. Meanwhile, the monitors practised with the pontoons and some infantry officers watched the naval manoeuvres on the River Medway. Some of the sailors visited Hush Camp to improve relations and a few were taken to see the trenches east of Ypres.

But the men of 1st Division became bored with their routine and while their correspondence was censored there was one major oversight: the men were allowed to go on leave. They were given strict instructions to say nothing to their friends and families in England but GHQ was taking a big chance.

The plan was for 10,000 troops to board on two monitors in Dunkirk harbour and sail through the hours of darkness. They would shell the coast while a smoke screen hid them as they pushed piers attached to the stern onto the shore.

Half the men would climb the sea wall while the rest unloaded the huge pontoons. Three tanks would also crawl ashore, dragging sledges full of equipment, while gun teams hauled the brigade artillery across the beach.

Operation *Strandfest*

The French had intended to abandon the trenches if their bridgehead on the east bank of the Yser was attacked, so when the troops moved into the trenches on 20 June they found there were no dugouts and the breastworks afforded little protection. The first British troops had dressed in French uniforms so as not to arouse suspicions. Unfortunately, German observers had noticed that the Allies were swopping their guns over and they planned an attack, codenamed Operation *Strandfest* (Beach Party).

Control was handed to XV Corps headquarters and while 1st Division settled in along the coast sector, 32nd Division took over the Nieuport area. Lieutenant General John du Cane was anxious that his men held the bridgehead until all his artillery arrived. General Henry Rawlinson's Fourth Army headquarters arrived on 5 July and the German bombardment began the following day. It was slow to begin with because of the poor visibility, so the Royal Flying Corps' aerial observers saw nothing unusual. There were fewer planes than normal in the air because twelve planes had recently been damaged during a bombing raid on Bray Dunes airfield. Inclement weather grounded the rest the following day.

The Germans postponed their attack by twenty-four hours due to the weather but their gunners started shelling in earnest on 10 July. The three floating bridges called Putney, Crowder and Vauxhall were destroyed, leaving only one bridge and a footbridge standing. All wire communications were cut with Brigadier General Kemp's 2 Brigade headquarters and the wirelesses had stopped working.

The shells kept pounding the 2nd KRRC and the 1st Northants, smashing the parapets and clogging everything with sand. The German guns fell silent for a time as the observers checked the results but low-flying planes strafed the battered trenches. The guns then smothered the bridgehead with two new types of gas. Sneezing gas, code named 'Blue Cross', made it difficult for the men to keep their gas masks on. Mustard gas, code named 'Yellow Cross', was a brown-yellow gas which blistered lungs. The gas became absorbed in clothing and equipment and created painful blisters on moist skin such as the armpits and the groin. It lingered in low-lying areas, like shell holes, trenches and dugouts for several days giving off a distinctive odour which gave it the name. The best defence was to stay calm, fix the gas helmet as quickly as possible and cover exposed skin, before moving away from the affected area. Drivers had to fit respirators over the faces of their animals and then lead them to a safe distance, without them panicking.

Mustard gas had been used before in small quantities before but it soon became known as *Ypreite* because of the large amounts used in the Salient. Few men died of the effects but many who came into contact with it would be affected for the rest of their lives. The British condemned the gas, only to use a stockpile of German shells captured at Cambrai in November 1917. GHQ would not receive its own version until September 1918.

XV Corps still only had one third of its complement of guns to reply with and they did little damage because the assault troops were waiting in concrete shelters. At 8 pm the first wave crossed no man's land, using flamethrowers to clear the British trenches. One party moved along the shore to infiltrate the trenches in the dunes but bad weather had stopped torpedo boats cooperating. Some of the support troops mopped up the dugouts while the rest consolidated the captured area. Most of the British troops had been hit by the barrage while the survivors were captured.

The 2nd KRRC's counter-attack in 2nd Division's sector ended in disaster while the 1st Northants' forward headquarters held out as long as they could. Around sixty KRRC men would swim back across the River

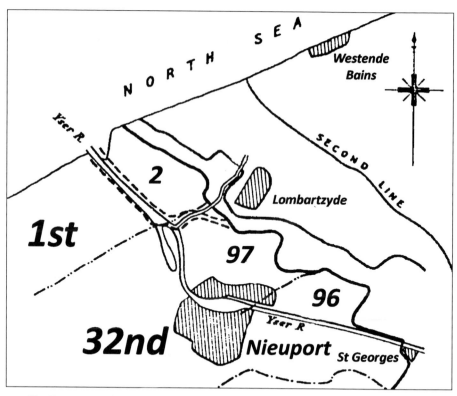

The German attack on the coast at Nieuport on 10 July.

Yser during the hours of darkness but only nine of the Northants escaped.

Brigadier General Blackadder's men held the Redan, a large triangular fort with a moat, in 32nd Division's area. The bombardment had destroyed the bridges while the attack drove 97 Brigade back towards Nieuport. The 11th Border Regiment regained some of the line with the help of the 17th Highland Light Infantry.

Rawlinson wanted the bridgehead retaken the following morning but Lieutenant General DuCane argued against the idea. He did not want to attempt a river crossing while the Germans had artillery superiority. He also pointed out that experience had shown counter-attacks made a day or two later usually failed. Rawlinson persisted and patrols swam across the Yser to reconnoitre the Germans' trenches. The 16th Lancashire Fusiliers were unable to retake any ground when they attacked while Captain Smith's raiding party was stopped by barbed wire. The German attack had cost XV Corps around 3,000 casualties. Brigadier General Kemp reported 1,300 missing, most of them from 2nd KRRC and the 1st Northants.

Haig explained the loss of the bridgehead to the War Cabinet blaming a mishandled relief of French troops by the British. He agreed not to try and retake the dunes area and said that Fourth Army could still advance from what remained of the bridgehead. The plans for the coastal landing remained unchanged and the date was set to coincide with the high tide on 7-8 August. The date for the offensive in the Ypres Salient was set for 25 July, giving Fifth Army time to get beyond the German defensive lines.

First Army, Lens

On 6 June, General Gough asked Fifth Army's corps commanders how long they needed to prepare their attack at Ypres. Both Lieutenant General Rudolph Lambart, the Earl of Cavan, and Lieutenant General Herbert Watts said they needed six weeks to organise XIV and XIX Corps while Lieutenant General Sir Ivor Maxse said XVIII Corps required eight weeks.

GHQ decided it would be a good idea to stage feint attacks on First Army's front, to distract attention from the Salient. But General Sir Henry Horne had to carry out the attacks during the last week of June because most of his artillery was about to head north.

The first attempt was planned for 24 June on I Corps' front, north of the River Souchez. But the Germans withdrew only hours before 46th Division was supposed to advance, so it occupied the forward slope of Reservoir Hill (or Hill 65) without a fight. A massive bombardment stretching fourteen miles from Hulluch, north to Loos, to Gavrelle, east of Arras, began on the evening of 28 June. Horne later commented, 'the Germans really thought that they were being attacked on a very wide front.'

A thunderstorm soaked the assault troops just before they advanced at 7.10 pm. This time 46th Division captured the rest of Reservoir Hill while the Germans withdrew opposite the 4th and 3rd Canadian Divisions. They moved forward to contact at 2.30 am, occupying the full length of Avion Trench. While 4th Canadian Division secured Eleu and part of Avion village, 3rd Canadian Division formed a defensive flank along the Avion–Arleux road. But the Germans had recovered and fought back while the heavy rain brought operations to a close.

Two attacks were planned against tactical points on First Army's right flank on the evening of 28 June. Observers saw the troops assembling and a short but heavy barrage caused the British 200 casualties just before zero hour. But the advance was a success and over 200 prisoners were taken. On 5th Division's front, Brigadier General Turner's 15 Brigade advanced into Oppy village. On 31st Division's front, Brigadier General Carter-Campbell's 94 Brigade captured Gavrelle mill, an important observation post.

German artillery was spotted withdrawing east of Lens following the attacks and while General Horne would have liked to keep pushing, his own artillery was heading north to Flanders. He would have to wait another two months before he could attempt to take Hill 70 north of Lens.

Chapter 6

Every Time a Coconut

The Flanders Plan

Field Marshal Haig submitted his plan for an offensive in Flanders on 4 May. Field Marshal William Robertson, Chief of the Imperial General Staff, had been considering the entire war and had given the War Cabinet a warning on 9 May. There had been a revolution in Russia in February and it had ended Czar Nicholas II's rule. Intelligence reported Bolshevik demonstrations and he believed the nation was likely to quit the war, meaning large numbers of German divisions could be sent west to the Western Front. An inconclusive end to the battle of the Isonzo, the tenth battle on the Italian front, added to the uncertainty.

The War Cabinet agreed in principle with GHQ's plan for an attack in Flanders but Haig was told he had to have French assistance before they would give their approval. The BEF would commit thirty-eight divisions to the Ypres area. Many had been sent north from Arras by First and Third Army while others had been engaged in Second Army's attack at Messines. General Rawlinson and his Fourth Army headquarters was given the Flanders coast sector. Pétain would eventually pledge twenty-two divisions for Group Dixmude, on the British left.

GHQ's head of intelligence, Brigadier General John Charteris, concluded the German army had suffered a huge number of casualties during the recent battles of Arras and Aisne. There had been talk of deploying 18-year-olds to the front (a year younger than normal) even though the German Minister of War, Hermann von Stein, did not think they were physically or emotionally fit enough for the trenches.

Charteris blamed the reported fall in German morale on their inability to maintain the strength of their divisions. He concluded that 'given a continuance of the existing circumstances and of the effort of the Allies, Germany might well be forced to conclude a peace on our terms before the end of the year.' There was no indication of a reduction in the German ability to wage war but Charteris concluded 'that offensive operations on our front would offer no chance of success'. As far as he was concerned,

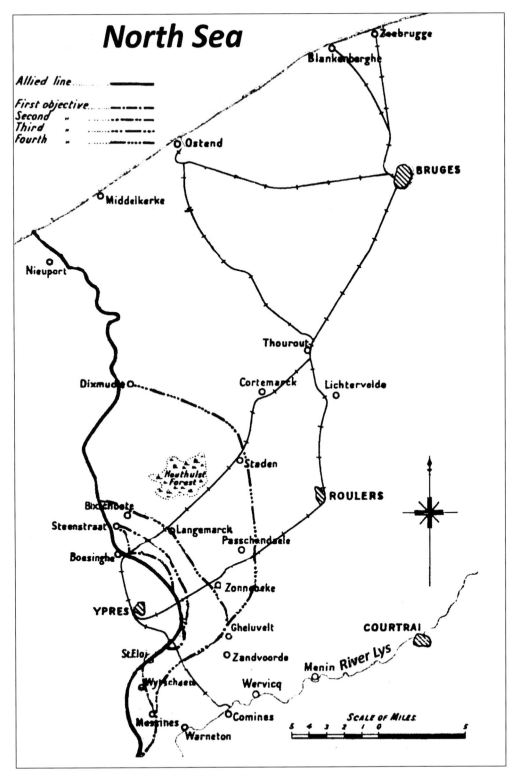

GHQ's plan to link the Ypres Salient offensive to the landings on the coast.

the wisest option was to wait for the Americans to arrive the following summer. Haig took the intelligence assessment seriously but disagreed with its conclusions. The Director of Military Intelligence at the War Office, Brigadier General George Macdonogh, went further; he disagreed with the assessment and its conclusions.

Haig told the Secretary of State for War, Lord Derby the Hon. Edward Stanley, that he wanted to keep the pressure on the Germans and urged him to 'send to France every available man, aeroplane and gun as soon as possible. We cannot tell how our Allies will stand another winter.' He thought there was 'no time like the present', and did not want to wait for the Americans.

GHQ's final instructions for the attack in Flanders were issued on 22 May, two weeks after the Arras campaign closed down. A streamlined Cabinet Committee on War Policy took over running the war two weeks later. The members were Prime Minister Lloyd George, George Curzon (the Earl Curzon of Kedleston), Alfred Milner, 1st Viscount Milner, Andrew Bonar Law and General Jan Smuts. Four days later they received a memorandum from Haig, stating he wanted to clear the Flanders coast while the German Army was at a low point. He went as far as to say a sustained offensive 'might quite probably lead to their collapse'. But Haig had shrewdly removed Charteris's intelligence summary from the memorandum, at Robertson's suggestion, fearing it would confuse the War Cabinet. Robertson had also told Haig: 'Do not argue that you can finish the war this year or that the German is already beaten, but argue that your plan is the best plan.' Quite simply, the Haig memorandum had been tailored to get the Cabinet's support for an offensive in Flanders.

On 19 June Haig told the Cabinet Committee he had chosen Ypres because the War Cabinet had asked for the Flanders coast to be cleared on 23 November 1916. The First Sea Lord, Admiral John Jellicoe, also wanted the coast cleared because the Royal Navy would be unable keep the Channel safe for shipping if the U-Boat threat increased. Shipping losses had already topped over two million tons in the six months since unrestricted submarine warfare had begun. Nearly 700 ships had already been lost and the Merchant Navy could not stand to lose many more.

Haig explained how the BEF only had to advance 15 miles to cut the railway behind the German front and another 15 miles to cut the second line. He suggested that Holland might even break its neutral stance if the BEF advanced in Flanders.

Lloyd George wanted to send troops and artillery to the Italian front but Haig wanted to keep all the BEF's resources on the Western Front. He believed the Italian front was far removed from France and Flanders and that the Germans could move their reinforcements quicker across a superior rail network. He still believed the Russian situation would take time to conclude and it would take months to move divisions across Europe.

Haig also suggested making step-by-step attacks rather than one 'big push', so progress could be monitored, avoiding an endless war of attrition as experienced the previous autumn. The BEF had a lot of experience from the Somme and Arras campaigns and it now had enough tanks to help the infantry capture achievable objectives.

Lloyd George opposed Haig's plan but it was difficult to argue against the wishes of both his army and navy commanders. The Cabinet Committee agreed the BEF could launch a summer offensive in Flanders but it would be closely monitored. The attacks would only continue if they met projections; a rare thing on the Western Front.

Haig returned to the Continent where he faced a busy month of July preparing for the offensive. Elsewhere, events unfolded apace as the Russian offensive (named the Kerensky Offensive after the Russian Minister of War) failed. Soldiers, sailors and workers took to the streets but the Bolshevists missed the opportunity to seize power. Even so, their popularity soared and Russia dropped out of the war as it was engulfed in a full-scale revolution. But all was not well in Germany where confidence in the blockade was falling as enthusiasm for the war waned.

On 5 July, Matthias Erzberger, an opponent of unrestricted submarine attacks, suggested to the Reichstag that Germany should again consider peace. Pope Benedict XV was also calling for peace terms to be discussed. However President Woodrow Wilson refused to deal with Kaiser Wilhelm II's autocratic style of government.

The Allied bombardment started in Flanders on 18 July but Robertson had to remind Haig that the War Cabinet had only agreed to his plan in principle 'as long as a step-by-step advance is adhered to'. They authorised the offensive on 20 July but again reminded Robertson and Haig that they would call it off if too little progress was made or if casualties were too high. They also instructed Haig to plan how to move divisions and heavy artillery to the Italian front if they chose to close down the offensive.

The War Cabinet asked what the first objective was, so they could measure the success of the offensive. Haig had chosen the Passchendaele Ridge, an advance of 5 miles on a 6-mile-wide front, adding that it would take several steps to reach it. That may have sounded optimistic but First and Third Armies had advanced up to 4 miles on a 10-mile-wide front in just four days at the start of the Arras campaign.

Haig was concerned and even annoyed that his plan had 'neither the confidence nor the full support of the War Cabinet'. On the day the offensive was supposed to have begun, 25 July, the War Cabinet finally pledged their support for the attack. They also made it clear they would consider the BEF's position and its commander-in-chief's views before changing any plans. Haig hedged his bets by replying, 'even if my attacks do not gain the ground as I hope and expect, we ought still to persevere with attacking the Germans in France. Only by this means can we win; and we must encourage the French to continue fighting.'

The Preparations

General Plumer had to hand over control of the Ypres Salient to Haig's favourite General Hubert Gough on 10 June, after holding the sector for eighteen months. Fifth Army headquarters had just finished the gruelling two-week battle at Bullecourt. Fifth Army was joined by four corps distributed across a 7-mile front. Lieutenant General Rudolph Lambart, the Earl of Cavan's XIV Corps and Lieutenant General Sir Ivor Maxse's XVIII Corps faced Pilckem ridge on the left. Lieutenant General Herbert Watts's XIX Corps had to cross the Frezenberg ridge in the centre while Lieutenant General Sir Claud Jacob's II Corps had to clear the woods on the Gheluvelt plateau.

Haig had told the War Cabinet and Robertson that he was not looking for 'a breakthrough nor for a rapid and spectacular success', but 'a series of carefully organised and prepared attacks, only gaining ground step-by-step.' The War Cabinet had sanctioned the offensive based on this promise. However, Haig and his Chief of the General Staff, Lieutenant General Kiggell, encountered a difference in opinion when they spoke to the two army commanders. Gough was happy to advance in short steps but Plumer suggested going deep, hoping to trigger a general withdrawal. Haig agreed with Plumer and the objective for the first day included Langemarck and Zonnebeke, an advance of 3 miles on a 5-mile-wide front.

Fifth Army was going to be supported by attacks on its flanks. Fourth Army was given another five divisions, over 580 howitzers and guns and around 200 planes for an attack on the coast. Half came from the Royal Flying Corps' IV Brigade and the rest from the Royal Naval Air Service, which specialised in attacking targets along the Flanders coast. The Belgian Army was poised to advance if the Germans withdrew from the flooded area around Dixmude. General François Anthoine's First French Army took over the line north of Boesinghe, on Fifth Army's left flank at the beginning of July. It would eventually have six divisions organised into two corps.

Gough and his chief of staff, Major General Neill Malcolm, asked GHQ to extend Fifth Army's front south of Mount Sorrel, so they could clear the whole of the Gheluvelt plateau. Haig agreed and it was extended another

1,200 yards south, as far as Klein Zillebeke. Gough also wanted Second Army to attack east of the Messines Ridge, to divert German attention from the Gheluvelt plateau.

Fifth Army's rear area was crowded with artillery batteries, infantry billets, ammunition dumps and all kinds of stores. Then there were the engineers, pioneers and labourers laying roads and light railways, building battery positions and installing communications. There was so much work to do, the infantry had to be called upon to help. One division alone had 2,000 men laying cables, building dugouts and carrying stores. The German gunners could hardly miss a target and there were many casualties across the salient in the days leading up to the attack, particularly amongst the gunners. One British gunner referred to the German bombardment with the fairground saying, 'every time a coconut'.

The roads were busy, particularly at night and there was always a line of slow-moving ammunition wagons between Ypres and the front line. The Germans shelled them relentlessly and road junctions were lucrative targets, as their names suggest: Hellfire Corner, Hellblast Corner and Shrapnel Corner. The procession frequently halted as men dragged smashed wagons and dead horses off the road and one padre said, 'many a man learned Christianity while waiting at Shrapnel Corner.'

The Bombardment
Second Army had to hand over all its tanks and more than half its medium and heavy artillery to Fifth Army. It left Plumer with only 243 heavy howitzers and 546 field guns and nearly half were deployed with X Corps around the Comines canal, so they could support Fifth Army's right flank. Meanwhile, Gough's artillery officer, Major General Grant, had 752 heavy howitzers and 1,422 field guns; a piece of artillery for every 5.5 yards of front or over 70 guns for every mile of front.

The RFC had assembled over 400 planes grouped under II Brigade, V Brigade and Ninth Headquarters Wing. Between them they would bomb short range and long range targets, carry out reconnaissance missions, reporting on enemy activity and the destruction of targets, particularly artillery batteries. Meanwhile, fighters would aim to drive the German Air Force from the sky. Fifth Army also had eighteen kite balloon sections for short range observation work.

The artillery and the aerial observers worked so well together that many German batteries had to be relocated. It meant the aerial observers had to find them again so they could be re-registered. It added three days to the bombardment programme. Haze also interfered with artillery observation and both Gough and Anthoine asked for extra time to find the relocated batteries. Z-Day (there were also W, X and Y-Days) was postponed to 31 July which also gave time to stockpile ammunition. The final three days would be devoted to counter-battery fire, neutralising many of the German guns. But the last week of July had been dry and while the significance of the late July weather was not understood at the time, it soon would be.

The repeated barrages and activity in the Salient made it obvious that an offensive was imminent. Arras had shown that the BEF was effective at smashing the front-line defences but it soon got into difficulties. The Germans believed it was more cost effective to use a small number of troops to break up the attack and then strike back at a disorganised enemy, so they deployed their artillery ready to support the counter-attacks.

The Tanks and Cavalry Deploy

Four days before the attack, the Heavy Branch of the Machine Gun Corps was renamed the Tank Corps. Brigadier General Elles' command had come a long way since its first battle on the Somme on 15 September 1916. It had expanded into three tank brigades, each with seventy-two tanks, and they were armed with the improved Mark IV which had proved its worth on Messines Ridge.

Tanks were now an integral part of the BEF's planning and experienced infantry were used to fighting alongside them. Fifth Army encouraged the infantry, officers and NCOs to visit the other's billets to learn from each other. The crews spent three nights driving the eight miles to their assembly points but there was nowhere to hide them close to the front line. Only two broke down, proving the Mark IV was a major improvement on earlier versions.

Fifth Army had been allocated 136 tanks for the attack but none were deployed in XIV Corps' sector on the left flank, because they could not cross the Yser Canal. Colonel Baker-Carr deployed twenty-four of I Brigade's tanks with XVIII Corps, ready to advance through St Julien; the rest were held as Fifth Army's reserve. Colonel Hardress-Lloyd shepherded around fifty of III Brigade's tanks to the Wieltje area, ready to move along the 's Gravenstafel and Zonnebeke roads in support of XIX Corps' advance. On Fifth Army's right, Colonel Courage moved a similar number of II Brigade's tanks to the Zillebeke area, ready to help II Corps' advance along the Menin road.

Experience showed that the tanks struggled to keep up with the infantry and they had proved to be far more useful for mopping up strongpoints. Fifth Army expected the artillery to deal with the strongpoints before the first objective but those beyond it were often out of sight. The tanks would

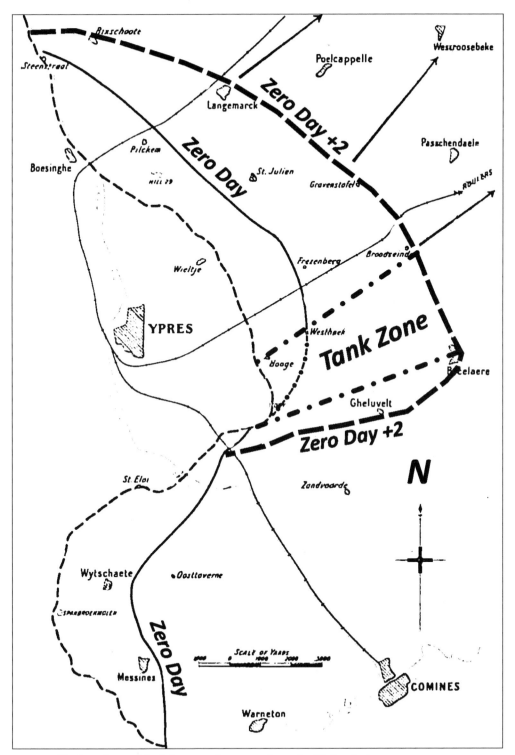

The first phase of the Salient attack using tanks on the Gheluvelt plateau.

be able to join the infantry as they waited at the objectives. Brigadier General Elles allocated one third of his tanks to mopping up strongpoints between the first and second objectives. Another third would silence the strongpoints between the second and third objectives. The rest would be held in reserve.

GHQ moved two cavalry divisions forward, deploying them behind the flanks of the attack front so they would be ready to exploit any breakthrough. Haig already had his advanced headquarters train forward at Blendecques siding, south-east of Saint Omer.

The Infantry Deploy

Fifth Army was given eighteen divisions. Each corps would have two divisions to make the initial assault and another two to continue the advance. Gough also had V Corps and VIII Corps in reserve and while they had one reserve division each, they would receive and train divisions when they arrived in Flanders. Meanwhile Second Army was left with twelve divisions, spread equally between X, IX and II Anzac Corps, to hold its 6-mile-long front facing the Warneton Line.

The BEF had learnt the importance of training during the battle of the Somme. It had refined its methods during the battle of Arras; each corps built large models which indicated objectives and had woods, buildings and pillboxes marked out. Officers and NCOs were given the opportunity to study the models from observation galleries.

Each brigade rehearsed their attack over taped-out courses. The men initially walked across at their own pace, so they could study the landmarks and they then advanced at the prescribed rate set by the creeping barrage, flag bearers being used to represent the moving bombardment while drummers signified enemy machine guns.

Platoon tactics concentrated on capturing pillboxes and the Lewis gunners and rifle grenadiers were taught to give covering fire to suppress the men inside. Riflemen and bombers used the safest approach until they were close enough to move in for the kill. The plan was simple enough over dry ground when no one was shooting but it was a deadly business when carried out under fire on a muddy battlefield.

Deserters and prisoners stated that their trenches were being battered by the bombardment. Aerial observers also reported there were few men west of the Steenbeek stream so Major General Feilding decided to see if it was true opposite the Guards Division. Lieutenant Colonel Crawford's 3rd Coldstream Guards crossed the canal, on 27 July finding that the water was up to their armpits. They found the Baboon trenches around Bois Crapouillots to be virtually deserted so they dug in between Wood 14 and

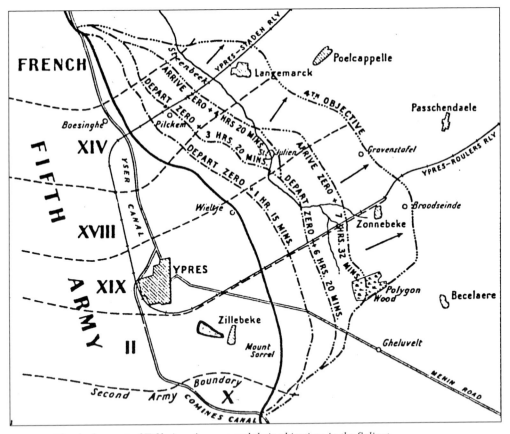

The deployment of Fifth Army's corps and their objectives in the Salient.

Artillery Wood. They stopped a counter-attack but some had to be withdrawn when the British artillery started shelling the area.

The same situation was reported on 38th Division's front. In the afternoon the 15th Welsh found empty German trenches but a company of the 15th Welsh Fusiliers was overrun. The Germans returned in force that night and the Guards had to form defensive flanks after the Welsh and the French withdrew. General Feilding reinforced the bridgehead and his pioneer battalion, the 4th Coldstream Guards, installed fourteen bridges across the canal.

The delay caused by the prolonged artillery bombardment meant the assault troops had to be relieved so they could rest. They began moving forward again on the night of 28 July and the brigades took over the front line the following night. The assault battalions moved into the assembly trenches on the night of 30 July ready for zero hour at 3 am. The Germans could see plenty of movement on the fields east of Ypres and the barrage alerted them to the imminent offensive. It appears they knew the original zero hour because they briefly evacuated their trenches in tunnelling areas, like Hooge and Hill 60, on 27 July, worried that mines would be detonated.

Overall the German response was subdued but it was still dangerous moving forward.

'It was extremely exciting going along in front of your platoon in single file, winding in and out of shell holes, hearing and seeing big black beggars [howitzer shells] bursting all around. Little by little you increased the pace, till by the time you had reached the halfway house your heart was fit to burst and your knees shaking with excitement and the fatigue of pulling your feet from the sticky mud each time.'

As the men prepared for what lay ahead, they had to get used to the evil smell which was 'a very ancient and fish-like smell, as of dirt, damp and stale humanity'.

Zero hour was approaching as the men checked their weapons, clambered over the parapet and lay on the ground. Officers and NCOs made sure their platoons were deployed correctly and then checked their watches; 'There was a faint glimmer in the sky. The silence was ominous. Five minutes to go: the order was passed to fix bayonets. One minute: officers and men crouched, ready to rush. The seconds passed and the guns began to open, one or two at first, and then swelling into the now familiar roar of the barrages.' The attack was on and there was no turning back as thousands of men began the long walk across no man's land.

Chapter 7

A Perfect Inferno

Zero Hour

Over 3,000 guns opened fire at 3.50 am, and the 'opening barrage and the corresponding German flares were probably the most wonderful displays of fireworks that were ever seen.' Simultaneously, thousands of men moved across no man's land on an 8-mile front. Mist meant the Royal Flying Corps could not observe for the batteries but the artillery still played a huge part in the opening advance. There were no less than eight gunners for every ten infantrymen. They would fire 23,000 tons of ammunition and this was the first day of many.

Major General Uniacke had instructed each corps to use two-thirds of the 18-pounder field guns for the creeping barrage. They hit the German front line for around seven minutes before moving forward at 25 yards a minute. A mixture of graze and standard fuses created a deadly curtain of ground bursts and air bursts for maximum effect. The guns fired four rounds a minute, reducing to two rounds a minute while the infantry reorganised on the objectives. All the time over 250 machine guns fired an overhead barrage.

The rest of the 18-pounders and all the 4.5-inch howitzers pounded the farmhouses and pillboxes in front of the first objective. They lifted each time the creeping barrage caught up with them. The 6-inch howitzers and 60-pounder guns shelled distant targets and ten minutes passed before most of the German artillery replied. The exception was on Fifth Army's right, where II Corps was crossing the Gheluvelt plateau.

XIV Corps, 31 July

Lieutenant General Rudolph Lambart, the Earl of Cavan's assault battalions would advance to the crest of the Pilckem Ridge and the support battalions would move beyond the summit. Reserve brigades would make the final 800-yard advance to the Steenbeek stream, west of Langemarck.

Guards Division, 31 July

Artillery fire had forced the Germans to abandon the Baboon trenches around Bois Crapouillots, allowing the Guards to cross the canal on 27 July. Zero was thirty-eight minutes later than the rest of Fifth Army, so XIV Corps advanced at the same time as the French troops on their left. It would also allow 38th Division to catch up on the right.

The engineers had built several bridges across the canal but they were vulnerable to artillery fire. So lightweight rafts made of chicken wire and canvas wrapped around wooden frames were prepared. They were launched across the canal at zero hour and while they sank beneath the water, a rope handrail guided the men as they waded across. They also made footbridges out of duckboards floated on petrol tins. The rafts and footbridges were ready in time for the support battalions to cross.

The Guardsmen moved across the canal and deployed facing Wood 15 and Artillery Wood during the hours of darkness. At zero hour 'boiling oil was poured on the enemy and the place became a perfect inferno' and it was followed by a 'magnificent combined artillery and machine-gun barrage.'

On 3 Guards Brigade front, the 1st Welsh Guards cleared the pillboxes around Wood 15 but Lieutenant Colonel Douglas Gordon's left became pinned down because the French were held up in front of Colonel's Wood. Sergeant Robert Bye crawled and ran from shell hole to shell hole when his platoon was stopped by one pillbox. He bombed the garrison into submission and then led a party of men along a line of pillboxes, taking many prisoners. The advance could then continue towards Wood 16; Bye would be awarded the Victoria Cross. Lieutenant Colonel Maitland's 1st Grenadier Guards kept up with the barrage on the right, crossing the wet ground around Caribou Trench. Brigadier General Lord Seymour was able to report that his two leading battalions had reached the objective on time, having killed or captured around 300 Germans on route.

The 2nd Scots Guards continued the advance behind a smoke screen. Lieutenant Colonel Orr-Ewing's men captured two field guns at Major's Farm but the Guardsmen were annoyed to see their fifty prisoners head into French lines because it meant they would not be added to their head count. Meanwhile, Lieutenant Colonel Gort's 4th Grenadier Guards outflanked Abri Wood, with the help of a smoke screen before clearing Fourche Farm.

In 2 Guards Brigade's sector, Lieutenant Colonel Greer was killed at an early stage leaving Captain Gunston to lead the 2nd Irish Guards under enfilade fire from Hey Wood. On the right, Lieutenant Colonel Romilly was wounded as the 1st Scots Guards silenced a machine-gun team concealed in Artillery Wood.

Lieutenant Colonel Brand's 1st Coldstream Guards continued the advance beyond the crest, coming under fire from Abri Wood on its left and

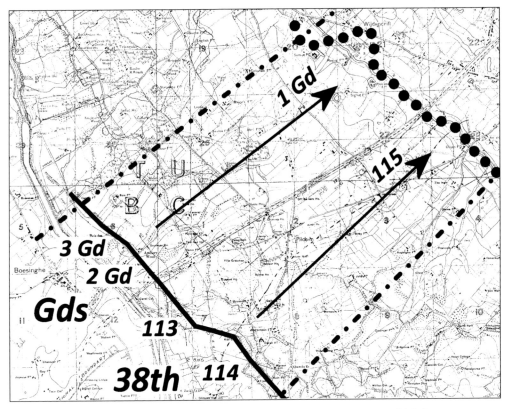

XIV Corps' advance across the Pilckem ridge to the Steenbeek stream on 31 July.

then from Captain Farm. Guardsman Thomas Whitham crawled beyond the British barrage to silence one machine-gun team; he would be awarded the Victoria Cross. Meanwhile, Lieutenant Colonel Thorne's 3rd Grenadier Guards cleared emplacements dug into the railway embankment, capturing fifty men in the main blockhouse. Brigadier General Ponsonby was then able to report that the Grenadier Guards had driven the Germans from Vulcan crossing, helping 38th Division's advance beyond the railway.

The advance was going to plan and the 1 Guards Brigade zig-zagged their way through gaps in the German barrage as they deployed, ready to advance to the Steenbeek stream. Brigadier General Jeffreys' men were supposed to move off at 8.50 am but the 2nd Coldstream Guards' left was pinned down because the French were still struggling around Colonel's Farm. The 2nd Grenadier Guards' left cleared Signal Farm and captured a battalion commander in Ruisseau Farm before reaching the stream. Lieutenant Colonel de Crespigny reported he had outposts on the far bank, facing Wijdendrift, but his right company was delayed due to problems on 38th Division's front.

<u>38th Division, Pilckem</u>

Major General Blackadder's message to the Welshmen under his command was *'Gwell angau na chywilydd'* – 'Better death than shame'. There would be plenty of opportunities to exhibit bravery because there were around 280 concrete shelters in the division's sector. Again, hundreds of thermite shells and blazing oil drums exploded among Cable, Cactus and Caddle Trenches at zero hour.

In 113 Brigade's sector, the 16th Welsh Fusiliers encountered resistance in Cancer Avenue before coming under enfilade fire from Telegraph House, as they moved past the north side of Pilckem. The 13th Welsh Fusiliers' first tough battle was for Caesar's Support but they then had to fight their way through the pillboxes protecting the village. Corporal James Davies advanced ahead of the barrage to silence one pillbox but he was mortally wounded leading bombers against Corner House, on the west side of the village; he was posthumously awarded the Victoria Cross.

The 15th Welsh Fusiliers suffered from the machine-gun fire coming from the houses and bunkers along the railway embankment before they cleared Battery Copse. Lieutenant Colonel Hodson's men were then thrown into confusion as British smoke shells exploded amongst them, causing them to lose the shrapnel barrage. A wounded Hodson reported he had dug in around Iron Cross redoubt but he told Brigadier General Price-Davies it was too dangerous to go any further forward.

On 114 Brigade's front, the 13th Welsh and 10th Welsh encountered resistance in Caesar's Support before crossing the Pilckem–Ypres road. They then suffered heavy casualties clearing the many fortified craters around Marousin House. The 14th Welsh then continued the advance east of Pilckem, tackling Stray Farm before having a tough fight around Iron Cross junction. On the right, the 15th Welsh came under fire from Rudolphe Farm in 51st Division's sector, so some men diverted to silence the garrison. The barrage had been lost but Brigadier General Mardon was pleased to hear his men had kept going to the objective in short rushes.

Brigadier General Gwyn-Thomas's 115 Brigade carried out the final advance to the Steenbeek. The 17th Welsh Fusiliers faced a tough fight to clear bunkers near Iron Cross crossroads but the men on the flanks kept going to the stream. Captain Jenkins and Lieutenant Sayce were hit as 11th SWB cleared The Ings and Varna Farm. Sergeant Ivor Rees silenced one machine-gun team and then charged a pillbox, killing five and taking another thirty prisoner; he would be awarded the Victoria Cross. Second Lieutenant Vizer took fifty prisoners at Chien Farm and then captured the Au Bon Gîte pillboxes on the far bank. The 38th Division had advanced over two miles and taken 700 prisoners, over half from the Guards Fusilier Regiment known as the Cockchafers.

XVIII Corps, 31 July

Lieutenant General Ivor Maxse's men faced a 2-mile advance across the Pilckem ridge to the Steenbeek stream. Eight tanks and a supply tank were allocated to both 51st and 39th Divisions while another five would support the advance between Langemarck and St Julien.

The Germans took a prisoner just before the attack and the 'unmitigated blackguard' gave away information on the attack. As luck would have it, the information meant the Germans were in the middle of a large-scale relief when the attack was launched and many were sheltering in shell holes when the barrage of burning oil and thermite shells lit up the sky.

51st Highland Division, Pilckem Ridge and Kitchener's Wood

Major General Montague Harper's men advanced from Cake Trench, Calabash Trench and Caledonia Trench. The German trenches had been nearly obliterated but there were plenty of snipers and machine-gun teams to deal with. The Scots silenced them, 'not by wild frontal, expensive charges, but by the skilful use of ground and their weapons, in accordance with their training'.

Lieutenant Colonel Hyslop had to take command of 153 Brigade after the death of Brigadier General Gordon. Lieutenant Colonel Sutherland's 7th Black Watch advanced from Five Chemins Estaminet and swept across the German trenches with 'unco precision' until they reached Cane Trench. The 7th Gordons captured Hindenburg Farm and then took twenty prisoners at Gournier Farm.

Lieutenant Colonel Booth's 6th Black Watch helped the 1/5th Gordons clear a strongpoint and take one hundred prisoners. Captain Menzies was killed clearing Cane Wood so Captain Lindsay led the advance beyond Rudolphe Farm and Kleist Farm to Varna Farm. The Black Watch then experienced 'one of the most exciting moments of their lives. Stumbling through the mud, falling, rising and pressing on, while the enemy, barely 100 yards away, stood up and took deliberate aim.' Second Lieutenant Drummond used a bridge to cross the Steenbeek but his men had to withdraw after fighting off three counter-attacks.

The Gordons had a lot of machine-gun emplacements to clear around Kleist Farm and François Farm. Second Lieutenant Maitland dealt with one by shooting two of the crew and stunning the third man with his rifle. Lieutenant Rutherland gathered all the men he could find and they engaged

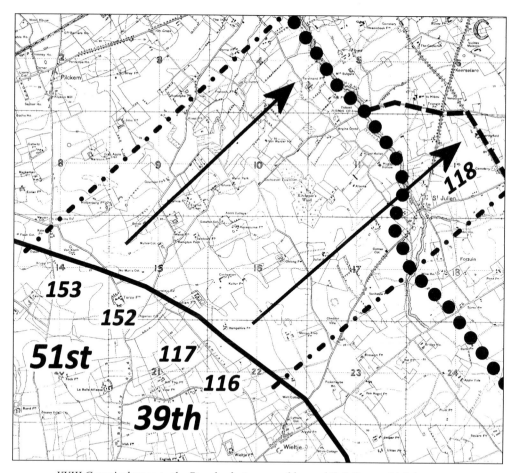

XVIII Corps' advance to the Steenbeek stream and beyond St Julien on 31 July.

a group of Germans on the right flank where they took one hundred prisoners and found many dead.

In 152 Brigade's sector, the 1/8th Argylls captured Turco Farm and then cleared a series of farms named after race courses (Kempton, Sandown, Ascot and Racecourse) with the help of a tank. They also faced a tough fight for Cane Wood. Another tank silenced the machine guns in Ferdinand Farm so the 1/5th Seaforths could occupy it.

The support battalions then headed for the Steenbeek while the artillery fired smoke shells to cover their advance. Lieutenant Colonel McDonald's 1/6th Seaforths had a hard time clearing MacDonald's Wood until some of the 1/6th Gordons outflanked the position. Sergeant Alexander 'Sandy' Edwards took control when his officer was killed and a barrage of rifle grenades and tank shells convinced the seventy men in McDonald's Farm to surrender.

The Seaforths bombed along Canister Trench while Edwards led his men towards MacDonald's Wood and cleared a pillbox. He was wounded by a sniper but later said, 'we could be doing without him and with a bit of luck, I attended to him. He is quiet enough now.' Edwards then led his men to the Steenbeek between Ferdinand Farm and Reid Farm.

General Maxse sent a squadron of the corps cavalry forward to investigate the situation beyond the stream. The King Edward's Horse came under fire as soon as they came close, so they had to dismount their horses and dig in. Sergeant Edwards rescued the troopers' commander, Major Swan, when he was injured checking the front line. Edwards' final deed was to lead a charge across a Steenbeek bridge. Brigadier General Burn later ordered him to withdraw behind the flooded stream because 39th Division was withdrawing from St Julien. Sanders would be awarded the Victoria Cross for his exploits.

The 1/6th Gordons were under fire from Maison du Rasta and Maison Bulgare, across the Steenbeek, so Private George McIntosh ran across a bridge and threw a grenade into a pillbox making the survivors flee. He brought back two light machine guns saying, 'somebody had to gae forrit!' McIntosh was awarded the Victoria Cross.

Eight tanks had ditched en route leaving two to prowl along the Green Line for two hours but there was no danger from the German infantry, the danger came from overhead. Planes swooped low, marking the Scots line, so they dug new slit trenches in front or behind the line and watched as the shells hit their original position. Altogether, 51st Division had taken nearly 650 prisoners, two field guns and nearly thirty machine guns.

39th Division, Regina Cross and St Julien

The 17th KRRC and 16th Sherwood Foresters found that most Germans had elected to stay in their dugouts once the barrage had passed over as they advanced towards Kitchener's Wood. The 16th Rifle Brigade killed or captured around forty men in the Regina Cross pillboxes before crossing the Steenbeek stream. Meanwhile the 17th Sherwood Foresters were pinned down in front of the Alberta pillboxes until two tanks crushed the wire and supressed the garrison. Brigadier Generals Armytage and Hornby were both able to report that 117 and 116 Brigades had reached their objectives.

The 12th and 11th Sussex only encountered light resistance around Mousetrap Farm and they kept pushing towards the Steenbeek. Two tanks drove through St Julien, silencing a gun battery, while the 13th Sussex found over 200 men cowering in the cellars. Nineteen-year-old Second Lieutenant Denis Hewitt had been badly burnt when a shell splinter ignited the flares in his backpack. Even so, he led his company of the 14th Hampshires to the Steenbeek on the division's right flank. Hewitt was killed while his men dug in on the far bank; he was posthumously awarded a Victoria Cross.

XIX Corps

All of III Brigade's tanks lined up XIX Corps as they deployed between Wieltje and the Roulers railway. The dark morning sky lit up at zero hour as hundreds of thermite bombs and barrels of burning oil exploded across the German trenches.

55th Division, North-East of Wieltje

The 1/5th King's Own and 1/5th Loyals of 166 Brigade found little to stop them around Pickelhaube House and Von Hügel Farm as they advanced astride the 's Gravenstafel road. All reports indicated that 'the resistance of the German infantry was quickly overcome and progress made on the greater part of the front of the main attack.' The 1/10th King's and 1/5th South Lancashires continued the advance across the Steenbeek and they cleared Border house and Spree Farm beyond the stream.

The 1/5th Loyals met little resistance advancing past Jasper Farm and Uhlan Farm, east of Wieltje, but the 1/10th King's came under fire from Capricorn Trench along the Steenbeek. The 1/6th and 1/5th King's also moved fast, surrounding Plum Farm and capturing 180 prisoners between them. Lieutenant Colonel Drew's 1/9th King's continued the advance and while Captain Richards and Roberts reached the Steenbeek, they only had a few dozen men between them; a tank helped clear the Bank Farm area for Captain Roberts. Second Lieutenant Elderd captured forty men around Pommern Redoubt, on the Hanebeek stream, with only six men of the 1/7th King's. Second Lieutenant Ellam took another fifty prisoners nearby while other men of the King's captured 130 prisoners in Square Farm's huge cellar. Unfortunately the farm was in 15th Division's sector and the prisoners were claimed by the Scots. Lieutenant Colonel Potter was able to report that Captain Heaton completed the consolidation of 165 Brigade's position with the help of a tank. Second Lieutenant Leach then occupied Hill 35, capturing a field gun en route.

Brigadier General Stockwell's 164 Brigade took over the next stage of the advance and two tanks helped Captains Mordecai and Bodington of the 2/5th Lancashire Fusiliers take Wine House and Spree Farm. Captain Briggs and Second Lieutenant Dickinson then brought the number of batteries of field guns captured to five as they closed in on Winnipeg with the 1/4th Loyals. Meanwhile, the 1/8th King's and 1/4th King's Own had cleared Somme Farm to reach the Langemarck–Zonnebeke road at Kanas Cross.

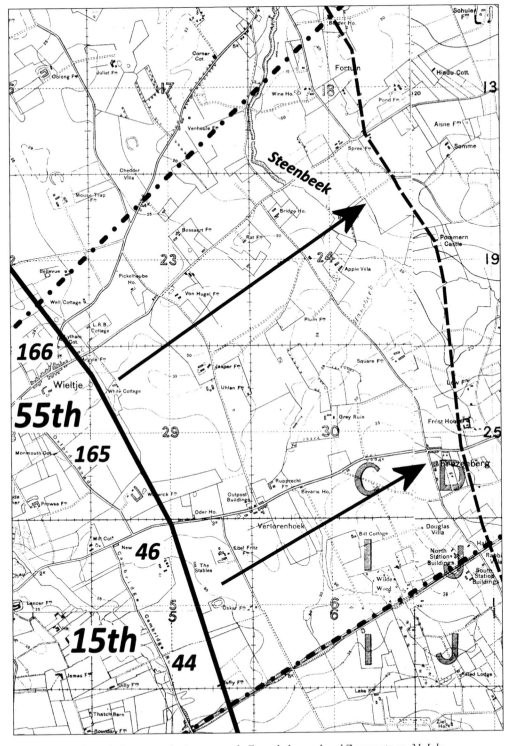

XIX Corps' advance to the Langemarck–Zonnebeke road and Zevencote on 31 July.

One officer even took a patrol half a mile across London Ridge to Aviatik Farm, finding few Germans.

15th Division, Verlorenhoek

The 10/11th HLI advanced through Verlorenhoek on the left but Lieutenant Colonel Dennis's 7/8th KOSBs veered south in the dark. Second Lieutenants Causley and Connachie were killed attacking Frezenberg Redoubt but Second Lieutenant Houston captured it with help from the 9th Black Watch. The Scots then came under fire as they crossed the crest of the ridge but 'the enemy's morale dropped to zero' when the tanks appeared. Over 150 prisoners were taken in a short time but the barrage had been lost. Second Lieutenant M'Kee led the survivors of the KOSBs from shell hole to shell hole and they eventually reached Frost House. The 10th Scottish Rifles were kept busy mopping up around places such as Eitel Fritz Farm, Rupprecht Farm and Bavaria House. Lieutenant Colonel Buchanan was able to report that 12th Highland Light Infantry was helping 46 Brigade consolidate the objective.

On 44 Brigade's front, the 9th Black Watch cleared Verlorenhoek but Captain Grant was hit during the attack on Bill Cottage, en route to Frezenberg. Lieutenant Colonel Innes's men advanced by section rushes to the trench covering Frezenberg Redoubt and then dug in beyond the village while a tank helped the moppers up take eighty prisoners. The 7th Camerons then waded across the Steenbeek and bypassed Pommern Castle before climbing the rise called Hill 35. Meanwhile the 8th Seaforths tackled Beck House and Borry Farm before closing in on Bremen Redoubt. Brigadier General Marshall was pleased to report that his men had taken their objectives and they were in touch with the troops on their flanks.

II Corps

Lieutenant General Sir Claud Jacob had responsibility for the 2-mile-wide sector between the Ypres–Roulers railway and Klein Zillebeke. His men had to capture three fortified lines on Fifth Army's flank. But they faced the tough task of clearing a 1-mile-deep belt of woods on the Gheluvelt plateau, starting with the outpost line which ran through Château Wood, Sanctuary Wood and Shrewsbury Wood. After six and a half hours they were expected to have cleared the Nonne Bosschen, Glencourse Wood and Dumbarton Woods. They then had to cross the Hanebeek and Bassevillebeek streams.

The Germans had defence zones tying together the three defensive lines and they also had plenty of artillery east of the plateau. The Tank Corps' II

Brigade had been given to II Corps but the tanks would not be able to get through the woods, so most would be restricted to the Menin road.

<u>8th Division, Hooge and Westhoek</u>
Major General William Heneker's men found most of the Germans 'too dazed to put up a fight', but they still came under a lot of sniper fire from the woods. Eight tanks crawled behind the infantry as they headed towards the thermite shells exploding along the banks of Bellewaarde Lake.

On 23 Brigade's front, Lieutenant Colonel Sutherland was killed as the 2nd Devons advanced from Railway Wood across Idea Trench and Iguana Lane. Lieutenant Colonel Jack was hit as the 2nd West Yorkshires went over the top, so Major McLaren led the advance beyond Identity Trench and along the north side of Bellewaarde Lake to Jacob Trench.

On 24 Brigade's front, Lieutenant Colonel Buckle's 2nd Northants crossed Ignis Trench and captured sixty prisoners along the banks of the lake. They then crossed the ravine which drained the lake in Château Wood and were seen 'ploughing through the mud' towards the crest of the ridge. Captain Thomas Colyer-Fergusson rushed Jacob Trench before stopping a counter-attack. He silenced a machine-gun team with the help of Sergeant Boulding and Private Ellis and then used the weapon against a second counter-attack. The three men captured another machine gun but Colyer-Fergusson was killed shortly afterwards; he was posthumously awarded the Victoria Cross.

The 1st Worcesters crossed Ignorance Trench before taking forty prisoners in the Hooge tunnel, which ran under the Menin road. Lieutenant Colonel Davidge's men lost the barrage clearing Château Wood and then faced a tough fight for James Trench until Second Lieutenant Frost of the Northants shot fifteen and dropped a grenade into a dugout which turned out to be a bomb store. The resulting explosion made the rest of the Germans surrender or flee, allowing the Worcesters to secure Jacob Trench. Brigadier Generals Grogan and Cobham were pleased to hear the Bellewaarde ridge had been taken and the Germans were falling back as the support battalions waited for the creeping barrage to move towards Westhoek ridge.

Lieutenant Colonel Hall's 2nd Middlesex and Lieutenant Colonel Stirling's 2nd Scottish Rifles advanced under fire from Kit and Kat but there was no one holding Jaffa Trench, so they could surround and capture the houses. Lieutenant Colonel Sherbrooke's 1st Sherwoods and Lieutenant Colonel Sharland's 2nd East Lancashire advanced to Jabber Trench, under fire from Surbiton and Clapham Junction to their right, where 30th Division had been held up. The objective was on the forward slope of Westhoek ridge and under machine-gun fire from across the Hanebeek valley to their front and from Glencourse Wood to their right. The Middlesex held on next to

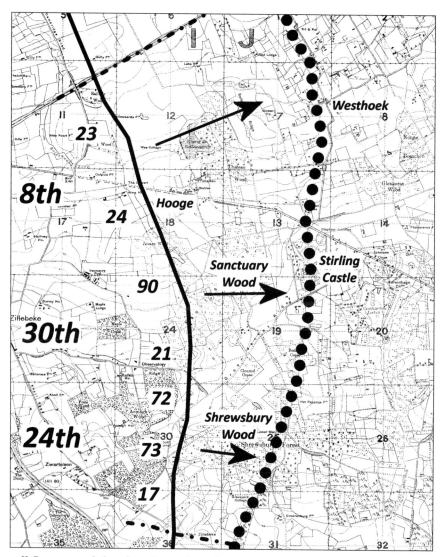

II Corps struggled to clear the woods on the Gheluvelt plateau on 31 July.

the railway but the rest withdrew behind Westhoek ridge, while the 1st Worcesters helped the East Lancashires form a defensive flank facing Glencourse Wood.

30th Division, Sanctuary Wood

Major General Weir Williams's division had been engaged twice during the battle of Arras in April and it was still under-strength. GHQ had wanted to deploy a fresh division in II Corps' centre but there had been insufficient time to train enough replacements. All General Jacob could do was to attach one of 18th Division's brigades to make the final advance towards Gheluvelt. To make matters worse, the tanks could not get through the mass of tree stumps that had once been Sanctuary Wood, while a request to slow the creeping barrage down was denied because it was too late to change the artillery plan.

In 90 Brigade's sector, the 16th and 18th Manchesters crossed the Jackdaw trenches in the north half of the wood. However the 2nd Scots Fusiliers veered across the Menin road and attacked Château Wood while the 17th Manchesters suffered casualties crossing the road at Clapham Junction. So only a few of Brigadier General Lloyd's men had reached the crossroads south of Westhoek, while none had entered Glencourse Wood.

Brigadier General Goodman's men faced a zig-zag line of trenches in 21 Brigade's sector. A German bombardment around zero hour delayed the deployment and the creeping barrage had moved forward before the men advanced through Sanctuary Wood. The 2nd Wiltshires struggled to clear the Jam trench system but pushed on nevertheless, taking forty prisoners en route to Stirling Castle. Captain Lund and Lieutenant Newbury worked their way through the Jeffrey trenches but the rest of the 2nd Green Howards came under heavy fire from Bodmin Copse when they left the wood. Captain Bunting and Lieutenant Watt's men were then pushed to the left as troops from 24th Division drifted across their front.

The German SOS bombardment hit the 18th King's and the 19th Manchesters and the divisional plan quickly unravelled as they became disorganised passing through Shrewsbury Wood. Captain Heywood and Second Lieutenants Graham and Futvoye fought for Jar Row south of Stirling Castle with men from four battalions. The King's left-hand companies drifted left into 90 Brigade's area but the right-hand companies went past Stirling Castle. Meanwhile, machine-gun fire had stopped the 19th Manchesters reaching Dumbarton Wood.

The infantry were disorganised and delayed. The telephone lines had been cut, the power buzzers did not work in the damp ground, the wirelesses had been damaged and bad light stopped visual signalling. So it was down to runners and pigeons to get messages back to General Goodman, and the barrage had moved forward before he found out what was happening.

The 6th Berkshires formed up in Jargon Trench and Lieutenant Colonel Clay's men then 'went gaily towards Glencourse Wood shouting and cheering, preceded by an officer guide who carried a yellow flag.' They came under fire from Surbiton Villas and Clapham Junction but the Lewis gunners gave covering fire as they dodged between shell holes. Captain Hudson was killed capturing a field gun while Captain Rochfort could not hold the south-west corner of the wood, so their men chose to hold Jargon Switch instead.

Fire from the Menin road and Stirling Castle killed Lieutenants Chibnall and Wheeler as the 8th Suffolks left Sanctuary Wood. Private Read led a charge which silenced the machine guns south of Surbiton Villas and Lieutenant Colonel Hill's men then used a captured field gun to supress nearby strongpoints. A British bombardment eventually forced the Suffolks to withdraw but the front was secured when 8th Norfolks and 10th Essex arrived.

General Williams contacted Major General Lee of 18th Division to make him hold back his brigade but it was some time before the four battalions moving through Sanctuary Wood could be contacted. Officer patrols went forward to find out what was happening but reports were confusing, so the 20th King's dug in south of Clapham Junction under fire from Glencourse Wood. The 17th King's immediately realised there were only German troops in front when they came under fire from Stirling Castle. The 2nd Lincolns and the 8th Norfolks reinforced the thin line astride the Menin road but it was several hours before Brigadier Generals Norman and Higginson realised what had happened.

The troops had formed a line in front of a 'tank graveyard', the result of II Tank Brigade's disastrous morning. Only four of the sixteen tanks in the first wave reached the front line. The artillery had failed to knock out an anti-tank gun hidden in a pillbox north-east of Clapham Junction and it hit them all as they crawled up the Menin road. Only fourteen of the twenty-four tanks deployed in the second wave went into action against Glencourse Wood, Inverness Copse and Dumbarton Wood. They too came under fire from the anti-tank gun and the few which left the road were bogged down. Only one survived the carnage. Only one out of eight from the third wave made it into action.

Fifty-two tanks had set off that morning; nineteen had been knocked out and twenty-two had ditched or had broken down. Only eleven returned to the deployment area. The only consolation was that the men in front of Glencourse Wood were able to strip the Lewis guns and ammunition from the hulks and use them to defend their position.

Captain Patten of the Norfolks was left in control of the mixed group of men facing Glencourse Wood. Low-flying German planes strafed the front line but the men had to conserve their ammunition, so they would be ready to deal with counter-attacks. All except for one man of the Berkshires. He fired a rifle grenade at one plane and, while he missed, the pilot thought better of flying over again.

Wounded men from eight battalions had gathered in the Clapham Junction dugouts on the Menin road by late morning. The 'stooping grey haired, bespectacled' figure of the 6th Berkshires' medical officer dealt with them all. Captain Harold Ackroyd had been a doctor at the Cambridge Research Laboratory but was now covered in mud and blood as he 'worked as stoically as if he was in the quiet of an operating theatre. Complete absorption in his work was probably his secret.' There would be twenty-three separate recommendations for his Victoria Cross. Unfortunately he was killed by a sniper eleven days later, without knowing they had been accepted.

Another medical officer, Lieutenant Colonel Pritchard Taylor, wanted forty prisoners to help 54th Ambulance carry 18th Division's wounded along the Menin road. He was warned they would escape overnight, so he told the German sergeant major he would shoot one man for every one that escaped and he would begin with him. There were forty-four German stretcher bearers by the morning.

24th Division, Shrewsbury Wood
Major General Louis Bols' men had to clear the huge Shrewsbury Forest, an irregular-shaped wood which was over one mile deep in places. On the left, 72 Brigade were pushed north as the troops on their right moved around Lower Star Post. The 1st North Staffords and 8th Queen's cleared Bodmin Copse in 30th Division's sector while the 9th East Surreys and 8th Queen's Own continued to the Bassevilleebeek stream. Machine-gun fire from Dumbarton Wood and Tower Hamlets forced them to withdraw from their isolated position and Brigadier General Sweny reported his men could not go beyond Bodmin Copse.

The 1st Royal Fusiliers were also pushed north because 73 Brigade was crossing their front, again to avoid Lower Star Post. Captains Cox and Doudney led them to the east side of Shrewsbury Wood while Lieutenant Flack rushed a strongpoint at Jeffrey Avenue after knocking out a machine gun with a rifle grenade. Some of the Fusiliers became involved with 73 Brigade's attack against Lower Star Post. The 12th Royal Fusiliers came under fire from Tower Hamlets and they fell back into Shrewsbury Forest where Lieutenant Colonel Hope Johnstone and Captain Leeming were hit as their men dug in. Brigadier General Stone sent the 3rd Rifle Brigade forward to reinforce the line facing Lower Star Post.

Brigadier General Duggan's 73 Brigade had to go through the heart of the forest and the officers struggled to stop their men bunching up. Lower Star Point was a formidable strongpoint which covered a clearing and the 7th Northants tried to avoid it. Lieutenant Colonel Mobbs and Second Lieutenant Berridge were mortally wounded making one last attempt to take the strongpoint and their men fell back to Jordan Trench. The 2nd Leinsters lost the barrage in the trees and all their officers were hit as they also swerved to avoid Lower Star Post. They crossed Jehovah Trench and cleared Groenenburg Farm but had to fall back to Jeer Trench inside the wood because of the problem at Lower Star Post.

Second Army

Although Second Army had been sidelined, General Plumer's men still had a part to play. Half of its artillery was deployed around the Comines canal and the gunners fired at targets on the Gheluvelt plateau, on Fifth Army's right. Others focused on counter-battery work, diverting *Group Wytschaete*'s attention away from the battle in the north. The rest gave covering fire for a number of small-scale attacks east of the Messines ridge while the infantry pushing closer to the Warneton Line.

X Corps

41st Division, Comines Canal

The 11th Queen's and 10th Queen's Own advanced 500 yards east of Battle Wood on the north bank of the Comines Canal until they were stopped by a line of pillboxes. But the 23rd Middlesex were delayed by flooded ground between the railway and the canal. The 11th Queen's Own crossed Oblique Trench south of the canal and then helped the 18th KRRC clear Hollebeke. The 12th East Surreys captured Forret Farm on 122 Brigade's front during the night.

IX Corps

19th Division, East of Oosttaverne

The 7th Loyals and 7th East Lancashires advanced the short distance to their objective, south of Hollebeke. The 7th King's Own captured Junction Buildings and Spider Farm, east of Oosttaverne, but they lost Tiny Farm on their right flank during a counter-attack.

37th Division, East of Wambeke

The 4th Middlesex and a company of the 8th Lincolns captured July Farm on the divisional boundary at zero hour. Four hours later, the Lincolns and the 8th Somersets captured Beek Farm, east of Wambeek.

II Anzac Corps

3rd Australian Division, East of Gapaard

The 43rd Australian Battalion captured the Windmill, near Kiwi Farm, while 42nd Australian Battalion advanced on its left. Fighting for the Windmill continued into the night.

New Zealand Division, La Basse Ville

The 1st Auckland Battalion raided the German line north of La Basse Ville. Lance Corporal Leslie Andrew silenced three machine-gun posts facing the 2nd Wellington Regiment at La Basse Ville; he was awarded the Victoria Cross.

Chapter 8

A Very Weak and Disorganised State

The Advance Continues

The offensive had started well. Three of Fifth Army's corps had reached their second objective and their reserve brigades were heading towards the third objective. They had advanced one mile, clearing the lightly held outpost zone, except on the right, where II Corps was struggling in Sanctuary Wood and Shrewsbury Forest, south of the Menin road. The capture of the Pilckem ridge and the west edge of the Gheluvelt plateau meant the British ground observers could see the German Third Line, the Langemarck–Gheluvelt Line. Meanwhile, German observers could no longer see the British rear areas in the salient. For the first time in over two and a half years, traffic could move safely during daylight hours.

GHQ's original plan had been to stop and consolidate the second objective for several days. The assault troops could then be withdrawn and rested while the artillery was moved forward. Haig had told the War Cabinet he was planning a step-by-step approach and they authorised his plan based on this promise. GHQ's Operation Branch advised a measured advance and while Gough agreed, Plumer advocated a deep advance, like that the First and Third Armies had made at Arras on 9 April. Haig agreed with Plumer because he was hoping a deeper advance would trigger a general withdrawal.

So Fifth Army's plan was to continue the advance after only a few hours, not two days. Both XIV and XVIII Corps would advance towards the Steenbeek around Langemarck four hours and twenty minutes after zero hour. XIX Corps would advance towards 's Gravenstafel two hours later. II Corps was supposed to advance at the same time as XIX Corps but it was in trouble on the Gheluvelt plateau. Twenty-four tanks had been allocated to the advance but only nine were able to cross the Steenbeek and the infantry had moved on before they were ready. A few would join them later on. The pause also gave the field artillery time to redeploy behind the

Pilckem and Frezenberg ridges. However the gun teams only moved forward at the trot having been given strict orders not to indulge in 'spectacular galloping'.

So the infantry and artillery were moving forward; but the plan to keep advancing had a problem: the British would become weaker the further they went while the Germans would become stronger.

XIX Corps
39th Division, North-East of St Julien and Winnipeg
Brigadier General Bellingham's 118 Brigade deployed beyond the Steenbeek and cleared St Julien before forming a protective flank astride the Poelcappelle road. The 4/5th Black Watch formed a flank between 51st Division, the stream and Triangle Farm while the 1/1st Hertfords reached Springfield Farm. Lieutenant Colonel Stanway's 1/6th Cheshires reached Winnipeg on the Langemarck–Zonnebeke road where they were joined by a tank. Enfilade fire virtually annihilated the Herts while no one from 55th Division had moved up on the brigade's right flank. The Black Watch and Cheshires were forced to withdraw and the Black Watch lost a lot of men crossing the Steenbeek near Regina Cross while the Cheshires had to abandon St Julien because it was a shell trap.

XIX Corps
55th Division, Winnipeg and Kansas Cross
The 164 Brigade had to advance to the Langemarck–Gheluvelt Line but it had to clear the pillboxes and machine-gun posts on the east of the Steenbeek first because the artillery had failed to silence them. The 2/5th Lancashire Fusiliers were disorganised moving up when a machine gun opened fire from a trench which was supposed to have been mopped up. Twenty-seven-year-old Lieutenant Colonel Bertram Best-Dunkley rallied his men and they captured the trench. They then cleared Spree House, south of St Julien, with the help of two tanks.

Captains Mordecai and Bodington led the 2/5th Lancashire Fusiliers as they struggled to clear Wine House and Pond Farm and they lost the barrage. Two tanks accompanied the advance to the Langemarck–Zonnebeke road but they had suffered many casualties. Best-Dunkley organised the survivors in an abandoned trench between Winnipeg, Schuler Farm and Kansas Cross. Captain Bodington advanced another 600 yards forward to capture Wurst Farm on London Ridge, while another platoon went further, capturing fifty prisoners at Aviatik Farm.

A few German batteries could not withdraw so they continued firing from their concrete emplacements until they were overrun. The 1/4th Loyals

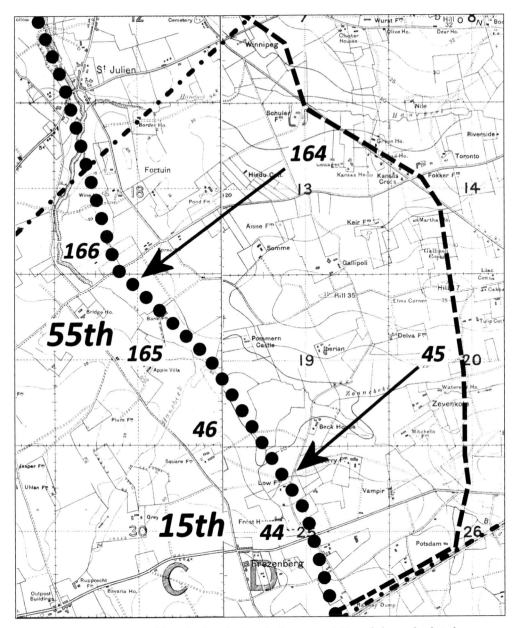

XIX Corps advanced from the Steenbeek to the Langemarck-Zonnebeke road only to be driven back to the Steenbeek stream and the Frezenberg ridge.

outflanked one battery so they could clear Somme Farm and they then crossed Hill 35. They had to do the same to capture Gallipoli Farm but they were 'in fine fettle' and advancing with 'clockwork motion'. One tank was knocked out but the tank commander led another one on foot to Kansas Cross under point-blank fire from an artillery battery.

Lieutenant Colonel Heath's 1/8th King's were enthusiastic on the left – 'everyone was in good heart and the men went over singing'. They cleared Border House, Pond Farm and Hindu Cott, with the help of a tank. There was then a hard fight for Schuler Farm and Keir Farm along the Langemarck–Zonnebeke road.

The 1/4th King's Own had become involved in the Loyals' advance and Corporal T. Mayson crept from shell hole to shell hole when his platoon came under machine-gun fire. He threw a bomb at the team and finished the survivors off with his bayonet. Mayson then helped round up 150 prisoners, who were 'poor specimens and very scared', around Kansas Cross; he was awarded the Victoria Cross.

15th Division, Hill 37 and Zevencote

Brigadier General Allgood's 45 Brigade deployed on the Frezenberg ridge before advancing towards the Langemarck–Gheluvelt Line around Zevencote. The 6th Camerons crossed the Steenbeek stream and advanced onto Hill 37, taking 150 prisoners. They established outposts at Otto and Dochy Farms, beyond the along the Langemarck–Zonnebeke road; a total advance of 2½ miles since zero hour. The 6/7th Royal Scots Fusiliers' left also crossed the stream and cleared Bremen Redoubt but the right was in trouble. It was pinned down around Potsdam Keep because 8th Division was struggling south of the Roulers railway.

General Allgood deployed the 11th Argylls and 13th Royal Scots along his open flank east of Frezenberg and they faced Beck House, Borry Farm and Potsdam. German planes flew low overhead directing artillery fire as they dug in and it was 'worse than any of us remember having received on the Somme'. One shell knocked out the Royal Scots headquarters, hitting all the staff.

II Corps

8th Division, Westhoek Ridge

The 25 Brigade suffered a lot of casualties while assembling on the jumping off line but observers saw Brigadier General Coffin's men 'going strong' over the Westhoek ridge. Unfortunately, the barrage had fallen beyond the German machine-gun teams in the Hanebeek valley and Lieutenant Colonel Brand's 2nd Rifle Brigade lost heavily as they advanced past Hanebeek Wood. Even more were hit as they approached the pillboxes on Anzac Spur.

Brigadier General Coffin deployed Lieutenant Colonel Haig's 2nd Berkshires to cover his exposed right flank but they had to endure enfilade fire from Glencourse Wood and Nonne Bosschen where 30th Division should have been. Lieutenant Colonel Reid was killed leading the 1st Irish

Rifles while Lieutenant Colonel Bastard of the 2nd Lincolns was wounded. Some men crossed the Hanebeek stream and climbed Anzac House spur but they soon had to fall back because the barrage had moved on. The 2nd Berkshires soon followed and General Coffin went from shell hole to shell hole to reassure his men as they consolidated Jabber Trench. His 'gallant conduct under the heaviest fire' contributed to his Victoria Cross award.

All the tanks had become bogged down so the crews handed over their weapons to the infantry. They reinforced the line of Lewis gun teams along the top of the Westhoek ridge and helped to stop three counter-attacks across the Hanebeek valley in the afternoon.

Counter-Attacks

By noon, XIV Corps was safely dug in behind the Steenbeek facing Langemarck. XVIII Corps' left was also established along the stream but its right was across the Langemarck–Zonnebeke road. Lieutenant General Watts' original plan was to end the protective barrage just after midday, so patrols could move forward accompanied by the corps cavalry, the North Irish Horse. If possible, the 55th Division would then to move onto the Wallemolen spur while 15th Division climbed Passchendaele ridge.

But General Gough countermanded the advance instruction because Fifth Army's situation was becoming precarious. The assault divisions had used up all their reserves while the corps reserves were still some distance away. Both XIX and XVIII Corps were weak after the morning's fighting and there was only a thin line of troops stretched out along the Langemarck–Zonnebeke road. Meanwhile, II Corps' failure to clear the Gheluvelt plateau meant Fifth Army's right flank was in danger.

Many of the tanks had ditched or had been knocked out while those which could still move had returned to rearm and refuel. The barrage had stopped at midday and the gunners were awaiting further instructions which was proving to be a problem because the weather had interfered with the air programme. The corps patrols had been busy reporting on progress while the army squadrons had concentrated on reporting stationary targets behind the German lines. But no planes had been detailed to look out for counter-attack troops and there were plenty.

A forward artillery observer working with the 15th Scottish Division was the first to spot 'a vast amount of German infantry going along the Passchendaele Ridge'. He was near Bremen Redoubt and they were only a mile away, heading towards Zonnebeke. The time was around 11.30 am and the front-line troops saw waves of men advancing towards the Langemarck–Zonnebeke road ninety minutes later. All the signalling cables had been cut and it took a runner two hours to get back to the signal centres; if he made it at all. The counter-attack was in full swing by the time Generals Jeudwine and Thuillier heard the news.

The rear observers could not see any targets through the heavy rain while the forward observers were too far forward to report the enemy positions. The divisional headquarters were not sure where their forward units were and the contact patrols had been forced to return to their airfields. The German observers meanwhile had watched Fifth Army approaching and their artillery fire was accurate. After a short bombardment, waves of infantry were seen heading for Winnipeg, Kansas Cross and Bremen Redoubt. Two *Eingrief* Divisions were about to fall on XIX Corps' weakened divisions.

XIV Corps
There were no attacks against the Guards Division, on Fifth Army's left. The Germans struggled to assemble to the north of Langemarck and the British artillery did not see the SOS flares when the counter-attack started. The 11th SWBs' machine guns in Au Bon Gîte stopped the advancing waves until 38th Division was forced to abandon all its bridgeheads across the flooding stream.

XVIII Corps
51st Division, Steenbeek Stream
Artillery and machine-gun fire broke up the attack against the Scots dug in along the Steenbeek. The 6th Seaforths and 8th Argylls countered by seizing the crossing at Ferdinand Farm and they captured Maison du Rasta and Maison Bulgare. The 6th Black Watch had to withdraw across the Steenbeek after the Welshmen abandoned their bridgeheads to the left. The Seaforths and Argylls followed when the heavy rain turned the stream into a torrent.

39th Division, The Retreat to St Julien
Major General Feetham's men were lined out along the Langemarck–Zonnebeke road between Springfield and Winnipeg but they had problems. The Hertfords were being forced back from Triangle Farm and Springfield after losing all their officers, compromising the 4/5th Black Watch's position next to the Steenbeek. The retirement allowed the Germans to get behind the 1/6th Cheshires' flank, inspiring others to attack the front. Captain Lee was killed leading the Cheshires' defence while a counter-attack by the Cambridgeshire Regiment allowed Captain Naden to arrange a fighting withdrawal to St Julien. The village turned out to be a shell trap so the mixture of Black Watch, Cheshires, Hertfords and Cambridge men fell back behind the flooded Steenbeek.

XIX Corps
55th Division, The Retreat to the Frezenberg Ridge
Brigadier General Stockwell's battalions were 'in a very weak and disorganised state' along the Langemarck–Zonnebeke road. They had done well but they had all suffered fifty per cent casualties and the survivors were low on ammunition. A few 2/5th Lancashire Fusiliers had reached Wurst Farm but 39th Division's withdrawal from Winnipeg had exposed 164 Brigade's flank. Brigadier General Stockwell planned to cover the gap but six waves of infantry came over the Zonnebeke spur just as the Lancashire men started to move.

Very rockets directed the German barrage while three aircraft strafed the withdrawing troops in an early example of combined air and ground combat. The planes 'will fly in front of the assaulting troops, they will stimulate the offensive spirit of our men by flying low and will weaken the enemy's power of resistance by dropping bombs and opening machine-gun fire.'

Chaos followed as groups of men tried to escape the onslaught. Jeudwine gave orders to form a new position which could be protected by a barrage but his chosen line had already fallen. Only thirty men of 164 Brigade's two left battalions made it back, the rest were killed or captured around Border House and Pond Farm. On the brigade's right, Captain Dodington escaped with fifty men after a desperate fight around Schuler Farm. Second Lieutenant Beesley used his Lewis guns to keep the Germans at bay until the two right battalions escaped across Hill 35. Lieutenant Colonel Best-Dunkley made the 2/5th Lancashire Fusiliers battalion headquarters staff and all the stragglers he could find form a line east of the Steenbeek. But he was mortally wounded and his adjutant Lieutenant Andrews was killed so their orderly room sergeant, Sergeant Haworth, organised the 120 survivors into a ragged line. They fought the Germans to a standstill because there was no escape; because the rainwaters had turned the stream into an impassable torrent.

General Jeudwine wrote to a dying Best-Dunkley, telling him that 31 July should be remembered 'with even more reverence than Minden Day. It was no garden of roses that you fought it.' He was referring to Minden Day which honoured the Battle of Minden during the Seven Years War, on 1 August 1759. Best-Dunkley was posthumously awarded the Victoria Cross.

15th Division, Frezenberg Ridge
Major General Thuillier cancelled any further advance when he heard about the delay at Potsdam House on his right flank. The problems on 8th Division's front endangered his right flank while 55th Division's retreat from Kansas Cross and Hill 35 exposed his left flank.

Lieutenant Colonel Hannay tried to reinforce the 6th Camerons and 6/7th Scots Fusiliers but the men at Otto and Dochy Farms were never heard of again. So Captain Craig and Second Lieutenant Henderson organised a line of stragglers along the Zonnebeke stream. Meanwhile Second Lieutenant Ogilvie had gathered some leaderless men of the 55th Division at Pommern Redoubt, securing the Scots left flank.

A wounded Captain Turner stopped the counter-attack so Captain Christie withdrew with the few Camerons and 11th Argylls he could find. An outpost at Iberian Farm kept the Germans at bay while they dug in along the Frezenberg ridge. Captain Christie withdrew 150 Scots Fusiliers into support and they cleaned their weapons as they waited. Artillery and machine-gun fire stopped the final attempt but the barrage continued throughout the night in case the Germans decided to attack again.

8th Division, Holding Westhoek

Lorries were seen delivering hundreds of troops to Zonnebeke and the first attack was made across the Hanebeek stream around 2 pm. The 2nd Rifle Brigade and 2nd Berkshires were driven back around Westhoek but Brigadier General Coffin saw to it that the 1st Irish Rifles and 2nd Lincolns retook the ground.

After the Battle

Heavy rain had started during the afternoon and it forced all wheeled transport onto the few roads, causing congestion. The downpour continued unabated and the blocked streams overflowed while the soil was churned into a thick, evil-smelling mud. The conditions made it difficult to rescue the wounded and many died awaiting evacuation.

Captain Noel Chavasse VC was the medical officer attached to the 1/10th King's. He spent all day searching for wounded, patching them up before carrying them to a collection point. He had his own wound bandaged up and then continued working into the night in the pouring rain. He was probably wounded again the following day, refusing to stop for rest or food. Early on 2 August Chavasse was mortally wounded when a shell hit his dugout and he died at Brandhoek casualty clearing station, west of Ypres. He was posthumously awarded a second Victoria Cross. His first had been awarded for the same type of brave work during the Somme campaign. He is the only man to have been awarded two Victoria Crosses for deeds both carried out in the First World War.

15th Division, Frezenberg, 1 August

The Germans wanted to drive Fifth Army's right flank off the Frezenberg

Ridge and recover the pillboxes of the Second Line. Artillery fire preceded the 3.30 pm attack while the infantry advanced behind smoke. The 13th Royal Scots held on around Square Farm, even after Captains Christie and Logan were hit, but the 12th Highland Light Infantry and the 8th Seaforths lost Beck House, Borry Farm and Vampir. Second Lieutenant Sandeman of the 6th Camerons held on but the Germans got behind the Royal Scots. Lieutenant Colonel Hannay resorted to calling down an SOS barrage on his position and his men held on until companies from the 6/7th Scots Fusiliers and the 11th Argylls reinforced the line around dusk.

XVIII Corps, 2 August
A prisoner warned a counter-attack was imminent early on the afternoon of 2 August. The order was issued to stand to, but it had been very difficult to clean weapons in the rain and mud. Troops were seen massing astride the Poelcappelle road but artillery fire stopped them reaching 39th Division's line along the Steenbeek. Lieutenant General Maxse instructed Major General Feetham to get his men into St Julien, where the ground was drier than it was around the Steenbeek. A second attack failed to drive the 1/7th King's from Pommern Redoubt, on 55th Division's front.

Summary and Plans
The attack on 31 July had many good points but it also had bad points. Fifth Army had advanced up to 4,000 yards in places but it was still short of the ambitious objective. The counter-attack had reduced the gains down to 2,500 yards on the left and centre, leaving Gough's troops in a difficult position along the Steenbeek. His right was embroiled in a tough fight for the woods on the Gheluvelt plateau.

Over 6,000 prisoners and 25 guns had been captured but Fifth Army had suffered 27,000 casualties and Second Army another 4,800. The attack had smashed the German divisions holding the front line but the nine British divisions had also suffered. One observer was shocked by the state of the men coming out of the line: 'Terrible indeed was the picture of a battalion coming back from battle. Wet through, cold, utterly worn out, and covered with mud from head to foot, it was impossible to keep any kind of formation, and in groups of twos and threes the men staggered along to their billets.'

The Tank Corps had endured a disastrous day because 42 of the 117 tanks which had gone into action had been destroyed, many of them by a single field gun on the Menin road. Another thirty-five had to be abandoned after becoming bogged down in the soft ground.

Haig met an optimistic Gough on the afternoon of 31 July. Early reports suggested the German Second Line had been broken through along a 7-mile front and troops were through the Third Line in places. The plan was to relieve the infantry while the artillery continued to hammer the German batteries with high-explosive and gas shells. They could then continue towards the Flanders I Line.

However, Fifth Army headquarters soon started to hear that counter-attacks had driven the left and centre back while the right was still in difficulties. Gough initially gave instructions to delay the attack to 2 August, to give his men time to reorganise. But when II Corps' true situation became known he changed his mind. Lieutenant General Jacob had to clear the German Second Line on the Gheluvelt plateau starting on 2 August. All four of Fifth Army's corps attacked the Third Line two days later.

GHQ initially supported Gough's plan but Brigadier General Davidson protested against making a hasty attack when his Operations Branch was given the details. They wanted to wait for several clear days so the artillery observers could capitalise on the recently captured observation points. They also wanted to give II Corps fresh divisions to put into the line because experience told them that tired troops usually failed.

Davidson's staff also thought it was wise to give Lieutenant General Jacob enough troops to clear all of the Gheluvelt plateau, which involved advancing another mile through a series of woods. The Germans believed the plateau was a key position as they lined up their artillery ready to support counter-attacks against II Corps.

Although Haig was confident, his staff were concerned about the outcome of the attack on 31 July and had held a meeting on 7 August to discuss the matter. It was clear that setting objectives to the artillery ranges was far too optimistic. They had to be chosen according to the infantry's ability to capture ground and then hold it against counter-attacks. The meeting was the foundation of the plan for the conduct of the later stages of the campaign. They would study how at conduct step-by-step attacks in quick succession. General Rawlinson explained how the BEF 'had never yet attempted to conduct a wearing-out battle with planned, logical methods but had always relied too much on its belief that a breakdown of the German army's morale was within sight.' He was no doubt referring to his experience on the Somme the previous year.

But the meeting was held too late to influence the 16 August attack and the weather meant it was another month until the ideas could be tested. Rawlinson was enthusiastic about the concept: 'We have never set ourselves to work to deliver a succession of carefully worked out hammer blows on the enemy at short intervals with the object of definitely beating him to his knees so that there is no question that his morale is finally broken.'

Chapter 9

Hard Going Through the Mud

Westhoek Ridge, 10 August

The heavy rain which had started late on 31 July continued for three days and nights, resulting in the soldiers calling it 'Haig's weather'. The network of ditches and streams had been damaged by the bombardments and they were soon overflowing with rainwater. The main problem was the Steenbeek, which ran along Fifth Army's front, but the rest of the battlefield was slowly turning into a bog which could only be crossed on the few roads and tracks. Unsettled weather followed, so the ground never had the chance to dry out.

Even Haig was concerned and on 4 August he wrote, 'as the rain still continues, I cannot yet say when it will be possible to continue the offensive.' Gough was against attacking in wet weather and urged the commander-in-chief to break off the offensive after consulting Plumer. Rawlinson doubted German morale would break soon but Haig was confident it might if they kept pushing.

Fifth Army's left was quiet because most of XIV and XVIII Corps' rear areas were hidden behind the Pilckem ridge. However German observers could still see XIX and II Corps' rear from the Westhoek ridge. While the German artillerymen knew where their targets were, the British gunners struggled to hit theirs because the rain interfered with aerial observation. They also suffered many casualties because their guns were obvious targets.

So General Gough instructed Lieutenant General Jacob to have his II Corps ready to seize the high ground astride the Menin road on 9 August; the whole of Fifth Army would attack four days later. A thunderstorm late on 8 August soaked the battlefield again, so II Corps' attack was postponed to 4.35 am on 10 August.

II Corps, 10 August

General Gough wanted 25th Division to capture the Westhoek ridge while 18th Division cleared the woods covering the Menin road, opening the way for the tanks.

25th Division, Westhoek Ridge

Major General Guy Bainbridge's men had to advance 500 yards around Westhoek. On the left, Second Lieutenant Grenier took most of the objective south of the Roulers railway 'by vigorous patrolling'. Lieutenant Colonel Martin's 11th Lancashire Fusiliers 'had won the battle the night before it happened' but Second Lieutenant Carruthers's men still faced a brutal battle around Kit and Kat. Sergeant Hall captured thirty-eight men but they killed the Lewis gun team covering them and ran. Hall's outraged men shot them all down.

Major Wienholt's 9th Loyals were pinned down and both Captain Green and Lieutenant Priestland were hit. Captains Loudon and Everett outflanked the offending pillbox and led their men towards the objective, where they then suffered many casualties from snipers hidden in Nonne Bosschen.

The 2nd Irish Rifles rushed two pillboxes in Westhoek hamlet but a third held out until an officer fired his pistol through the firing slit. Major Rose's men did not pause to take aim, they just kept walking as they fired from the hip. The objective was taken but it had cost the Irish Rifles dearly; 350 out of 485 men were casualties, the majority of them wounded. Around 150 prisoners had been taken while the rest had to run through the British barrage which bracketed the Hanebeek valley.

Captains Payne and Wilkinson were hit leading the 13th Cheshires' advance south of Westhoek and one large shell explosion hit all but fifteen men of one wave. Lieutenant Colonel Finch and Major Nares were both injured as the battalion dug in under enfilade fire after 18th Division was forced out of Glencourse Wood; these were just a few of nearly 400 casualties.

The four battalions of 74 Brigade had taken most of their objectives and the flooded Hanebeek persuaded the Germans not to counter-attack. However planes flew low over the Westhoek ridge, strafing Brigadier General Bethell's men.

18th Division, Glencourse Wood and Inverness Copse

The Germans had established a line of machine-gun posts covering the approaches to Glencourse Wood and Inverness Copse but many were silenced by the creeping barrage. The 7th Bedfords crossed the tank graveyard north of the Menin road and then 'leapt through gaps in the wire and rushed on cheering'. Captains Driver and Colley led their men past a line of ten pillboxes at the south-west corner of Glencourse Wood before 'they surged through the morass inside the wood, the trees of which had been rendered naked and mutilated by shell fire.' Unfortunately Lieutenant Colonel Mills' men then came under enfilade fire because there was a gap on their right.

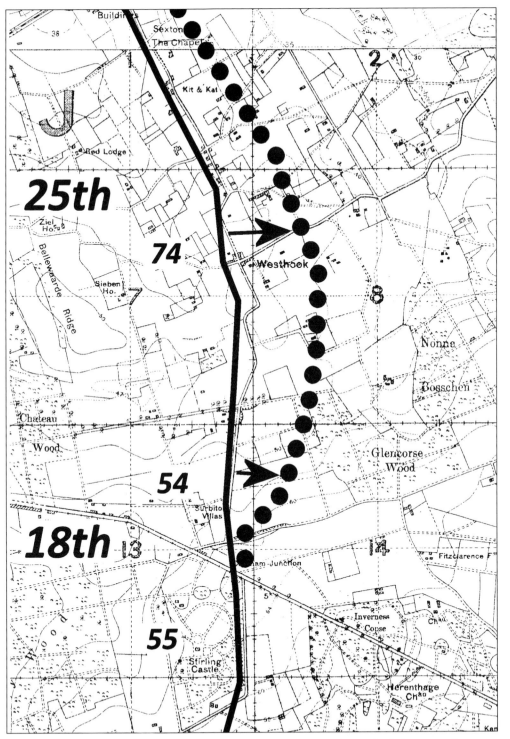

II Corps captured Westhoek ridge but could not clear the woods astride the Menin road on 10 August.

The 11th Royal Fusiliers suffered heavy casualties passing between Glencourse Wood and Inverness Copse but Captain Gray led them as far as Fitzclarence Farm. Captain Hoare was the last officer to fall, leaving Sergeant Major Burch to lead the survivors. Signalling officer Lieutenant Pearcy took all the servants, runners and pioneers forward to reinforce the line and they held on until Captain Shepheard of the 6th Northants and Captain Minet, a machine-gun officer, arrived to take charge. Captain Grace also led the Fusiliers' final company forward but the battalion was too weak to hold on. Major General Lee refused to send any more reinforcements and the afternoon counter-attack infiltrated along Jargon and Jap Trenches, forcing 54 Brigade to withdraw to its start line.

The German outposts facing 55 Brigade's front hit many of the 7th Queen's but Second Lieutenant Wilson led the survivors through Inverness Copse. They found themselves in an isolated position and under fire from three sides but held on until they were counter-attacked at dusk. The 'barrage smashed the attack in the space of a minute. It seemed as though the front line was annihilated. Survivors of the others could be seen flying in all directions.' Lance Corporal Jelly's Lewis gunners stopped the rest but the Queen's had to fall back during the night because no one could reach them with ammunition.

Both Brigadier Generals Cunliffe Owen and Price reported their men had reached their final objective but they had not got there at the same time; if they got there at all. They also complained the creeping barrage had been too weak and the gunners were sometimes slow at responding to SOS flares, if they replied at all. It was clear that more wireless planes were needed to speed up the response time.

24th Division, Lower Star Post
Major General Louis Bols wanted to capture Lower Star Post, in Shrewsbury Forest, ahead of the main attack. However one battery lifted ninety seconds late and it disorganised Lieutenant Lowles' men, giving the Germans time to man their weapons. Lance Corporal Simson led the 8th Buffs' final charge but his men had to fall back when their Lewis gun jammed.

18th Division, Glencourse Wood, 11 August
There was a morning raid on the trenches west of Glencourse Wood while the 10th Essex and 8th Norfolks relieved the 7th Bedfords and 11th Royal Fusiliers. Captains Rochfort and Hollis of the 6th Berkshires reinforced the Norfolks while Captain Morgan rescued several soldiers who had been taken prisoner when he recaptured a pillbox. Brigade Major Captain

Higginson proudly reported the counter-attack had been 'carried out without any artillery preparation and entirely on the initiative of the commanders on the spot. The assaulting troops advanced by rushes, under the cover of fire from Lewis guns and rifles.'

Fifth Army's Preliminary Actions

General Gough's rear areas were hidden behind the Pilckem ridge, so the shelling had been less intense, but mustard gas was causing many casualties. The Steenbeek ran along Fifth Army's front and the combination of shelling and heavy rain had turned the stream into a bog. Both XIV and XVIII Corps had to establish bridgeheads on the far bank and patrols had to locate submerged bridges and culverts in advance. The first crossing was made at Passerelle Farm by 29th Division on the night of 10/11 August but the 1st Border Regiment failed to capture the pillbox covering their crossing site the following night. Temporary bridges, made by floating duckboards on petrol cans, were installed the night before the attack so Major General Sir Beauvoir de Lisle's men could deploy on the far bank.

The 10th KRRC were spotted crossing the Steenbeek on 20th Division's front on the night of 11/12 August and machine-gun and artillery fire disorganised them. Two companies were overrun on the far bank and few men returned. The 10th and 11th Rifle Brigades crossed either side of the Langemarck road early on 14 August but Captains Edwards and Irvine were killed trying to capture one pillbox while Lieutenant Martin was killed at another. Many casualties were caused by the machine guns in Au Bon Gîte and the two surviving officers withdrew the 10th Rifle Brigade. The 11th Rifle Brigade surrounded Au Bon Gîte but the Germans had locked the steel door and Captain Slade fell back when his men ran out of grenades. Lieutenant Colonel Troughton had to report no gains for the loss of 200 casualties while plans to blow open the pillbox door with explosives were cancelled because the assault team assembled too late on 15 August. Major General William Douglas Smith instead had to make a plan to seize Au Bon Gîte at zero hour.

In 11th Division's sector, the 8th Duke's captured Wellington Farm in 'one of the prettiest little stunts you can imagine', south of Langemarck. But one company advanced too far and Private Arnold Loosemore had to give covering fire so his comrades could escape a counter-attack. He threw German grenades and then fired his revolver to keep them at bay after his Lewis gun was damaged. He ran when that too jammed, having saved his company. Loosemore later engaged in sniping before rescuing a wounded man; he would be awarded the Victoria Cross.

Fifth Army, 16 August

Rain had made life very difficult in the salient and Second Lieutenant Essame of the 2nd Northants explained that 'all the holes were full to the brim with water. Everywhere it was hard going through the mud. In some places duckboard tracks sank out of sight almost as soon as they were laid.' Fifth Army was also short of men, making it difficult to keep the tracks open, so Gough postponed the attack until 15 August to give the divisions time to prepare. A thunderstorm late on 14 August resulted in a second postponement to 4.45 am on the 16th. The assault troops then found it difficult to negotiate the water-filled shell holes on the misty night and officers were relieved to get their men into position before zero hour.

The plan was for XIV Corps to clear Langemarck while the French advanced on its left. As XVIII Corps advanced north-east of St Julien, XIX Corps would do the same towards 's Gravenstafel and Zonnebeke. Meanwhile, II Corps had to clear the woods east of Westhoek and form a flank between Polygon Wood and Stirling Castle. Most of the divisions faced an advance of 1,500 yards but Gough had halved the battalion frontage, so they would have double the number of troops to clear the ground.

XIV Corps

Lieutenant General Lambart, the Earl of Cavan, faced the marsh between the Steenbeek and Kortebeek streams. Fortunately, most the Germans had no stomach for a fight across the marsh; some surrendered while others ran.

<u>29th Division, North-West of Langemarck</u>

Major General de Lisle's men were on the 'the worst patch of the battlefield' and they only just formed up in time. On 87 Brigade's front, Captain Pierson and Lieutenant French led the 2nd SWB across a swamp to clear Cannes Farm. Captain Ross and Lieutenant Haydon then outflanked Montmirail Farm and Craonne Farm under fire from Champaubert Farm, where the French were held up on their left.

The 1st KOSBs were clearing Wijdendrift when Company Sergeant Major William Grimbaldeston saw a neighbouring company pinned down. He crawled forward while his men gave covering fire and captured the pillbox after threatening the thirty-six men inside with a grenade. He would capture two more pillboxes and another twenty-four prisoners with the help of a few men. Grimbaldeston was wounded, the eighth wound of his career; he was awarded the Victoria Cross.

An injured Company Sergeant Major John Skinner crawled seventy yards through the mud with six men to get to their enemy. They outflanked

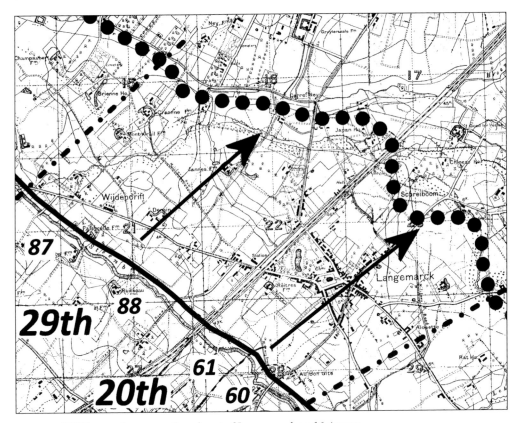

XIV Corps advance north and east of Langemarck on 16 August.

three pillboxes, taking sixty prisoners, three machine guns and two trench mortars. Skinner was also awarded the Victoria Cross. All was going well for the KOSBs until one large shell hit the crowded battalion headquarters causing over one hundred casualties. The 1st Borders and the 1st Inniskillings continued the advance and Brigadier General Lucas was able to report they had breached the Langemarck–Gheluvelt Line, close to the Kortebeek stream.

The Newfoundland Regiment took Denian and the pillboxes along the Bixschoote road with help from the 2nd Hampshires. Captain Day cleared pillboxes around the railway station while Sergeant Finch killed four and captured twenty single-handedly. The Hampshires' Lewis gunners scattered the Germans fleeing from Langemarck, allowing the 4th Worcesters and 1st Essex to reach the Kortebeek stream. Lieutenant Colonel Stirling's Essex cleared Martin's Mill and then silenced the snipers who were pinning the Worcesters down. Brigadier General Cayley was pleased to hear that 170 prisoners had been taken en route to the Kortebeek. A counter-attack was stopped by 88 Brigade but the men could do little against the low-flying German planes directing artillery fire against their position.

<u>20th Division, Langemarck</u>

Major General Douglas Smith's men were across the Steenbeek but they still had to cross a bog to reach Langemarck. Lieutenant Colonel Wood of the 6th Shropshires sank up to his waist in mud en route to the front while his battalion diary noted that five men were 'missing – drowned in the mud'.

On 61 Brigade's front, the 7th KOYLIs were hit by fire from the railway station and Reitres Farm, west of Langemarck. Private Wilfred Edwards threw bombs through a firing slit in Reitres Farm pillbox and over thirty men surrendered. He then climbed on the roof and shouted 'come on KOYLIs, we've got them'. He was nearly shot later on as he entered a dugout. He said the German 'nearly gave me a wooden cross instead of the one that I have got' when he was awarded the Victoria Cross.

The KOYLIs had to skirt the Château's lake to reach the outskirts of Langemarck. Second Lieutenant Robinson continued to the objective on the far side of the village while the moppers up detailed by Major Janson set about clearing the Château. The 7th Somersets suffered many casualties as they approached the south-west side of Langemarck but they still fought their way past the church.

The 7th DCLI and the 12th King's ditched most of their equipment to make it easier to walk through the mud but Lieutenant Colonel Burges-Short's DCLI still had to follow the railway line in single file. Captain Eary's men captured the battalion commander and the forty staff responsible for Langemarck in a bunker at the far side of the village. Brigadier General Banbury was relieved to hear that both battalions had cleared many pillboxes of the Langemarck–Gheluvelt Line.

Au Bon Gîte, on the east bank of the Steenbeek, 'was the key to the enemy's defences' in 60 Brigade's sector. A company of the 11th Rifle Brigade had crossed the stream under cover of darkness and then crawled up to the bunker. A plane flew low overhead with its guns blazing, one minute before zero hour, to distract the garrison. Lieutenant Colonel Cotton's men threw smoke grenades at the bunker and then captured the fifty-strong garrison. The 6th Ox and Bucks had advanced to the St Julien road, south-east of Langemarck, while the fight for Au Bon Gîte was underway.

Sergeant Ned Cooper of the 12th KRRC saw his officer fall in front of Aloutte Farm, so he took his map and worked out how to approach a strongpoint before arranging covering fire. He ran forward and fired his officer's revolver through the firing slit forcing forty-five men to surrender their seven machine guns; he would be awarded the Victoria Cross. Other Germans nearby were so angry to see their comrades surrendering that they shot at them.

The 12th KRRC and 6th Shropshires 'advanced to the attack under very heavy fire in as perfect order as if on Salisbury Plain' towards the Langemarck–Gheluvelt Line. Lieutenant Hannah's men cleared Alouette but he was killed capturing the White House. Captain O'Connor was one of many hit by enfilade fire from the Rat House, where 11th Division was pinned down to their right. Many Germans had chosen to run but Brigadier General the Hon. Butler was pleased to hear 135 prisoners had been taken en route to the objective.

An afternoon counter-attack forced Lieutenant Colonel Prioleau's KRRC out of the pillboxes north-east of Langemarck and Lieutenant Colonel Vince had to withdraw some of the King's as well. The rest of the King's abandoned Schreiboom during the night after losing all their officers and senior NCOs. Some of the Langemarck–Gheluvelt Line would be retaken the following afternoon.

XVIII Corps
There was a narrow bridgehead across the Steenbeek but it was too dangerous to deploy on the east bank. So Lieutenant General Maxse deployed his troops on the west bank and tapes led them to the footbridges floating in the muddy water.

11th Division, South-East of Langemarck
Major General Henry Davies had deployed 34 Brigade, and the 5th Dorsets and 8th Northumberland Fusiliers both advanced past Hannixbeek Farm to get to the Langemarck–Zonnebeke road. Second Lieutenant Goss moved ahead of the 9th Lancashire Fusiliers to reach the White House, but he was wounded when the British barrage passed over his position and had to withdraw. Captains Dawson and Granger were wounded and Sergeant Hodkinson was left to deal with contradictory orders which told him to withdraw to the Dorsets' position. Brigadier General Pedley heard that enfilade fire from 48th Division's sector had stopped the 11th Manchesters taking Bülow Farm and the Cockcroft so Lieutenant Colonel Thurston was told to pull the Lancashire Fusiliers' flank back.

48th Division, North-East of St Julien
Major General Robert Fanshawe had 145 Brigade deployed in a bridgehead around St Julien as a starting point but tanks failed to capture the strongpoint at the north end of the village. The 1/4th Ox and Bucks could not take Maison du Hibou while the 1st Bucks failed to reach Hillock Farm. A few of the Bucks reached Springfield Farm on the Langemarck–Zonnebeke road but they were never seen again. The 1/5th Gloucesters took Border House

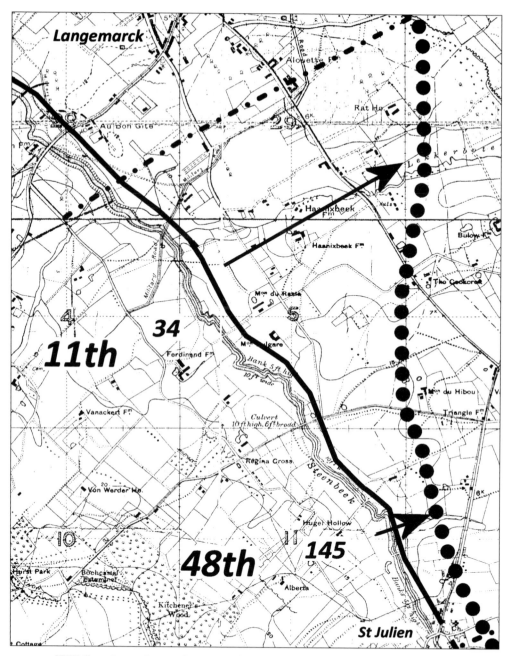

XVIII Corps' struggle to make progress between Langemarck and St Julien.

but were pinned down by fire from Janet Farm. Captain Norrish of the 1/4th Berkshires also failed to capture Hillock Farm while Captain Tripp was killed trying to reach Winnipeg. Second Lieutenant Brooke had to reinforce the right flank where 36th Division had been unable to clear Fortuin Hill, south-east of St Julien.

XIX Corps

Two divisions from Ireland, the 36th and 16th, were fighting side by side for the second time in ten weeks. The men had spent the two weeks building roads across the Frezenberg ridge while living alongside the flooded Steenbeek. The men were tired and each division had lost 150 men a day due to sickness, leaving battalions at half strength.

The artillery had to remain behind the Frezenberg ridge, leaving the gunners struggling to hit the pillboxes in front of the Langemarck–Gheluvelt Line at long range. Platoons had been trained to deal with them but the shortage of men meant that each wave was only 150 strong. Casualties further reduced each wave until they 'looked more like a big raiding party than anything else'.

36th Division, Fort Hill and Hill 35

Major General Oliver Nugent's men had to cross the Steenbeek and deploy on the east bank in the dark. Lieutenant Colonel Pratt was killed as the 11th Inniskillings advanced towards Border House and onto Fortuin Hill, otherwise known as Fort Hill, alongside the 14th Irish Rifles. Lieutenant Ledlie surrounded Pond Farm but he had too few troops to capture it and his call for reinforcements went unanswered by 109 Brigade's headquarters.

Brigadier General Griffiths' men faced a new entanglement which ran diagonally across 108 Brigade's front and machine-gun fire cut down many as they bunched up to pass through the few gaps. The first wave of the 13th Irish Rifles bypassed Somme Farm and Captain Belt's second wave could not take it. Lieutenant Colonel Maxwell was wounded as his headquarters staff tried in vain to capture it. The 9th Irish Rifles cleared Pommern Redoubt and then advanced onto Hill 35, where Lieutenant Colonel Somerville was mortally wounded.

16th Division, Beck House and Borry Farm

Major General William Hickie had wanted the artillery to fire gas shells at the many pillboxes before zero hour but his request had been ignored. There were early successes in 49 Brigade's sector where the 7th Inniskillings captured Iberian Farm and Delva Farm while the 8th Inniskillings took Borry Farm. But again casualties weakened the battalions so much that they could go no further. The 2nd Irish Regiment moved up in support but they could not reach Hill 37 nor Zevencote either.

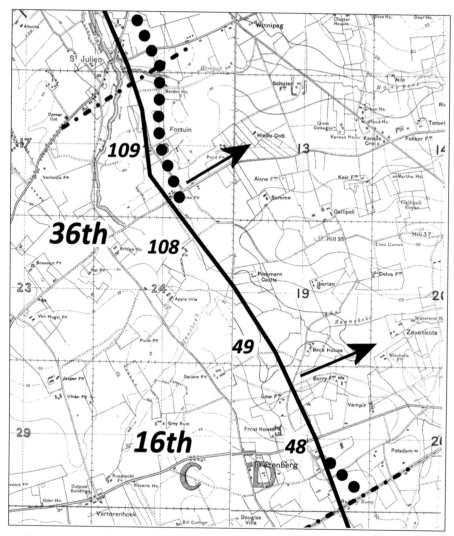

XIX Corps failed to gain any ground east of the Steenbeek stream.

A shortage of men also hampered the 9th Dublin Fusiliers and 7th Irish Rifles in 48 Brigade's sector. They had lost more before Borry Farm, Vampir and Potsdam were cleared, leaving too few men to mop up effectively. It left many Germans free to fire into the backs of the Irishmen as they approached the Langemarck–Gheluvelt Line.

The Counter-Attack

All the battalions had suffered many casualties and there were few spare men to reinforce 36th or 16th Division. The skies were clear but the battlefield was covered in smoke, so the aerial observers failed to spot the counter-attack, leaving the Ulstermen and Irishmen to fight on alone. Their weapons were clogged with mud and they had little ammunition left, so they had to withdraw to their start line.

The Ulstermen had advanced 109 Brigade's line 400 yards but they were in an impossible position, so they withdrew nearly back their start line where Brigadier General Ricardo had deployed the 9th and 10th Inniskillings to help them dig in. It was the same for 108 Brigade on 36th Division's right.

The 2nd Irish Regiment reinforced 49 Brigade while the 12th Irish Rifles helped 48 Brigade hold on. Many were needed to evacuate the wounded because it took eight men to carry a stretcher across Steenbeek. Private Freddie Room took charge of the 2nd Royal Irish stretcher bearers and he saved many lives under fire; he would be awarded the Victoria Cross.

By 10 am Lieutenant General Watts knew the attack had failed and both divisions were in danger of being driven back across the Steenbeek. So he decided to pull the barrage back to the start line, knowing that many men, many of them wounded, were still out in front. Early in the afternoon, General Gough told Watts to organise a short advance to Hindu Cottage, Hill 35 and Borry Farm, to improve his position. Both Generals Nugent and Hickie argued their assault brigades were finished and they needed their reserve brigades to hold the front line. Both divisions had suffered around 2,000 casualties on top of the 2,000 they had lost over the previous weeks. Later that evening Watts told Gough the 36th and 16th Divisions would not be able to attack again.

II Corps
Lieutenant General Sir Claud Jacob faced the Hanebeek valley on his left and Nonne Bosschen, Glencourse Wood and Inverness Copse on his right. Only then could his men tackle the Langemarck – Gheluvelt Line.

<u>8th Division, Hanebeek Stream and Anzac Spur</u>
Major General Heneker had wanted 56th Division to advance earlier, to clear Nonne Bosschen on his right flank, but his request was denied. When the attack began, the 2nd Middlesex moved faster than 16th Division next to the Roulers railway and many of Major Cade's men were hit by enfilade fire from Potsdam. The 2nd Scottish Rifles faced the same problem as they carried portable bridges forward to cross the Hanebeek stream so they could climb Anzac spur. On 23 Brigade's right, the 2nd West Yorkshires used smoke bombs and mills grenades to clear Sans Souci. Lieutenant Colonel Jeffries' men were the joined by the 2nd Devons and they worked together to clear Zonnebeke Redoubt.

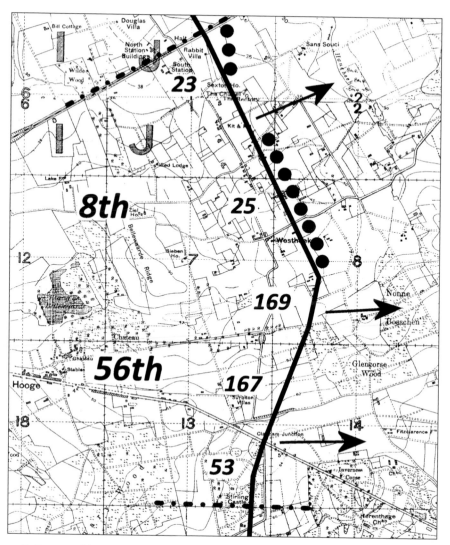

II Corps could not cross the Hanebeek stream or clear the woods astride the Menin road.

Brigadier General Coffin's men crossed the Hanebeek using bridges placed by the 22nd Durhams, the division's pioneer battalion. Lieutenant Colonel O'Leary's 1st Irish Rifles climbed Anzac Spur and Captain Cahill cleared Anzac House as the 2nd Rifle Brigade reinforced the line. The 2nd Berkshires captured Iron Cross Redoubt and some men even continued far enough to see Zonnebeke, to the north-east.

Despite the success, 8th Division's left flank was exposed because 16th Division was still struggling around Potsdam. The Middlesex covered the danger area while Major Smith of the Scottish Rifles called down a barrage to give them support. The Berkshires were under enfilade fire from Polygon

Wood, where 56th Division should have been on their right. Lieutenant Colonel Hanbury-Sparrow deployed a company to cover the flank until Lieutenant Colonel Richards' 2nd Lincolns reinforced the line.

The Irish Rifles lost Anzac Farm to the first counter-attack and then 56th Division was driven from Nonne Bosschen, allowing the Germans to get behind the Berkshires' two flanks. Captains Young and Hales were both wounded as casualties mounted and a wounded Colonel O'Leary staggered back to report 25 Brigade's precarious situation.

Brigadier General Coffin sent reinforcements from the Rifle Brigade and the Lincolns as the Germans closed during the afternoon. The ground observers saw them approaching but smoke obscured the SOS signals and the air observers relayed only one message so the artillery fired too late to help. It resulted in a retirement to the Hanebeek where Brigadier General Coffin encouraged Lieutenant Colonels Hanbury-Sparrow and Latham as well as Major Cole to make a stand.

The withdrawal of 25 Brigade forced the West Yorkshires to withdraw on 23 Brigade's front. Lieutenant Colonel Coleman also held on along the Hanebeek but the Germans were closing in. The few Lincolns and Berkshires were running out of ammunition and Captain Blake and Second Lieutenant Frost were hit taking two 2nd Northants companies forward while Second Lieutenant Bailey was hit four times while saving the right flank.

The division withdrew to the start line during the evening due to enfilade fire from Nonne Bosschen. Coffin also sent his headquarters staff forward to the crest of the Westhoek ridge so they could give covering fire: he would later be awarded the Victoria Cross for saving the day.

56th Division, Nonne Bosschen, Glencourse Wood and Inverness Copse

Major General Frederick Dudgeon faced several complaints about the plan to clear the woods north of the Menin road. Brigadier General Freeth thought too many instructions were being produced and they were being issued too late. Brigadier General Higginson argued that 53 Brigade (attached from 18th Division) was too weak to attack Inverness Copse on his right flank, so it was reinforced with the 1/4th London Regiment and 7th Bedfords.

Whereas other divisions had been in the line for several days, 56th Division had less than twenty-four hours to take over, leaving no time to study the ground. In Dudgeon's own words:

'The darkness of the night, the boggy state of the ground, heavy shelling of all approaches, and the fact the division was strange to the ground and had little opportunity for reconnaissance and preparation presented great difficulties in carrying out the assembly.'

The 1/1st London Regiment was hit by the German barrage as it advanced off Westhoek ridge. It was then pushed north because the 8th Middlesex was forced to skirt around a marshy area at the head of the Hanebeek. The disorganised Londoners failed to mop up, leaving snipers free to shoot into their backs. Meanwhile, Lieutenant Colonel Ingpen's Middlesex men were left with a gap on their right caused by the bog.

Some men headed for the Langemarck–Gheluvelt Line but none returned. Bad ground meant the 1/3rd London and 1/8th Middlesex could not keep up with the barrage and only a few reached Anzac Farm spur. Brigadier General Freeth's men withdrew across the Hanebeek to their start line after the Germans recaptured Glencourse Wood, to their right.

On 169 Brigade's front, both Lieutenant Colonels Husey and Kellett were wounded at an early stage of the 1/2nd and 1/5th London Regiments' advance. The 1/2nd London Regiment skirted the same bog at the head of the Hanebeek, pushing the 1/5th London Regiment south, widening the gap on the division's front. The 1/2nd London Regiment cleared Nonne Bosschen but the 1/5th London Regiment faced a tough fight for the pillboxes in Glencourse Wood.

The first wave of the two battalions entered Polygon Wood but the rest were pinned down before they reached it. The Londoners became disorganised moving through the smashed up trees and groups became isolated. One officer reported, by pigeon, that he had reached the racecourse in the centre, but the note also said, 'ammunition and bombs exhausted. Completely surrounded. Regret no course but to surrender.' No one returned from Polygon Wood.

Smoke meant the aerial observers did not see the Germans infiltrating behind the Londoners, driving them back through Nonne Bosschen and Glencourse Wood. Brigadier General Coke deployed the 9th London to hold the line but they were forced to withdraw to their start line because they were running out of ammunition.

On the right, 53 Brigade had to cross the Menin road but the tanks ditched on the boggy ground. The German barrage fell quickly and the 1/4th London Regiment were hit by the pillboxes in Glencourse Wood. The 7th Bedfords were stopped by crossfire from Fitzclarence Farm and Inverness Copse while the 6th Berkshires could not get into the copse either. Brigadier General Higginson wanted a pillbox at the north-west corner of Inverness Copse shelled again but it never happened due to a misunderstanding. The second advance just added to the carnage astride the Menin road. The division had suffered over 2,100 casualties; a third of them were missing. Captain Steven led only fifty men of the 1/2nd London Regiment out of the line.

Chapter 10

Bite and Hold

19 to 22 August Operations

There had been success around Langemarck on 16 August but the attack had been a disaster elsewhere. A lot of questions were asked and answers suggested about how to deal with the dozens of pillboxes the Germans were building. The general agreement was to 'not try and penetrate too deeply'; and they had to allocate more troops to mop up and consolidate the captured position. The ease with which the Germans counter-attacked was also worrying. The number of aerial observers to watch for counter-attacks was doubled to two per division, so one was always in the air. Each level of command also had to consider how many men to hold in reserve.

Gough was happy about the situation around Langemarck but he wanted his centre and right to push forward for two reasons: he wanted to be closer to the Langemarck–Gheluvelt Line and he wanted to get away from the Steenbeek. The stream was only 500 yards behind XIX Corps' front and a counter-attack could easily reach it, splitting Lieutenant General Watts' front. On 17 August, Gough told his corps commanders to be ready to make several 'bite and hold' attacks.

<u>XVIII Corps, Keerselaere Crossroads, 20 August</u>

After three dry days, 11th Division made a preliminary attack at 4.45 am on 20 August. Twelve tanks had been allocated but five ditched around St Julien. The rest followed the Poelcappelle road and a male tank fired fifty shells into Hillock Farm while a female tank fired its machine guns as the garrison fled. The plan had been to do the same to Maison du Hibou but the ground was too soft so the tanks stayed on the road.

One tank kept the garrison of Triangle Farm pinned down until the infantry stormed it. Another ditched near the Cockcroft but the crew were able to shoot the garrison as they fled. The 7th South Staffords were able to occupy the ground for only a handful of casualties while the five tanks returned. It was a small-scale example of how tanks could dominate ground so that the infantry could occupy it. Unfortunately, the Germans knew the tanks were limited to the roads.

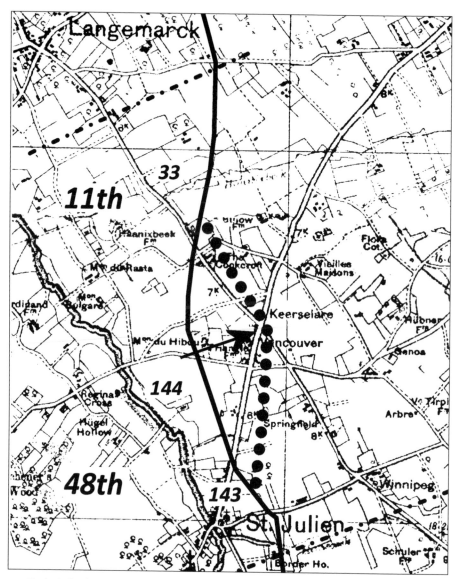

Tanks helped XVIII Corps clear the roads between Langemarck and St Julien.

Fifth Army, 22 August

The success meant Lieutenant General Sir Ivor Maxse's XVIII Corps would try to move its flanks forward while Lieutenant General Herbert Watts' XIX Corps advanced away from the Steenbeek. But the late decision to attack meant there was little time to reconnoitre the ground. The deployment was rushed and, to make matters worse, there was no morning mist when they advanced at 4.45 am on 22 August. The Germans had built new pillboxes during the lull in the fighting, working at night and camouflaging them with mud during the day. The men inside waited for the next attack to begin before opening fire.

XVIII Corps

Orders for the attack were issued late and Lieutenant General Maxse's officers had not had time to explain the operation to their men.

11th Division, East of Langemarck

The 6th Border Regiment was pinned down as it advanced towards Pheasant Trench, east of Langemarck. Two tanks helped Captain Sutherland's company of the 6th Lincolns capture Bülow Farm but Captain Jones's men hesitated after all their officers and sergeants were hit. Sutherland rallied them and they reached Keerselaere crossroads.

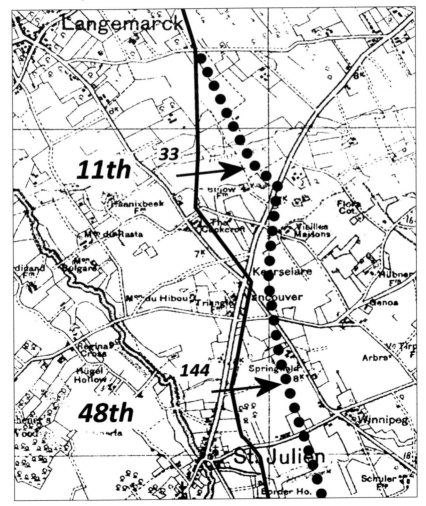

XVIII Corps edged towards the Langemarck–Gheluvelt Line.

48th Division, North-East of St Julien

For a second time, tanks were to spearhead the advance north-east of St Julien but the Germans were waiting for them this time. Six tanks were hit or ditched as they crawled towards Keerselaere crossroads but three silenced Vancouver Farm and Springfield Farm. But they were alone because the 'men struggling forward could be seen hoisting one another out of the glutinous mud which had engulfed them to the middle.' The Gloucestershire and Worcestershire territorials waded past Maison du Hibou and Triangle Farm to Keerselaere and Vancouver Farm but the 1/6th Gloucesters could not hold Springfield Farm on 144 Brigade's right. The Warwickshire territorials dragged themselves closer to Winnipeg on the Langemarck–Zonnebeke road on 143 Brigade's front.

XIX Corps

Lieutenant General Watts' corps held a narrow foothold on the east side of the Steenbeek on its left but its right straddled the boggy stream.

61st Division, 's Gravenstafel road

The 184 Brigade held a long sector astride the 's Gravenstafel road. Second Lieutenants Davis and Blythe were killed during the 2/4th Ox & Bucks' struggle for Pond Farm. It took until the afternoon to capture the fifty-strong garrison but Lieutenant Colonel Wetherall's men then pushed as far as Hindu Cot. Lieutenant Colonel Muir's 2/1st Bucks pushed towards Kansas Cross but the moppers suffered heavy losses dealing with Somme Farm and Aisne Farm. A counter-attack retook Aisne Farm from the Bucks but Brigadier General White released the 2/5th Gloucesters to help the rest of the brigade hold on.

15th Division, Steenbeek Stream

Four tanks ditched around Pommern Redoubt, on 44 Brigade's left flank. The other two tanks led the 7th Camerons onto Hill 35 but machine-gun fire from Gallipoli Farm stopped them going any further. The 8th Seaforths were unable to reach Iberian Farm either.

All four tanks supporting 45 Brigade ditched on the Zonnebeke road. Few of the 11th Argylls made it past Beck House while Major Mitchell's 13th Royal Scots advanced towards Bremen Redoubt as the 6/7th Scots Fusiliers mopped up Borry Farm, Vampir and Potsdam. None of the men who made it to the Langemarck–Gheluvelt Line came back. Captain Young led the 9th Black Watch across Hill 35 to Gallipoli Farm on 25 August but they had to withdraw. The battalion headquarters was knocked out when a shell hit the door of their pillbox. The Scots' dreadful situation is

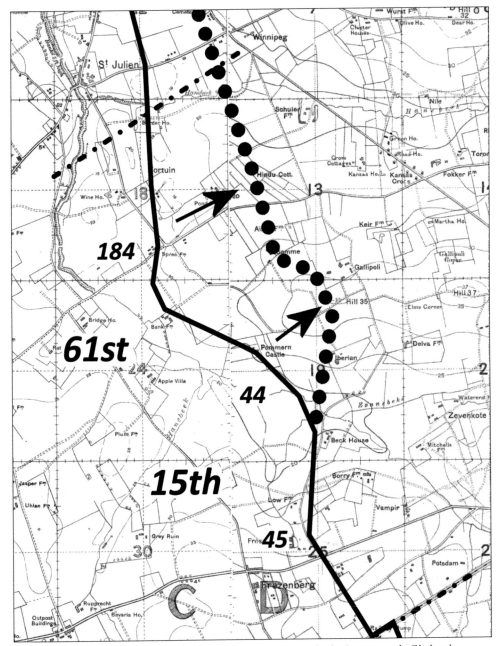

XIX Corps moved away from the Steenbeek and towards the Langemarck–Gheluvelt Line.

summarised with the following words: 'All accounts as to what took place are vague. Few men from attacking formations were able to tell what occurred as nearly all were either killed or wounded.'

Second Army, 22 August
II Corps
<u>14th Division, Astride the Menin Road</u>
Major General Victor Couper was given orders to clear the woods either side of the Menin road. All but one officer of the 5th Shropshires' two leading companies were hit in the first five minutes so Captain Lloyd and Second Lieutenant Cooke took over the advance towards Glencourse Wood. A tank headed for L-Shaped Farm, but the 6th DCLI were pinned down as they followed the other tanks towards Fitzclarence Farm. Lieutenant Whitby went the furthest but the rest of the DCLI dug in along Jargon Drive and Jap Avenue and the tanks turned back without their infantry support. The 6th Somersets advanced through Inverness Copse, under fire from three sides. They were later driven back to the centre of the copse where two tanks and the 10th Durhams helped them hold on.

General Jacob wanted to attack the following morning but one tank got stuck, the second had engine trouble and the third was knocked, so the attack was cancelled. It was the Germans who attacked first, tackling Inverness Copse early on 24 August with flamethrowers. The 6th DCLI were driven back to their start line while the 6th Somersets fell back when the British guns fired short; they could not rectify the problem because all the telephone wires had been cut.

Fifth Army, 27 August
XIV Corps
<u>38th Division, Eagle Trench</u>
Brigadier General Gwyn-Thomas's men were 'lying in shell holes that were gradually filling with water' where they 'found great difficulty in getting out and keeping up with the barrage'. The 16th Welsh Fusiliers were unable to capture Eagle Trench while the 11th SWB failed to take White Trench.

XVIII Corps
<u>11th and 48th Divisions, East of St Julien</u>
The plan was to advance a short distance towards Pheasant Farm astride the Lekkerboterbeek stream. Three tanks crawled out of St Julien and along the Poelcappelle road with 48th Division. They helped 144 Brigade capture Vancouver Farm while 143 Brigade took Springfield Farm, both on the Langemarck–Zonnebeke road. Some Germans intended to surrender until they saw the British soldiers struggling in the mud on 11th Division's front, so they picked up their weapons and fired at them.

XIX Corps
61st and 15th Divisions, Astride the Steenbeek

On the left, 61st Division could not reach Schuler Farm on the Langemarck–Zonnebeke road. Equally, 15th Division could not reach Gallipoli Farm, beyond Hill 35.

Second Army, 27 August
II Corps
23rd Division, Glencourse Wood and Inverness Copse

Seven tanks were detailed to drive down the Menin road but two broke down and the other five sank into the mud as they waited for zero hour around Hooge Crater. Meanwhile, the men waited ten hours in two feet of water in heavy rain for zero hour at 1.30 pm only to lose the barrage as they negotiated the shell holes. It meant that hardly any of Brigadier General Skinner's 41 Brigade (attached from 14th Division) reached the woods.

Summary

Haig wrote to the War Cabinet after the disaster on 16 August to say he was 'well satisfied with them [his men], although the gain of ground would have been much more considerable but for the adverse weather conditions'. He said he wanted to keep the pressure on and that he was still hoping to clear the coast. The Admiralty supported his view.

Haig told his army commanders that the German 'army was beginning to fail' only three days later. He believed 'a decision might be reached this year' if they kept on the offensive in the Ypres Salient and he told the government the same. He believed the Germans had already suffered 100,000 casualties in the offensive, on top of what they had suffered in the spring offensives at Arras and on the Aisne. There was evidence they were already sending 18-year-olds to the front line; they were referred to as the class of 1919.

Various intelligence sources estimated that the Germans had deployed thirty-seven divisions against the BEF and French. Prisoners and documents suggested twenty-three had been worn out. It was an optimistic assessment but the Germans had cancelled their attacks against the French, fulfilling part of the strategic aim. Ludendorff himself described August as 'a period of tremendous anxiety' because his troops suffered the same privations as the British and French soldiers. The salient was an unhealthy, dangerous place where 'the defenders cowered in the water-filled craters without shelter from weather, hungry and cold, abandoned without pause to overwhelming fire.' There 'were no trenches and no shelters except the few concrete blockhouses'.

However, the BEF was also suffering heavy casualties, and Fifth and Second Armies had engaged twenty-two divisions while fourteen of them had been exhausted. Neither army had reached the objectives set for the first day. Many of the BEF's divisions were still understrength after their exertions at Arras and the recent casualties had made the situation worse. Haig doubted the War Cabinet would send any more replacements and he told Gough and Plumer so at a conference on 21 August. So he issued instructions to comb support units to find men fit enough to serve in the infantry. Staff officers inspected cavalry, labour, construction, transport, medical, forestry and clerical units for men who could be transferred and trained as replacements.

Meanwhile, the War Cabinet and the Chief of the Imperial General Staff had many things to consider. The Americans were committed to sending a large number of troops to France but it would be a year before they would be ready to fight. The Russian Kerensky Offensive had already collapsed on the Eastern Front. The good news was that the mutinies in the French armies had calmed down, but Pétain warned it would be some time before they could stage another attack. The Italians were also having some success along the River Isonzo.

On 2 September Haig told the War Cabinet that he regretted the delay in operations, which was down to the bad weather and a shell shortage. However he still wanted to continue the offensive to help the French. Lloyd George had mixed feelings because he wanted to send heavy artillery to Italy where he thought they would have better results for fewer casualties.

Two days later Haig told Lloyd George that he did not want to lose any divisions or any guns because it would hand the advantage to the Germans. He wanted to keep pushing and most of the Cabinet Committee supported him. Haig also had to consider Brigadier General Elles' request to withdraw half of the tanks for training. The salient was too boggy and he hoped they would be able to prove their worth on dry, firm terrain.

Haig was confident the Germans were being worn down but the generals and war correspondents knew it was the BEF that was being worn down. The censors stopped the soldiers writing home about the mud and casualties but they could not stop the wounded telling their stories when they returned to England. Crown Prince Rupprecht was also hearing that British troops were surrendering more readily than they had before and many were blaming their officers for the failures.

The heavy casualties and lack of clear success had also worried the War Cabinet. They did not want another drawn-out campaign like the Somme or Arras. On 23 August Lloyd George said he wanted to close down the Flanders offensive as quickly as possible and send divisions to the Italian front. Meanwhile Haig was disappointed with the lack of progress by Gough's Fifth Army, so he gave II Corps back to General Plumer. He met his two generals on 25 August and told them he wanted to advance in small stages in quick succession. Plumer's request for three weeks to prepare his artillery and logistics was granted but the wet weather returned three days later and further operations were cancelled until the ground dried out.

Supplying the Battle

The British artillery alone had fired over ten million rounds (around 340,000 tons) in August, using up most of GHQ's artillery reserve. The Germans had fired a huge number as well, churning up the battlefield. There had been nine days of rain, which was average for the time of year, but it was sometimes heavy and prolonged. Each downpour flooded the cratered streams, turning the soil into thick mud which stuck to men, equipment and weapons.

Another 54,500 tons of ammunition would be delivered through two railheads, Pacific and Fuzeville, in the first two weeks of September. Endless convoys of horse-drawn wagons then hauled the shells to the front as the engineers and labourers fought a constant battle to keep the roads open.

Everything had to be carried across the Steenbeek stream and up to the front line. Tracing parties marked out routes with tapes on wooden posts or steel barbed-wire pickets painted white. Duckboards were laid in pairs (up and down traffic) while notice boards guided the men to their destinations. They were fast to lay, quick to mend and easy to move if an area came under shell fire. Mats made of wire netting and strips of canvas stretched around wooden slats were used to cross boggy sections. Mules were often used and it was discovered that they were happy to follow their leader across the mud. The main problem was stopping them congregating on the tracks.

Roads were always busy with traffic and repairs had to be made quickly to limit congestion, but there was never enough crushed stone to mend all the damage. The daily logistics situation was a nightmare because everyone had to leave according to a strict schedule, with the vehicles which had to go the furthest leaving first.

All the plank roads and light railways had to be extended by around 1,500 yards, creating a one-way system so the endless lines of wagons would keep moving. Road surfaces were made of beech slabs and sleepers while split logs were used on slopes to give a better grip. A train delivered 240 planks to Ouderdom siding, south-west of Ypres, every day and a convoy of eighty lorries carried them through the ruins of Ypres in the darkness to drop-off points along the Menin road.

The next stage of the journey was the most dangerous. Around 120 two-horse-drawn wagons each carried thirteen planks the three miles to the end of the road. The German gunners had the road well targeted and the column of wagons halted if a shell hit the road. The poor horses came to know what the sound of the shells meant and they would nuzzle their noses into the chests of their drivers. After dropping off the planks, the wagons returned along the return road ready to make a second journey before dawn.

Pioneers, engineers and tunnellers carried the planks by hand to the end of the road in the dark where the infantry were preparing the ground by digging the mud and filling in shell holes. Longitudinal planks were dug into the soil so that planks could be bolted to them side-by-side. Split logs were laid like kerb stones, to stop wheels slipping off. Water collected in ditches, dug to keep the road dry.

Three hundred yards of tramway could be laid every day and could carry large amounts of material, but they were easily broken. It was also an engineering feat to get them across the many steams; one trestle bridge north of Poelcappelle was eighty yards long. It took a lot of organisation to load the right items onto the trains and despatch them in the right order. A breakdown stranded crews in the open until a train was repaired and the railway units had to cannibalise rolling stock to keep trucks on the move.

Chapter 11

A Killing by the Artillery

The Battle of Hill 70

Haig had encouraged General Sir Henry Horne to take offensive action around Lens, to keep the German reserves opposite First Army's front. But his plan to capture Hill 70, two miles north of the town, was cancelled because so many heavy batteries had been moved to Flanders. General Sir Arthur Currie's Canadian Corps was instructed to take control of the sector on 10 July. Currie was the corps' new, Canadian born, commander who had taken over following General Julian Byng's recent promotion. Command of the 1st Canadian Division had, in turn, passed to Major General Archibald Macdonell.

Over the next few days the 1st Canadian Division took over the line facing Hill 70 while the 3rd Canadian Division took over the sector west of Lens. Currie's plan was to capture Hill 70 and the high ground at Sallaumines, south-east of the town. At 1 am on 23 July, 3rd Canadian Division carried out their first raid against Méricourt trench. The 116th Canadian Battalion reached the trench, destroyed dugouts and returned with over fifty prisoners.

The rain which started on 31 July delayed the main Canadian Corps' attack for two weeks. The Canadian artillery fired nearly 1,000 gas shells at Lens while Livens projectors launched over 3,500 drums filled with gas at the German trenches when the weather eased. The rest of the Canadian artillery benefited from new wirelesses fitted to the spotting planes. It allowed them to instantly relay targets to the relevant corps headquarters. Another squadron specialised in strafing targets as soon as they were spotted. The two innovations shortened registration time and reduced the quantity of shells required to neutralise targets.

General Currie was an advocate of clearing ground with the artillery so the infantry could occupy it with the minimum of casualties. He wanted the attack to be 'a killing by the artillery' and he kept the objectives within reach of the guns, to help the infantry deal with counter-attacks. Currie also supported the deployment of dummy tanks to upset the Germans; all the real tanks were still in Flanders.

Patrols spotted the infantry assembling in no man's land during the early hours but the Canadian artillery neutralized the German guns which tried to disperse them. Drums of burning oil were launched across no man's land to create a thick smokescreen and then the creeping barrage crashed down 'with beautiful accuracy' at zero hour.

1st Canadian Division, Hill 70

On 3 Canadian Brigade's left, 15th Canadian Battalion cleared the ruins of the *Puits 14 bis* colliery and then advanced through Bois Hugo. The 13th and 16th Canadian Battalions cleared Chalet Wood and reported they had taken the rest of Hugo Trench to Brigadier General Tuxford. The 10th and 5th Canadian Battalions cleared Hill 70 but the smoke created by the burning oil had cleared by the time the second part of the advance started.

Both 7th and 8th Canadian Battalions had to advance by rushes between the shell holes under machine-gun fire from Cité St Auguste housing estate. The 7th Canadian Battalion had a tough fight for the Chalk Quarry on the left flank while its right flank had to withdraw because 8th Canadian Battalion was pinned down in front of Norman Trench. Brigadier General

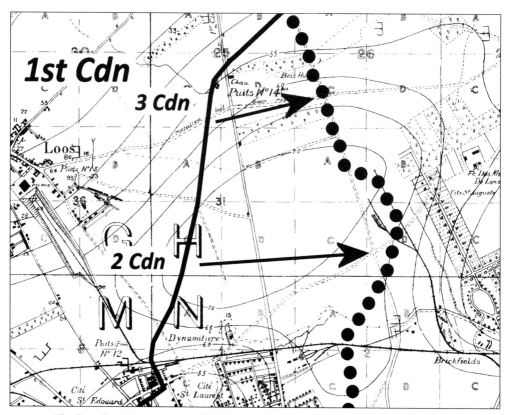

The Canadian Corps' capture of Hill 70 on 15 August.

Loomis had to report that 2 Canadian Brigade was in a difficult position in front of Cité St Auguste.

2nd Canadian Division, North-West of Lens

Major General Burstall's men faced the difficult task of clearing the suburbs north of Lens. On 5 Canadian Brigade's front, 22nd Canadian Battalion worked its way through Cité St Edouard while 25th Canadian Battalion fought through Cité St Laurent. The 24th Canadian Battalion passed through *Fosse 14* colliery to reach Norman Trench. Meanwhile 26th Canadian Battalion moved through the ruins of Cité St Emile to Nun's Alley. On 4 Canadian Brigade's sector 20th Canadian Battalion cleared Cité Ste Elisabeth and reached Commotion Trench. On the division's right, 21st and 18th Canadian Battalions advanced to Chicory Trench, facing the north-west outskirts of Lens.

Early counter-attacks were stopped because the aerial spotters warned the artillery as soon as they appeared. A larger attack faced 'fountains of

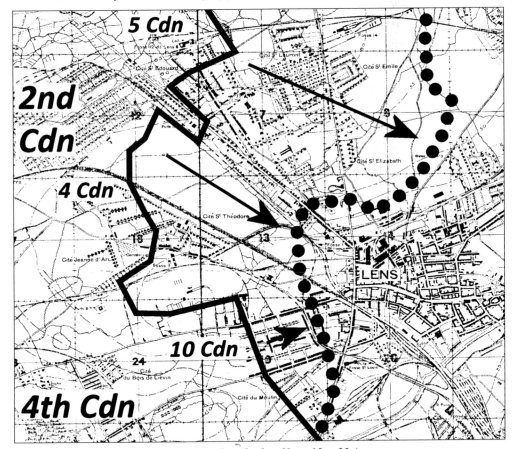

The Canadian Corps attacks into the suburbs of Lens 15 to 25 August.

earth sent up by the heavy shells and then went through a hail of shrapnel and machine-gun bullets.' Chicory Trench was lost until Brigadier General Rennie organised a counter-attack to secure it. Another attack from Cité St Auguste against 7th and 8th Canadian Battalions was broken up by artillery fire. Private James O'Rourke spent three days and nights rescuing 7th Canadian Battalion's wounded around the Chalk Quarry; he would be awarded the Victoria Cross.

<u>1st Canadian Division, 16 August</u>
The 2 Canadian Brigade made its postponed attack at 4 pm and while the 10th Canadian Battalion killed or captured around 230 in the chalk quarry area, Lieutenant Colonel Ormond was desperate for help. He sent back two runners with the same message and while one was killed, a badly injured Private Harry Brown made it to Brigadier General Loomis's headquarters. He collapsed on the dugout steps but managed to whisper the words 'important message' before he died; he was posthumously awarded the Victoria Cross. The 5th Canadian Battalion captured fifty prisoners in Norman Trench but casualties had been heavy and they had to fall back because they were running out of ammunition. Bombers would return to clear the trench the following evening while the 4th Canadian Battalion held onto the chalk quarry.

At dawn on 18 August, the Germans attacked Chicory Trench on 2nd Division's right flank. Sergeant Frederick Hobson, 20th Battalion, took over a Lewis gun when its crew were hit. He used it to keep the Germans at bay, getting an injured Lewis gunner to fix the weapon when it jammed. Hobson was wounded but he fought on with his bayonet and rifle until reinforcements arrived. He was mortally wounded and would be posthumously awarded the Victoria Cross.

Bombers and flamethrower teams broke into 2nd Canadian Battalion's trenches at Bois Hugo, north of Hill 70. A badly injured Major Okill Learmonth took command after the company commanders were hit and he stood on the parapet directing his men, hurling back the German grenades until he could no longer stand. Learmonth then instructed his subalterns until he passed out; he was posthumously awarded the Victoria Cross.

The Canadians had taken most of their objectives but their position was far from secure. Norman Trench was abandoned on 1st Canadian Division's front, so the safer Noggin Trench could be held, but General Currie was still not happy. He wanted to advance to a better position, next to the Cité St Auguste road.

2nd Canadian Division, Cinnabar Trench

Zero had been set for 4.35 am but the Germans shelled the Canadian trenches as they assembled. On 6 Canadian Brigade's front, 29th Canadian Battalion's left charged in no man's land where there was a hand-to-hand battle. But the right company lost all its officers and it was left to Sergeant Major Robert Hanna to capture part of Cinnabar Trench before stopping several counter-attacks; he would be awarded the Victoria Cross. The 28th Canadian Battalion moved forward to clear Nun's Alley and more of Cinnabar Trench, however it could not clear the centre of the position, leaving Brigadier General Ketchen's men in a precarious position. A plan for 29th Canadian Battalion to clear the rest of Cinnabar Trench in the afternoon was cancelled when the Germans counter-attacked. Both the 29th and 27th Canadian Battalions had to withdraw to their original lines.

4th Canadian Division, Cinnabar Trench

The 27th Canadian Battalion advanced from Chicory Trench towards Cinnabar Trench, on the north-west side of Lens. They were struggling to dig into the rubble when the Germans emerged from their cellars to strike back from Bombay Trench.

Meanwhile, 50th Canadian Battalion had a problem because a feint attack the day before had alerted the Germans in Aloof Trench. The assault companies suffered from artillery fire as they formed up and the support companies had to lead instead. Only three small groups reached Aloof Trench and everyone eventually withdrew to the start line. The 46th and 47th Canadian Battalion spent all day battling to reach and then hold Aconite and Alpaca Trenches, on the west side of Lens. Corporal Filip Konowal silenced three machine guns in Alpaca Trench and another one the following day. The Lithuanian emigrant would be awarded the Victoria Cross, the only East European to receive the award.

4th Canadian Division, 21-25 August

Aloof Trench formed a troublesome salient on the Bethune railway line and Major General Watson wanted it clearing late on 21 August. The 50th Canadian Battalion sent three bombing parties towards the ends of the trench but the artillery was inaccurate and only one made any progress. A large attack planned for the following day was cancelled 'because of a misunderstanding'.

At 3 am on 23 August, 44th Canadian Battalion attacked the Green Crassier slagheap and pithead, south of Lens railway station. The Germans around the St Louis colliery hid their tunnels and called down their heavy artillery until the Canadians could stand the shelling no more. The men on the slagheap had to withdraw when they ran out of ammunition. An accurate barrage by Stokes mortars and rifle grenades at 2 am on 25 August allowed the 50th Canadian Battalion to capture the north half of Aloof Trench at the cost of only a few casualties.

Summary

The Canadian Corps had only suffered 3,500 casualties and they took around 970 prisoners on 15 August while gaining a lot of ground. But they suffered another 5,700 casualties over the next nine days for only a few more gains. One consolation was that they had stopped five German divisions moving to Flanders. General Currie later wrote that the battle for Hill 70 'was altogether the hardest battle in which the Corps has participated'.

Medics evacuate wounded of the 36th Division during the battle for Messines ridge.

Wounded Australian soldiers await evacuation during the battle for Messines ridge.

Men of 42nd Division keep a watch on the German trenches on the coast near Nieuport.

Guardsmen march to the front line before the attack against the Pilckem ridge on 31 July.

Stretcher bearers deal with casualties of the Irish Guards near Pilckem on 31 July.

The engineers build a bridge across the Yser Canal, behind Fifth Army's front.

Troops use a planked road to get to the front line.

Men of 23rd Division wait to advance near the Menin road on 20 September.

Australian troops extend a duckboard track east of Zonnebeke early in October.

Australian gunners shell German positions in Polygon Wood.

An Australian dressing station inside a German bunker in Polygon Wood in late September.

A working party follows a duckboard track across the flooded crater fields.

A light railway carries men and material to the front line.

Walking wounded gather in Wieltje after the attack on 4 October.

A team of horses struggles to haul an 18-pounder gun through the mud.

Mules struggle to carry artillery ammunition across the flooded battlefield.

Chapter 12

Like Spectres Out of the Mist

Preliminary Attacks, Early September

Lieutenant General Watts wanted to improve his position between St Julien and Frezenberg. He wanted to increase his bridgehead across the Steenbeek on the left flank and get close to the stream on the right. The attack was made on 6 September.

The 2/5th Warwicks were unable to advance towards Somme Farm or Aisne Farm on 61st Division's front due to enfilade fire from Hill 35. The machine guns on Hill 35 also stopped Lieutenant Colonel Hammond-Smith's 1/6th Lancashire Fusiliers reaching Iberian Farm in 42nd Division's sector. The 1/5th Lancashire Fusiliers captured Beck House but they could not take Borry Farm due to machine-gun fire from Vampir Farm. Beck House was lost before midday but Lieutenant Colonel Holberton did not know until two wounded survivors staggered back late in the afternoon. The men in front of Iberian House were then forced to retire and everyone was back on the start line by dusk.

A few nights later, a patrol discovered an exhausted man of the Inniskilling Fusiliers who had been lost in no man's land for thirty-one days. He had remained hidden in shell holes during the day and crawled around during the night looking to get back to safety. He had survived off rations taken from the dead.

Major Ferguson was uneasy about the 2nd Irish Guards' bridgehead across the Broembeek stream, north of Langemarck. Early on 13 September, Lieutenant Manning was killed trying to expand it around Ney Copse, so Captain Redmond instructed Lieutenant Smith to withdraw. Sixteen men were left behind and Lance Sergeant John Moyney ordered them to fire when the Germans attacked; around 150 were hit. Moyney's group returned three days later, 'tired, very hungry but otherwise in perfect order'. Private Tom Woodcock covered the withdrawal but he then waded back through the mud to rescue an injured Private Hilley. Both Moyney and Woodcock were awarded the Victoria Cross.

Preparations, 20 September

By mid-September, GHQ's Operations Branch was considering halting on a line between Poelcappelle, 's Gravenstafel, Zonnebeke, Broodseinde and Polygon Wood; a further advance of only one mile. Troops could then be used elsewhere and General Sir Julian Byng was even considering an attack towards Cambrai. But GHQ's plans would be shelved after Pétain asked Haig to keep the Germans focused on Flanders on 19 September.

Haig's staff had been planning step-by-step attacks, each involving a short advance and to be made a few days apart. The hope was that the constant pressure would break the German morale. Fifth Army had to advance across the muddy wastes towards Poelcappelle, 's Gravenstafel and Zonnebeke. Second Army had to cross the drier Gheluvelt plateau and General Plumer submitted his overall plan on 29 August. He planned four attacks, each only 1,500 yards deep. There would be six days between each one, giving time to build tracks so the artillery could move forward. He had given up hope of crossing the Bassevillebeek valley on his right, where Tower Hamlets was too tough to crack. Haig agreed that Fifth Army would take control of 800 yards of front south of the Roulers railway, so each of Second Army's divisions had smaller sectors to cover.

GHQ finally thought it had a winning formula for infantry advances. A short, strong attack through the lightly held outpost area left the infantry in a condition fit to deal with counter-attacks while the artillery was still able to give cover. The planners also chose objectives favourable to their own troops and not to enemy trench lines, which had been dug to benefit the Germans. The British and Australian troops would dig their own position which was not on the German artillery's list of targets.

Plumer had issued a memorandum on infantry tactics on 12 August. An advance would be led by a line of skirmishers who would find routes across the mud and locate enemy positions. They were followed by platoons moving in worms, columns or diamonds towards specific objectives. Groups of moppers up would deal with pockets of resistance while consolidation troops would fortify captured positions. Each division drew a massive allocation of 3.1 million rounds of ammunition, 36,000 grenades and 16,000 rifle grenades for the attack.

The first wave of battalions had to advance 800 yards to get to the first objective. They then waited forty-five minutes before the second wave, advancing a shorter distance to the second objective. During the waits, the heavy howitzers hit specific targets while four of the barrage layers crept forward to disrupt counter-attacks. The guns recreated one deep barrage and field guns fired smoke shells to notify the infantry that the barrage was about to move.

The advance to the final objective was only 300 yards but each brigade sent two battalions forward to hold it against the larger counter-attacks which came several hours later. Company commanders usually kept one platoon in reserve and battalion commanders held one company back. Divisions kept a brigade on hand to deal with any large-scale counter-attacks and each corps had a division ready to take over the captured position during the night.

The Royal Flying Corps

The Royal Flying Corps had twenty-six squadrons. Three squadrons of bombers hit billets, roads and bridges during the day while two squadrons attacked the only two railway lines supplying the Flanders area at night. A squadron reported damage in each corps area on behalf of the artillery. Another two squadrons of fast moving fighters were dedicated to reconnaissance. Wireless communications had been installed at the army report centres and planes regularly dropped messages in the adjacent target areas.

Twelve squadrons of fighters kept the German planes from the skies above the salient and they controlled the skies during the bombardment period, forcing the Germans to rely on balloon observers. However there were many complaints of German fighters swooping low over the front line on the day of the attack. They strafed the troops as they dug in, guiding the gunners by a variety of means including flares. Pilots flew low under the arch of artillery shells fired by both sides, as the infantry fired machine guns, rifles and even the occasional rifle grenade at the biplanes.

Both Fifth and Second Army had to make sure that their forward areas did not become overcrowded, to keep casualties from artillery fire to a minimum. But night after night, twin-engine *Friedrichshafen*, and *AEG G.IV* bombers flew overhead, looking for targets. They were joined by the *Gotha G.IV* and the new *Gotha G.V.* The BEF responded by installing searchlights and anti-aircraft guns while the RFC established a network of observers to warn their night fliers.

The Bombardment

The month-long delay in operations had allowed GHQ to stockpile 3.2 million shells, including 43,300 tons of large-calibre shells. That was four times as many as were used before the 31 July attack; the artillery was literally going to batter the Germans into submission. Fifth and Second Army had organised their heavy and medium guns into three types of group. The first was dedicated to counter-battery fire and the second focused on hitting other stationary targets, like strongpoints, billets and roads. They worked to target lists and returned to them time and again until the aerial observers reported they had been destroyed.

The third type of group was silent, waiting for what was called a 'fleeting opportunity', usually troops moving forward to counter-attack. Communications were prepared and the gunners were on standby, ready to shoot at lucrative targets when they were spotted by aerial or ground observers.

Artillery liaison officers were billeted with the infantry officers, so they could learn about each other's tasks. The liaison officers also had telephone links to the groups, so they could call the gunners if the infantry needed help. The field artillery officers also billeted with the infantry and their guns were organised into groups which focused on targets up to 6,000 yards away.

Fifth Army was in a difficult position between Langemarck, St Julien and Frezenberg. Its rear area straddled the Steenbeek valley and was under observation from Passchendaele ridge. Fifth Army's casualties were nearly double Second Army's in the three weeks before the attack; 10,500 compared to 5,500. Each division was suffering around 100 casualties a day and they were not receiving any replacements.

Gough wanted the attack to be a surprise and his artillery officer, Major General Uniacke, planned a 'really intense and hurricane bombardment'. Many of Fifth Army's guns remained silent and camouflaged until twenty-four hours before zero. The heavy barrage cheered up the assault troops as they waited around the Steenbeek.

Major General Buckle chose a different approach for the bombardment of the Gheluvelt plateau because Second Army's guns were hidden from German observers. His gunners spent two weeks methodically destroying targets as soon as they were spotted and the reduced volume of shelling made it easier for the sound-ranging sections to locate batteries. Each time a battery was spotted, it was isolated from its supplies before the guns were destroyed. The amount of artillery fire doubled at night, when there was plenty of movement behind the enemy line.

A five-day intense bombardment began on 13 September after two weeks of 'softening up'. The gunners repeatedly fired creeping barrages, sometimes by corps and sometimes by the entire army, confusing the enemy. The infantry raided the enemy line during the barrages, checking the defences, and took prisoners. Uniacke and Buckle were sure the German guns were in their final positions forty-eight hours before the attack began, so all the heavy and medium guns hammered them with a mixture of gas and high explosive shells.

The Final Hours

The assault troops followed cross-country tracks and tapes over the course of two nights, leaving the roads free for the horse-drawn wagons. Drizzle dampened spirits as the men covered the final stretch, while GHQ's weather officer, Lieutenant Colonel Ernie Gold (who operated under the codename *Meteor*), had reported occasional thunderstorms. The first one struck at 11 pm and Gough telephoned Plumer to ask for a postponement in case prolonged rain flooded the Steenbeek. Plumer found his corps commanders were optimistic about the ground conditions and he convinced Gough they should go ahead.

It was a well-known fact that the German gunners were quick to react, shelling the British front line within a few minutes of zero hour. All along the line the assault troops huddled together in shell holes in no man's land. Officers had orders to spread the first wave out to a strict timetable at zero hour, a process known as 'shaking out'. The second wave had to shelter in the trenches while the third wave waited 1,000 yards behind the front line.

Mist hid the troops as they deployed but disaster struck three hours before zero hour. An Australian machine-gun officer was given incorrect directions and was captured by an enemy patrol near Nonne Bosschen. To make matters worse, he had an operation order on him. The German field artillery began shelling I Anzac Corps area but, fortunately, there was insufficient time to tell the heavy howitzers about the targets. Flares lit up no man's land four minutes before zero hour and the German guns fired again.

Second Army's artillery orders stated that the creeping barrage would 'teach the enemy to lie at the bottom of shell holes or dugouts wherever any barrages are going on. After one barrage has passed over him he must always expect others.' In other words it would make the Germans too afraid to leave their shelters. The creeping barrage would be composed of five 'curtains' of shells passing over the trenches at 200 yard intervals as follows:

    a. 60-pounders and the 8 and 9.2-inch howitzers firing high explosive
    b. 6-inch howitzers firing high explosive
    c. Machine-gun barrage, enticing the Germans into the open
    d. 18-pounders and 4.5-inch howitzers firing high-explosive
    e. 18-pounders followed closely by the troops firing shrapnel

All the guns would fire a mixture of graze and delay fuses, creating a deadly mixture of ground and air bursts.

Precisely at 5.40 am, the heavy artillery smothered the enemy battery positions with gas. The creeping barrage simultaneously began moving across the German lines as the infantry advanced as fast as they dared, appearing 'like spectres out of the mist'. The guns fired two shells a minute when the infantry were moving, reducing to one round a minute while they paused on objectives. They increased the rate of fire to four shells a minute when it was time for the infantry to advance again. The RFC observation planes were in the air before zero hour and arrangements had been made to switch some of the guns to lucrative targets while others could respond to SOS calls without leaving gaps in the creeping barrage.

Fifth Army, 20 September
XIV Corps
20th Division, Eagle Trench

Major General Douglas Smith had not received drafts to replace the casualties from 16 August, so his battalions were only 350 rifles strong. The division held the sector north-east of Langemarck, between the Staden railway and the Poelcappelle spur. At zero hour 290 Livens protectors fired oil drums but they exploded harmlessly beyond Eagle Trench, which lay between two embankments astride the Schreiboom road junction. All the flames did was illuminate the men crossing no man's land.

Major Cockburn's 10th KRRC reached Goed ter Vesten Farm on 59 Brigade's left but Brigadier General Hyslop had to report that the 11th Rifle Brigade could not reach Eagle Trench. Brigadier General Butler heard that 12th KRRC could not take Eagle Trench in the centre but it had captured White Trench alongside the 6th Oxford and Bucks, giving 60 Brigade a footing on the Poelcappelle spur.

Douglas Smith ordered another attack at 6.30 pm, only this time the artillery would fire smoke shells, to mask Eagle Trench. The smoke failed to hide the 11th Rifle Brigade but they still reached Eagle Trench. Captain Lloyd was killed and his company of the 6th Shropshires were pinned down but Captains Craigie and McKimm used the Lewis guns normally used for anti-aircraft duties to cover their men as they cleared the south end of Eagle Trench.

Lieutenant General Lambart, Earl of Cavan, wanted the rest of Eagle Trench clearing but an operation planned for 22 September was cancelled because the tanks could not get through Langemarck. Major General Douglas Smith retimed it for 7 am the following morning and the 10th Rifle Brigade and 12th KRRC took the Germans by surprise because they had just stood down. Captain Ashwell was at the head of the bombing attack which captured nearly one hundred prisoners and ten machine guns.

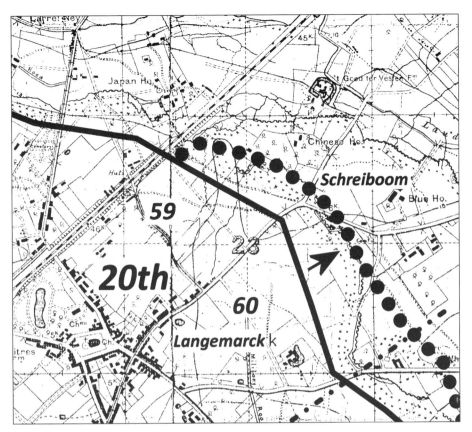

XIV Corps' capture of Eagle Trench on 20 September.

XVIII Corps
51st Division, Pheasant Trench
Major General Harper's men faced thick belts of barbed wire astride the Lekkerboterbeek stream. White Trench and Pheasant Trench had been hammered by an incredible 100,000 shells in just twenty-four hours; more than one shell every second. Many Germans sought cover in no man's land but over 200 dead would be counted in a stretch of Pheasant Trench measuring just 120 yards.

Captains Dane and Jackson led the 1/4th Seaforths as 154 Brigade skirted the shell holes to reach Pheasant Trench. Jackson personally captured the White House pillboxes but Lieutenant MacKenzie was killed clearing outposts in front of White Trench. The Germans mounted their machine guns on the top of their shelters as Lieutenants Davidson and Monroe cut through the wire but they still cleared their part of the German line in a fierce hand-to-hand fight.

Lieutenant Colonel Unthank's Seaforths could not advance any further because of 20th Division's problems around White Trench. The 1/9th Royal

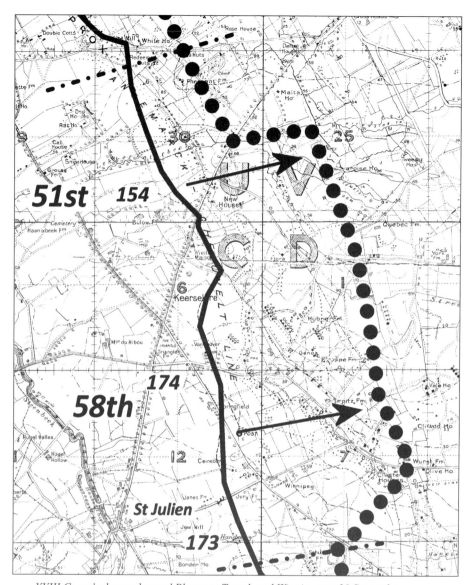

XVIII Corps' advance beyond Pheasant Trench and Winnipeg on 20 September.

Scots' left company was also pinned down until Corporal Horne silenced a machine gun in Pheasant Trench. Lieutenant Scott then led his men forward to join Captain Urquhart's company and they advanced along the Lekkerboterbeek. Urquhart cleared Hübner Farm outside the division's area and Private Flynn then captured Flora Cot. Brigadier General Hamilton was pleased to hear that Lieutenant Colonel Green's men were keeping up with the division on the right.

Both the 1/4th Gordons and 1/7th Argylls advanced onto the Poelcappelle spur where they faced a tough fight for Pheasant Trench. Only one of D Battalion's ten tanks had reached the front line but it helped the Gordons capture Malta House, Pose House and Delta House, while the Argylls cleared Quebec Farm and Bavaroise House. Both battalions had suffered many casualties and the first counter-attack hit the Gordons' left, where 20th Division should have been. General Hamilton sent the 1/8th Argylls forward but the Scots were forced back to Delta Huts and Pheasant Farm cemetery when the Lewis guns ran out of ammunition. The men then resorted to stripping ammunition from the casualties to keep the Germans at bay.

Captain MacDonald arrived with reinforcements and ammunition carried in Yukon packs. The Canadian backpacks were made from two pieces of wood and canvas while a strap around the forehead increased the weight that could be carried. Unfortunately, the heavy loads resulted in some men becoming stuck in the mud while others toppled over. Their comrades had to put their own load down before they could pull them to their feet.

58th Division, London Ridge

Twenty of E Battalion's tanks had been allocated to Major General Hew Fanshawe's division but none reached the front line. The Londoners faced a difficult time crossing the Steenbeek and they then had to assemble in the boggy crater field, east of St Julien.

Three of 174 Brigade's battalions advanced in column through smoke and mist along London Ridge. The 2/8th London Regiment found many Germans hiding in shell holes and Sergeant Alfred Knight killed three in one as the nine others abandoned their machine gun and ran. The Londoners cleared the pillboxes around Springfield, and Knight forced over seventy men to surrender near Hübner Farm; he would be awarded the Victoria Cross.

The 2/5th London Regiment continued the advance south-east of the spur, capturing Von Tirpitz Farm. The 2/6th London Regiment then outflanked the pillboxes around Wurst Farm before establishing a line of outposts overlooking the Stroombeek stream to the north. Brigadier General Higgins's men had advanced over 1,000 yards, taking nearly 300 prisoners and 50 machine guns.

The ground around the Hanebeek stream was so boggy that Brigadier General Freyberg's 173 Brigade was only expected to advance a short distance. Two tanks became bogged down helping the 2/4th London Regiment capture Winnipeg crossroads but it was unable to capture Schuler Farm, even with help from the 1/8th King's, on the divisional boundary.

V Corps

Lieutenant General Sir Edward Fanshawe's staff had recently taken over responsibility for the sector astride the Zonnebeke stream. The pillboxes either side of the stream, including Iberian Farm, Beck House, Borry Farm and Potsdam, had defied several attacks over the past five weeks. The corps' front was double the width of other corps and there were only enough guns to create three belts of fire.

<u>55th Division, Kansas Cross and Hill 37</u>

Major General Jeudwine's division was also short of men because there had been insufficient time to train the replacements sent to replace the casualties suffered on 31 July. German observers on Hill 35 had seen the white tapes laid out in no man's land, so they relieved their tired front-line troops while their artillery hit the assembly area.

Brigadier General Stockwell's 164 Brigade had to advance along the south side of the Hanebeek. Captain Hodson led the 1/8th King's through the crater field but Captain Monks could not clear the north end of Schuler galleries because all his Lewis guns had been knocked out. The 2/5th Lancashire Fusiliers handed over one Lewis gun and the 'Liverpool Irish rallied and swept like an angry flood over the shell holes and took up position in front of the galleries, shooting down or bayoneting the Germans who refused to surrender.' Around one hundred prisoners were taken. The delay meant the King's had lost the barrage and they were unable to capture Schuler Farm. The King's chose to ignore a white flag over the pillbox in the afternoon and it soon disappeared.

Captain Mudie and Second Lieutenant Smerdon lost many men as they led the 2/5th Lancashire Fusiliers towards the south end of Schuler galleries. They used rifle grenades to silence the machine-gunners on top of the bunkers and then charged, killing and capturing many. Captain Kerr was pinned down beyond the galleries because the King's had been unable to advance on their left but Second Lieutenant Stafford advanced along the Hanebeek to the final objective.

The adjutant, Second Lieutenant Cridland, consolidated the galleries after Major Cochrane was killed, but there were concerns they could be lost after Hill 37 fell to the Germans in the afternoon. Lieutenant Colonel Brighten had no reserves left so he deployed his headquarters staff to meet the counter-attack. Brigadier General Stockwell sent the 1/5th King's Own forward to reinforce the line but the galleries were soon lost. Second Lieutenant Allerton of the 1/8th King's would capture Schuler Farm the following morning.

The 1/4th King's Own led the advance across Hill 35 under fire from

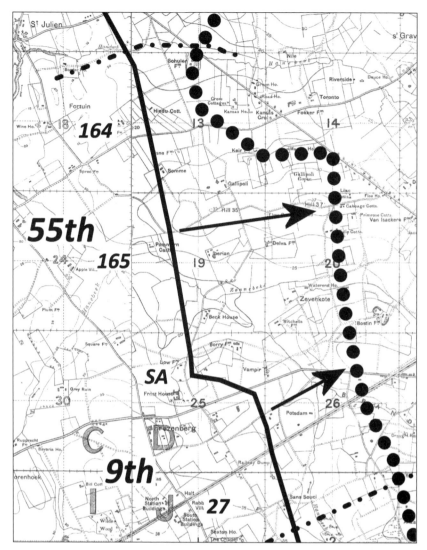

V Corps' capture of Hill 37 as it advances closer to Zonnebeke on 20 September.

Gallipoli Farm. They cleared Somme Farm but overlooked Aisne Farm in the mist and machine guns cut down many of the 1/4th Loyals, including Captains Baker and Captain Tautz, as they pushed towards Kier Farm. The two battalions became mixed up and Aisne Farm was again missed, so it was down to the 1/4th South Lancashires to clear it. Brigadier General Stockwell deployed the 1/5th South Lancashires to reinforce his line when he heard his brigade had fallen back after Hill 37 was lost.

Brigadier General Boyd-Moss's 165 Brigade faced Hill 35 and the 1/9th King's cleared the forward slope while Captain Wilde took thirty prisoners around Gallipoli. Lieutenant Colonel Drew's report remarked that it was 'pleasing to note that the bayonet was widely used'. Captain Eastwood was killed as the 1/6th King's cleared Hill 35 and both Major Gordon and Captain Phillips were wounded consolidating the summit. The 1/7th King's took time to capture Iberian Farm on the south slopes of Hill 35 but the South African Brigade provided covering fire while they cleared Kaynorth, next to the Zonnebeke stream. The King's then cleared Delva Farm and Ditch Trench.

The 1/5th Loyals and the 1/5th South Lancashires pushed east across Hill 37 but the moppers up failed to clear all the dugouts in the mist and the Germans emerged to shoot at the supporting waves. The first wave hesitated when they heard the firing and they lost the creeping barrage, just as the mist was clearing. Wires had been cut, Hill 37 was hidden by smoke and none of the runners made it back, so the gunners unwittingly kept extending their range according to the barrage timetable.

The Loyals and South Lancashires were driven off Hill 37 in the afternoon but Captain Roberts reported that the survivors were 'standing cheerfully to their posts and had no intention of retiring' from Hill 35. A couple of times they saw a German stretcher under a white flag 'protecting' a machine-gun team carrying their weapon forward, so they shot at them. The 1/5th Loyals and 1/10th King's managed to retake Hill 37 before nightfall.

9th Division, East of Frezenberg

Major General Lukin's men had to advance across the Hanebeek valley, a boggy strip of land crossed by the Roulers railway. The creeping barrage had a mix of high explosive and smoke. The heavy guns were detailed to target the strongpoints while the infantry outflanked them.

Brigadier General Dawson's South Africans faced a line of fearsome strongpoints between the Zonnebeke stream and the road. Lieutenant Colonel Macleod's 4th South African Regiment followed a smoke screen through lanes left in the artillery barrage while high explosive shells hammered Beck House and Borry Farm. Captain Sprenger led the 3rd South African Regiment to Vampir before helping the 12th Royal Scots take Potsdam House, on their right.

The 2nd South African Regiment came under enfilade fire from across the Zonnebeke, where 55th Division was delayed, but it secured Kaynorth on the stream before clearing Zevencote. Lance Corporal Billy Hewitt was ordered to capture a pillbox enfilading the regiment while the rest of the regiment cleared Waterend House and Bremen Redoubt. All his men were hit as they approached so he continued alone only to be wounded by a bomb blast near the pillbox. Hewitt crawled around the front and was wounded again as he shoved a grenade through a firing slit. Only three men survived the bomb blast and they surrendered; Hewitt was awarded the Victoria Cross. Major Cochran's 1st South African Regiment encountered less resistance, advancing along the south side of the Roulers railway towards Brand's Gully.

The 27 Brigade had to advance across the Hanebeek valley where the ground was 'frightfully cut up, very wet and the going very bad'. Brigadier General Maxwell instructed his battalion commanders to advance in section lines, with each section tackling the nearest pillbox to its route, while the rest kept pushing forward.

Lieutenant Colonel Ritson's 12th Royal Scots advanced astride the Roulers railway where Captain Harry Reynolds organised the clearing of five pillboxes. He dodged from shell hole to shell hole to get to the first one but a backpack pushed against the firing slit stopped his first grenade. Undeterred, Reynolds squeezed a phosphorous grenade past the obstruction and the exploding 'devil's fire bomb' convinced the garrison to surrender. Reynolds then led his company and some of Captain Sprenger's South Africans against Potsdam. Second Lieutenant Kerr's men hit the four pillboxes with rifle grenades and Reynold's then led a charge which captured seventy men; Reynolds was awarded the Victoria Cross.

Lieutenant Colonel Lumsden's 9th Scottish Rifles advanced alongside the railway to the Langemarck–Gheluvelt Line. Meanwhile artillery fire turned Hanebeek Wood into 'a gigantic furnace shooting up blazing roots and trunks to an enormous height' as Captain Bird's men attacked from the front and rear, capturing fifty prisoners. Lieutenant Colonel MacLean's 6th KOSBs followed a lane left in the barrage onto Anzac Spur and two companies of the 11th Royal Scots joined the KOSBs as forty men surrendered to the 'dour Scotsmen and lusty Australians' around Zonnebeke Redoubt.

The mist was clearing as the advance to the final objective began and a German observation plane began flying low overhead, directing the artillery onto the Scots. General Gough was pleased to hear Hill 37 and Anzac Spur had been captured because the German observers could no longer see into the Steenbeek valley, allowing Fifth Army batteries to move forward. But the triumph was dampened in 9th Division's sector when Brigadier General Maxwell was killed by a sniper while assessing the new line the following day.

Chapter 13

Everything is Absolutely Très Bon

Second Army, 20 September
General Plumer had six divisions deployed along a 3½-mile front between the Westhoek ridge and the Comines Canal. The I Anzac Corps and X Corps had their four divisions squeezed into 1,000-yard-wide sectors astride the Menin road.

The advance progressed at 25 yards a minute through the outpost zone and most of the Germans were taken by surprise in the mist. Assault teams 'wormed' their way forward through the craters, finding dazed Germans waving anything white so they could surrender. The guns fired four rounds a minute, each shooting a single smoke shell to tell the infantry when they had reached their objective. The advance through the defensive zone was slowed to 17 yards a minute while the guns only fired two rounds a minute.

I Anzac Corps
The Australians were visiting the Salient for the first time. Lieutenant General William Birdwood's wish to have all four Australian divisions deployed together had been granted and he reckoned the rivalry would improve their efficiency by thirty per cent. However, 4th Australian Division had just received hundreds of men who had recovered from wounds received at Bullecourt and Messines. It had also accepted hundreds of inexperienced replacements from the base camps but was still a couple of thousand men below strength.

By this stage in the war the word 'digger' was becoming the popular slang word for the Australian and New Zealand soldier. It originated from New Zealand and referred to the 'gum diggers' who collected a fossilised resin collected from the kauri tree.

<u>2nd Australian Division, Anzac House Spur</u>
Major General Nevill Smyth had his assault troops deployed in no man's

land while the battalions detailed for the final advance assembled some distance back, to avoid the German barrage. Brigadier General Smith's 5 Australian Brigade moved forward three minutes early because the German barrage was hitting no man's land. Captain Barlow led the 20th Australian Battalion as they cleared pillboxes, in a sometimes brutal battle:

> '...the first the German came out with his hands up but another behind fired between his legs and wounded a sergeant. A Lewis gunner shouted "Get out of the way, I'll see to the bastards" and fired three or four bursts into the entrance, killing or wounding most of the crowd inside.'

Barlow's company took time to bypass the Hanebeek swamp and the Germans had time to deploy their weapons, hitting many including Major Hosking and Captain Broadbent. Captain Appleby was killed by machine-gun fire from a pillbox beyond the objective, so his men dealt with it; others did the same as their comrades dug in.

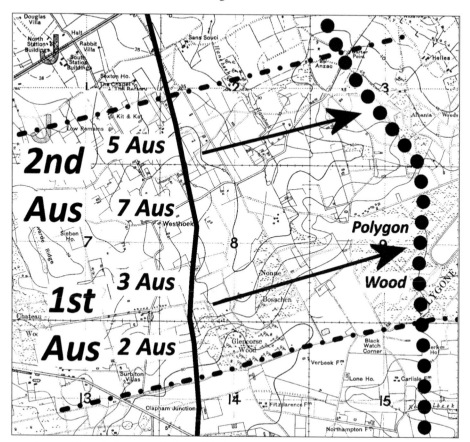

I Anzac Corps' advance to Polygon Wood on 20 September.

The 18th Australian Battalion headed for the Wilhelm Line, on Anzac House Spur, but most Germans had just fired 'a few shots and run away'. Lieutenant Hull's men reached the two storey Anzac House observation post before the machine-gun teams could deploy their weapons. It was the main artillery observation post overlooking the Steenbeek and Hull raised an Australian flag on top to celebrate.

Brigadier General Wisdom's 7 Australian Brigade had to cross the Hanebeek before clearing the Wilhelm Line north of Polygon Wood. The 25th Australian Battalion's Lewis gunners fired from the hip as they advanced through the mist and while many Germans sheltered from the fire, five machine guns were silenced as soon as they opened fire. The 27th Australian Battalion continued up the slope, finding many of the Germans waiting with their hands up. Smoke grenades blinded the men in Iron Cross and Albert Redoubts and the Lewis gunners shot them down as they ran. Meanwhile, 18th Australian Battalion cleared snipers from Garter Point, finding an abandoned dressing station full of wounded men. A breeze dispersed the mist as the Australians waited on the reverse slope of Anzac Spur and their artillery scattered the counter-attacks in Brand's Gully.

The advance to the final objective began at 9.45 am. The objective had already been cleared on the left but 27th Australian Battalion still had to clear the pillboxes in the north end of Polygon Wood. They then set about building new strongpoints while prisoners were questioned about arrangements for further counter-attacks.

1st Australian Division, Glencourse Wood, Nonne Bosschen and Polygon Wood

Major General Harold Walker chose to deploy his assault troops forward, so they could 'shake out' into lines quickly and avoid the German bombardment. They did but some of the Australians kept too close to the creeping barrage and were hit by the corps' heavy howitzers who were firing short. The 3 Australian Brigade faced Nonne Bosschen but all of 9th Australian Battalion's company commanders were hit before zero, so it was down to the subalterns to lead their men through the maze of tree stumps. Fortunately, the creeping barrage stunned many Germans, leaving them eager to surrender.

The 11th Australian Battalion reached Nonne Bosschen under fire from bunkers along the sunken track, north of Glencourse Wood. Lieutenant Fordham was killed leading his men through the trees but Lieutenant Colonel Wilder-Neligan told Brigadier General Bennett that 'everything is absolutely très bon'. Lieutenant Leaver was killed as 10th Australian Battalion approached the bunkers in Nonne Bosschen and his men 'went mad' with rage when the Germans then tried to surrender. They 'filled the place with bombs until they tired of killing' and then sent forty terrified prisoners to the rear. Captain Cornish then led the battalion towards Polygon Wood. Private Roy Inwood went through the barrage protecting 10th Battalion, to silence one troublesome bunker on his own. He later spent the night scouting deep into enemy territory, reporting on the enemy positions around the mound called the Butte in Polygon Wood. The following morning he crawled behind a German machine-gun team and killed all but one with his bombs before making the survivor carry the weapon back. Inwood would be awarded the Victoria Cross.

Brigadier General Heane's 2 Australian Brigade faced the south side of Glencourse Wood. Lieutenant Ward alerted his men of an approaching flamethrower team just before he was killed. Lieutenant Green's men shot the team before the 6th Australian Battalion moved through the south side of Glencourse Wood. Second Lieutenant Frederick Birks led a charge against one pillbox, killing ten and capturing fifteen men. He then fired rifle grenades into Fitzclarence Farm strongpoint while his men took forty prisoners as they filed out of the back door. Birks was killed the following morning; he was posthumously awarded the Victoria Cross.

The second stage of the advance towards Polygon Wood was much easier and many Germans came out of their shelters waving white cloths. The 12th Australian Battalion took nine dazed machine-gun crews prisoner in the Wilhelm Line bunkers alone; none of them had fired a shot. The 5th Australian Battalion attacked Black Watch Corner, at the south-west corner of Polygon Wood where Captain Moore's men captured a two-storey bunker. Tragedy followed because they did not see the Germans hiding on the top storey and one shot and mortally wounded Moore. His outraged men started indiscriminately killing soldiers who wanted to surrender, until Company Sergeant Major Collins restored order and took the rest prisoner. Lieutenant Laxton sums up the futility of the conflict with the words: 'such incidents are inevitable in the heat of battle and any blame for them lies with those who make wars, not those who fight them.'

Some shells fell amongst the advancing Australians as they approached the final objective but it was difficult to identify which guns were firing short. Major Frederick Tubb of the 7th Australian Battalion may have been mortally wounded by such a shell; he had been awarded the Victoria Cross for heroism displayed during the Gallipoli campaign. Even so, the 8th and 7th Australian Battalions cleared the pillboxes south of Polygon Wood and then dug in as German planes flew low overhead, strafing and spotting for the artillery. The counter-attacks took a long time to organise and the artillery scattered them all before they came close.

X Corps

23rd Division, Tower Hamlets

Four tanks were supposed to drive down the Menin road, however one broke down before zero hour and another was hit shortly after zero hour. The remaining two were late, so they carried ammunition and engineering equipment to the infantry. Stokes mortars silenced the strongpoints in Inverness Copse for Major Hudson's 11th West Yorkshires on 69 Brigade's front. The 11th Northumberland Fusiliers picked their way through the south side of Inverness Corpse, avoiding the marshy area north of Dumbarton Lakes on 68 Brigade's front.

Some dugouts had been overlooked in the mist and the Germans started sniping at the 9th Green Howards and 12th Durham Light Infantry as they

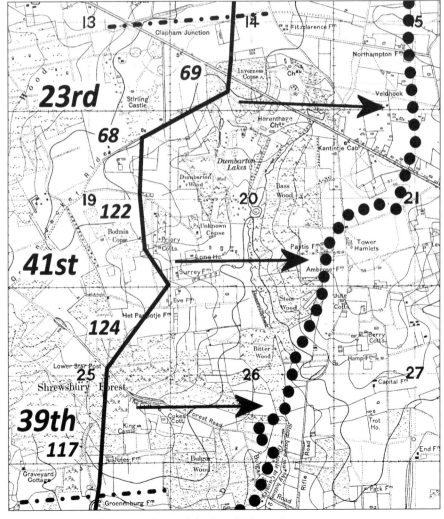

X Corps' struggle to cross Bassevillebeek on 20 September.

moved up in support. It took some time before the moppers up had cornered and killed around sixty of them. The 9th Green Howards took the pillboxes of the Albrecht Line around Fitzclarence Farm in the flank, shooting at the Germans as they fell back towards the Wilhelm Line. Their haul included ten machine guns, fifteen flamethrowers, five howitzers and four mortars.

The creeping barrage had fallen beyond a strongpoint in Dumbarton Wood; it hit most of the 10th Northumberland Fusiliers' officers. There were more casualties during the clearing of the Albrecht Line bunkers around Herenthage Château but Captain Steele led the Fusiliers in a tough engagement for Veldhoek. Captain Payne was the last officer standing but he led the 10th Dukes to Brigadier General Lambert's final objective, taking 200 prisoners in a tough fight for Veldhoek. Captain Tilly led the 13th Durhams along the Menin road, under enfilade fire from Tower Hamlets, where 41st Division was supposed to be. So Brigadier General Colville instructed the 12th Durhams to cover the exposed flank, where they were reinforced by some of the Northumberland Fusiliers.

41st Division, Bassevillebeek
Brigadier General Towsey's 122 Brigade advanced down a long open slope under fire from the Tower Hamlets bunkers, on top of the steep rise across the Bassevillebeek. The 11th Queen's Own and 12th East Surreys became mixed up with the 15th Hampshires and the 18th KRRC during the fight for Java Avenue along the stream and the barrage had moved on by the time they had reorganised. Lieutenant Colonel Corfe led the Hampshires and Queen's Own to Tower Trench under tremendous fire from the right where the KRRC and East Surreys were pinned down in front of the Quadrilateral. They soon had to withdraw and General Towsey had to report that his men had been unable to clear Tower Hamlets spur.

The 15th Hampshires were ordered to attack Tower Hamlets spur again at 6.40 pm but Second Lieutenant Moore could only find 130 men. He was one of the few to reach the summit but he still sent back nearly forty prisoners including a battalion commander. He stayed all night on the spur, driving off several counter-attacks even though only a couple of dozen men were left standing.

Brigadier General Clemson's 124 Brigade deployed around Lower Star Post in Shrewsbury Forest. The 26th Royal Fusiliers suffered horrendous casualties from the Quadrilateral as it crossed Bassevillebeek, losing all but one of its twenty officers in a few minutes. Major Maxwell took command when Lieutenant Colonel McNichol was killed but it was down to Lieutenant Firth and a wounded Second Lieutenant Jones to lead the survivors forward. The 32nd Royal Fusiliers came under enfilade fire from the Quadrilateral and it too lost most of its officers. Second Lieutenant Christie was encouraged by the sight of Germans waving white flags but the Fusiliers were too weak to take the Wilhelm Line. The Germans had decided to fight on by the time the 20th Durhams arrived.

Another attempt by 123 Brigade to take Tower Hamlets early on 21 September failed because the Germans in the Quadrilateral again refused to give in. The barrage had forced Second Lieutenant Moore to withdraw a short distance and he eventually returning with just ten men, most of them wounded, on 22 September. Twenty-year-old Monty Moore later wrote, 'I have been through a hell I hope never to face again.' He was awarded the Victoria Cross.

39th Division, Bulgar Wood

Major General Edward Feetham's men deployed in Shrewsbury Forest ready to capture Bulgar Wood. Lieutenant Colonel Coke's 16th Rifle Brigade suffered many casualties because 41st Division was delayed crossing the Bassevillebeek and two companies were eventually led by corporals. The same happened to the 17th KRRC in support, jeopardising 117 Brigade's attack. The 10th Queen's were delayed until Sergeant William Burman of the Rifle Brigade dealt with the group of men pinning them down. Burman also single-handedly silenced a machine-gun team and carried the weapon to the objective so he could use it; he was awarded the Victoria Cross.

The 17th Sherwood Foresters crossed a swamp to outflank the dugouts protecting the west side of Bulgar Wood. Major Webster's 16th Sherwood Foresters were moving through the wood when the mist started to clear and they came under fire from Welbeck Grange, behind their line. Nineteen-year-old Corporal Edward Egerton volunteered to go back; he shot three men and another twenty-nine surrendered. He probably did it out of revenge for his brother, who had recently been killed. Whatever his motive, Egerton would be awarded the Victoria Cross. Despite the difficulties both Brigadier Generals Armytage and Hornby were able to report their objectives had been taken.

IX Corps

19th Division, Belgian Wood

Major General Tom Bridges' men had to advance between Klein Zillebeke and the Ypres–Comines canal, to capture Belgian Wood and Hessian Wood. The division had fewer batteries than the rest so the artillery fired a smoke screen to blind the observation posts on Zandvoorde hill. More smoke shells hid the advancing troops.

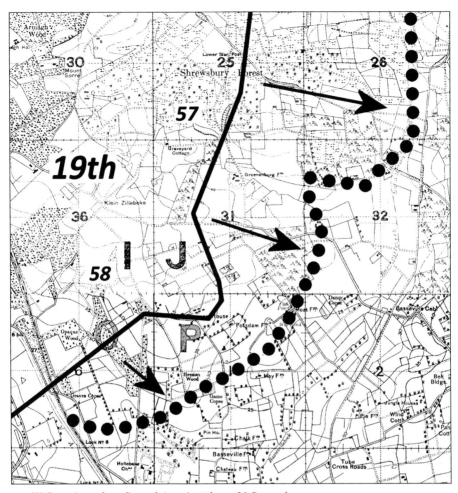

IX Corps' attack on Second Army's right on 20 September.

Brigadier General Cubitt's 57 Brigade lost the barrage crossing a belt of thick mud south of Groenenburg Farm. The 8th Gloucesters and 8th North Staffords were also delayed wading through thick mud but they still cleared Belgian Wood, so the 10th Worcesters could secure it.

Brigadier General Glasgow's 58 Brigade was hit by enfilade fire from across the Comines canal and Lieutenant Colonel Southey's 9th Cheshires lost the barrage due to machine-gun fire from Hollebeke Château on the canal bank. Major Jones was hit while clearing Jarrocks Farm and Pioneer Farm but the Cheshires continued towards Potsdam Farm and Hessian Wood. Second Lieutenant Hugh Colvin entered several dugouts on his own and took fifty prisoners, helping the 9th Welsh to continue its advance. When fifteen Germans ran at him, he shot five and held one hostage before forcing the rest to surrender. Colvin then took command of two companies because Captains Wood and Jones had both been injured. He was later forced to withdraw his right flank because it was under fire from the railway embankment, which ran parallel with the canal. Colvin would be awarded the Victoria Cross.

Major General Bridges had gone forward to congratulate Generals Cubitt and Glasgow when he was severely wounded by a shell splinter near Hill 60. He was succeeded by Major General George Jeffreys.

The Counter-Attacks

Both Generals Gough's and Plumer's plans included measures to stop the counter-attacks. The final objective was turned into an outpost line covered by snipers and Lewis guns. The second objective, around 500 yards behind, had been chosen as the main line of defence. Captured pillboxes were turned into strongpoints while men converted shell holes into defensive positions. Some of the Australian troops chose to dig trenches and while they made it safer to move about, they became targets for the German artillery as soon as the aerial spotters saw them.

Communications had been difficult to establish east of the Steenbeek. It had been impossible to get cables deep enough, while power buzzers were difficult to use when there was a lot of noise. Signalling was used when visibility was good but otherwise it was left to the runners to get messages across the stream. Second Army tried tanks fitted with wirelesses and while the one sent to X Corps did good work, the one given to I Anzac Corps was knocked out.

Each corps had two wireless-equipped planes circling above and one checked the front line while the other watched the German rear. The local counter-attacks soon ended but the aerial observers spotted columns of men marching forward while they were still four miles from the front line. The infantry had been provided with a new sort of SOS flare which floated in the air for several minutes. The combination of three lights (red, green and yellow) meant the observers would not confuse them with enemy flares.

The British and Australian artillery forced three battalion-sized attacks to deploy in the afternoon. The German gunners overshot their targets because they did not know where Fifth Army's front line was. One column advanced down the Poelcappelle road towards 51st Division, forcing the 1/8th Argylls and the 1/4th Gordons to fall back to Pheasant Trench when they ran out of ammunition. They collected what they could from casualties and recaptured their trench. An SOS artillery barrage was fired when the second column was only 150 yards from 58th Division's line and the Germans 'stampeded'. The artillery also dispersed another group which had assembled in Zonnebeke ready to attack 9th Division. An attempt by 55th

Division to take Hill 37 failed because artillery fire and enfilade fire from the Schuler Galleries and Keir Farm 'tore great gaps' in the ranks of the Lancashire men.

There were several evening attacks against Second Army and the artillery stopped the first body of troops advancing towards 2nd Australian Division on Anzac spur. The next attack was made against Polygon Wood but the Diggers of 1st Australian Division 'simply sat back and laughed. They knew the Germans could not get through it [the barrage], yet they were praying for them to get through' because they wanted their revenge. The same thing happened in front of 23rd Division around Polderhoek and opposite 39th Division's position in Bulgar Wood. By nightfall the *Eingrief* divisions were withdrawing, having failed to dislodge the British and Australian troops.

Summary
Fifth Army had advanced around 1,200 yards on a 5-mile front and Second Army had pushed forward a little across four miles. The first try at making a short advance followed by a solid defence had been successful but it had cost 20,000 casualties. The Germans stated 'this new English method of attack had proved its effectiveness' and they immediately looked at how to counter it. Meanwhile, all the British and Australian divisions were being relieved and fresh ones were preparing for an attack on 26 September.

Chapter 14

Men Plunged Onward into the Sticky Gloom

The next advance towards the Passchendaele ridge was going to be narrower. Fifth Army would only attack on a small, 2-mile-wide front, with General Fanshawe's V Corps aiming to capture Abraham Heights around 's Gravenstafel and Zonnebeke. Second Army reorganised across its 3-mile-wide front so General Birdwood's I Anzac Corps could clear Polygon Wood and General Morland's X Corps could advance astride the Menin road.

Haig outlined his plans for future advances on 22 September. He wanted Fifth Army to capture Poelcappelle and Wallemolen spur while Second Army climbed the Broodseinde ridge. Fifth Army would then push north towards the Houthulst Forest and east towards Westroosebeke. Second Army would advance north along the ridge, clearing Passchendaele. Haig was still hoping the Germans would break and five cavalry divisions were waiting west of Ypres. General Rawlinson was also told to put Fourth Army on standby in case there was a general withdrawal across Belgium.

The guns had started moving forward as early as the afternoon of 20 September, so they would be ready as soon as possible. The five-layer creeping barrage was to be used again but each corps fired fewer practices than before because the guns were busy cutting the wire in front of the Flanders I Line.

Counter-attack South of Polygon Wood, 25 September
The German guns started shelling the line between Polygon Wood and the Menin road early on 25 September. At 5.30 am waves of German infantry advanced through the mist, aiming to recapture the pillboxes of the Wilhelm Line as 33rd Division relieved 23rd Division.

The 1st Middlesex fell back 600 yards along the north side of the Reutelbeek before making a stand between Black Watch Corner and Lone House, alongside the 2nd Argylls. The 1/9th Highland Light Infantry were driven back 400 yards but Captain Gelsthorpe's machine-gun teams held their fire until each wave of infantry were close before opening fire. Lance Corporal John Hamilton repeatedly ran back and forth carrying messages and ammunition through sniper and machine-gun fire; he would be awarded the Victoria Cross. Flamethrower teams drove the 1st Queen's 200 yards back along the north side the Menin road and 'the stream of burning oil thrown from these devilish weapons reached a length and height of 100 yards and set fire to the trees, which were as dry as tinder.'

As 33rd Division's line crumpled, the flanks were holding. Major Freeman had 58th Australian Battalion throw back a flank along the south edge of Polygon Wood. Brigadier General Elliot sent Lieutenant Cahill's company of the 60th Australian Battalion forward to prolong the flank back to Black Watch Corner. Meanwhile, the 1/4th King's held on south of the Menin road.

Some of the Middlesex and Argylls counter-attacked with Cahill's company of Australians during the afternoon. Lieutenant Colonel Marshall and Captain Dickson reinforced the line with the rest of the 60th Australian Battalion before Elliott sent Lieutenant Colonel Stewart and the 57th Australian Battalion to help them.

The Battle of Polygon Wood, 26 September

Zero hour was set for 5.50 am and the first wave of infantry crossed no man's land as the creeping barrage threw up clouds of dust into the mist over a 1,000-yard-deep area. Officers led their men along compass bearings and while most of the machine-gun posts in the outpost line were silenced, a few were missed and they caused many casualties before they were silenced.

Fifth Army
XVIII Corps

Lieutenant General Sir Ivor Maxse's men had to clear the pillboxes of the Langemarck–Gheluvelt Line on the west end of the 's Gravenstafel spur.

58th Division, 's Gravenstafel Spur

Major General Hew Dalrymple Fanshawe had deployed 175 Brigade to secure more of London Ridge. The 2/9th London Regiment became disorientated as they advanced through the smoke and mist from *Wurst* Farm but it reached Aviatik Farm. The 2/12th London Regiment took time to clear Dom Trench but they reached Dale House on the north side of the Hanebeek. A counter-attack pushed Brigadier General Jackson's Londoners back from Aviatik Farm and Vale House but the 2/9th London Regiment reinforced the line, allowing the 2/12th London Regiment to retake Nile House during the evening.

V Corps
Lieutenant General Sir Edward Fanshawe's left would only advance 600 yards because it was too dangerous to get any closer to Abraham Heights. The right had to go twice that distance to secure Hill 40 and Zonnebeke.

59th Division, Kansas Cross
The 2/7th Sherwoods led 178 Brigade's advance south of the Hanebeek while two tanks helped the 2/6th Sherwoods take Kansas Cross and Fokker Farm. Captain Bampton captured Toronto Farm for the 2/8th Sherwoods but they then came under fire from Abraham Heights, across the Hanebeek. Captain Broad was wounded capturing Riverside Farm, then had to abandon it because the British barrage was falling on his position. The 2/5th Sherwoods suffered many casualties capturing Otto Farm but the survivors were 'smoking and laughing when they successfully extricated comrades from the mud, which in several places was thigh deep'. Brigadier General Stansfeld reported his men had reached their objective before a counter-attack recaptured Otto Farm.

The 2/5th and 2/4th Leicesters advanced from Hill 37 to the Langemarck–Zonnebeke road around Van Isackere Farm on 176 Brigade's front. Captains Hill and Newsum of the 2/5th Lincolns captured fifty men around Dochy Farm en route to the final objective but Lieutenant Colonel Johnson's 2/4th Lincolns' encountered little opposition. Brigadier General Cope's men had captured 300 prisoners but the ground was too wet to dig deep while the German guns were targeting the pillboxes.

3rd Division, Hill 40 and Zonnebeke
Major General Cyril Deverell's men advanced astride the Roulers railway towards Windmill Cabaret, north-west of Zonnebeke village. Officers struggled to keep their men together because 'a grey mist hung over the ground so dense that even the outline of the railway embankment could not be distinguished and when the men plunged onward into the sticky gloom they had great difficulty in preserving direction.'

On 8 Brigade's front, the 8th East Yorkshires and the 2nd Royal Scots cleared Bostin Farm but lost the barrage as they waded across the Zonnebeke stream. Captains Powell and Topham were wounded leading the 7th Shropshires across the Langemarck–Zonnebeke road but their men captured seventy prisoners around Jacobs Farm and Israel Farm. Lieutenant Colonel Teacher was killed as the 1st Scots Fusiliers prepared to attack and his death disrupted Captain Orr's advance onto Hill 40.

Brigadier General Holmes had wanted the 12th West Yorkshires to take the hill but they were only given an hour's notice. Only a few were in place

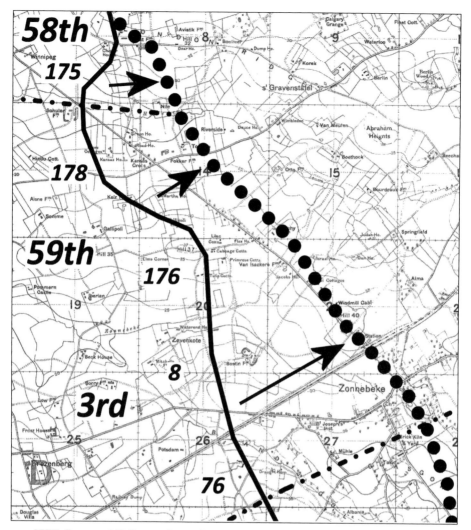

XVIII Corps and V Corps advanced astride the Hanebeek and Zonnebeke streams on 26 September.

when the barrage crept forward and they were driven back by a better organised counter-attack, taking the Shropshires with them. Major Lumsden and Captain Stuart of the Scots Fusiliers stopped the retirement while the 1st Northumberland Fusiliers formed a defensive flank along the railway, facing Hill 40.

South of the railway, Brigadier General Porter's 76 Brigade were delayed crossing the boggy Steenbeek. The 1st Gordons cleared St Joseph's Institute, on the west side of Zonnebeke, while the 8th King's Own tackled Mühle Farm. The 10th Welsh Fusiliers' left was pinned down by machine-gun fire from Hill 40 but Captain Fish led the right as far as Zonnebeke church. Captain Walker was killed leading the 2nd Suffolks in a tough fight for the village but his men reached the Château. Lieutenant Colonel Compton Smith's Welshmen ended up 'down to their last clip', stopping a counter-attack from the station but the Germans were too exhausted to take advantage of the situation.

Major General Deverell's plans to capture Hill 40 the following day were thwarted when the Germans launched their own attack. A bombardment hit the 4th Royal Fusiliers and 13th King's as they assembled and while they held their line, they had suffered too many casualties to clear the hill.

Second Army
I Anzac Corps
Lieutenant General Birdwood's men had just cleared the Hanebeek valley and 4th Australian Division now faced the upper reaches of the Steenbeek valley before it could get onto the drier ground overlooking Zonnebeke. On the right, 5th Australian Division had to clear the rest of Polygon Wood.

<u>4th Australian Division, Tokio Spur</u>
Major General Sinclair-MacLagan's men had to cross the Steenbeek between Zonnebeke and Polygon Wood. On the left, 50th Australian Battalion led 13 Australian Brigade to the stream in Brand's Gully. The 51st Australian Battalion and 49th Australian Battalion then climbed Glasgow Spur and cleared Tokio before digging in close to Retaliation Farm.

The 16th Australian Battalion led 4 Australian Brigade along the north side of Polygon Wood. The 14th and 15th Australian Battalions then tackled the pillboxes of the Flanders I Line on the Glasgow Spur. Brigadier General Brand's men were digging in facing Molenaarelsthoek when a machine-gun team opened enfilade fire on their position. Sergeant Jack Dwyer of 4th Australian Machine Gun Company went forward and silenced it with his Vickers gun. He returned with the enemy weapon and displayed a 'contempt of danger, cheerfulness and courage' as he used it to disperse counter-attacks from the Flanders I Line; he would be awarded the Victoria Cross.

<u>5th Australian Division, Polygon Wood</u>
Major General Talbot Hobbs had made sure all the officers had seen the ground in the smashed up jumble of tree stumps that had once been Polygon Wood. Brigadier General Hobkirk wanted 14 Australian Brigade to be quick off the mark, to avoid the German barrage which would hit no man's land. All twelve waves of men deployed in a narrow strip just sixty yards deep ready to spread out quickly.

Lieutenant Colonel Croshaw of 53rd Australian Battalion had a premonition he would be killed and said 'gentlemen, your men before

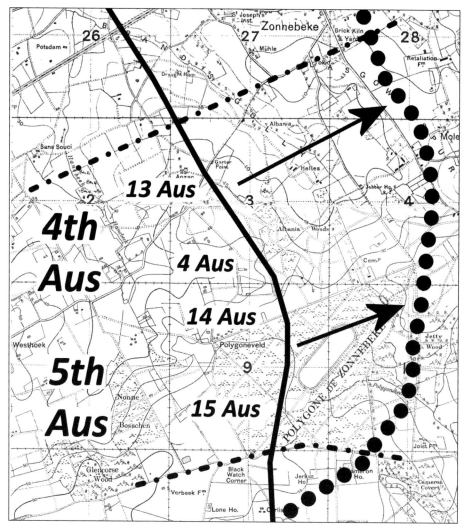

I Anzac Corps cleared Polygon Wood on 26 September.

yourselves, look to your flanks, God bless you lads, till we meet again' before they advanced. Croshaw died leading his men through the north side of Polygon Wood as most of the Germans ran before them. Lieutenant Geldard's men found sixty medical personnel caring for wounded, waiting to surrender in the dugouts under the Butte.

The 55th and 56th Australian Battalions pushed to the north-east edge of the wood and Captain Cotterell was seen 'walking easily, cigarette in mouth, map in hand, behind him the thick line of worm columns, each led by an NCO'. They were under enfilade fire as they cleared the pillboxes of the Flanders I Line around Jetty and Juniper Trenches, until 15 Australian Brigade had cleared the area to their right. Captain Smythe and Lieutenant

Slater then seized pillboxes beyond the objective but they had to withdraw when the British barrage began hitting the area.

Brigadier General Elliott's 15 Australian Brigade had been mauled during the German attack the previous day. Major General Hobbs had given him two battalions from 8 Australian Brigade but there had been insufficient time to brief them about the situation in the south half of Polygon Wood.

The 33rd Division was in no fit state to advance and Lieutenant Colonel Stewart could not to find the Argylls on his flank when he took 57th Australian Battalion forward.

The barrage stirred up a dust cloud 'like a Gippsland bushfire', because it reminded the Diggers of the regular fires in an area in Victoria. But there were problems from the start. Elliott always made his battalions wait three minutes when the creeping barrage crashed down, so his officers had time to warn their men. It also made sure they did not walk into the curtain of shells in their eagerness to get at the Germans. Unfortunately no one had told Lieutenant Colonels Toll and Purser and the 29th and 31st Australian Battalions walked through the 59th Australian Battalion as it waited, causing confusion as the barrage moved forward.

Navigation was difficult in Polygon Wood and officers had to count their paces as they followed compass bearings. The Germans ran in many places but the 59th Australian Battalion still mistook the 'racecourse' (an artillery training area) in the centre of the wood for the final objective for a time. Captain Neale and Lieutenant Pentreath eventually led them to the edge of the wood before Captain Cate led the 29th Australian Battalion to the final objective.

Lieutenant Thompson led his company of the 31st Australian Battalion to the south-east corner of Polygon Wood. Twenty-year-old Private Paddy 'Tank' Bugden twice captured pillboxes by pushing grenades through the firing slits before using his bayonet to make the survivors surrender. Bugden was killed two days later while rescuing his sixth wounded man; he was posthumously awarded the Victoria Cross. Meanwhile, Captain Hibbs had veered south out of the wood and was killed trying to stop Jerk House firing into the battalion's flank.

Major Tracy was concerned about the enfilade fire from Cameron House, where 33rd Division should have been. He formed a flank facing Jerk House with help from 60th Australian Battalion and waited for Lieutenant Thompson to silence the position with his Lewis guns. Lieutenant Colonel Toll had told his men to wait until the British moved up on his flank but Elliott told him to keep moving or he would be sacked. Both 29th and 31st Australian Battalions resumed their advance when their halt order was countermanded.

X Corps

Lieutenant General Morland's line was astride the Menin road. The Germans were quite happy to hold onto Tower Hamlets opposite 39th Division, south of the road. However, they were determined to drive 33rd Division back to the south of Polygon Wood.

33rd Division, South of Polygon Wood

Major General Phillip Wood was anxious to recapture the ground lost the previous day. He told Brigadier General Heriot-Maitland to send his 98 Brigade forward but there was no moon and the mist meant the guide taking the 5/6th Scottish Rifles along the Menin road got lost. Captains Hardie and Arthur eventually found the assembly area but Captain McChlery remained

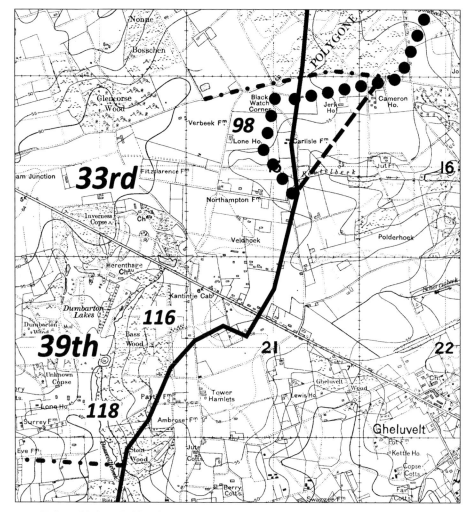

X Corps' fight to hold its line astride the Menin road on 26 September.

lost. Most of the 1/4th Suffolks lost their way in Inverness Copse but Captains Lake and Scrimgeour reached the front and deployed the few men they had. What was left of the two battalions advanced from Verbeek Farm at 5.15 am but the German barrage was heavier than the British one and the two battalions were pinned down alongside the Middlesex and Argylls.

Major General Wood instructed Lieutenant Colonel Garnett to move through the Australian area so the 2nd Welsh Fusiliers could advance south-east from Black Watch Corner. There were no maps to explain the situation and Captain McLennan of the 31st Australian Battalion had to guide the Welsh Fusiliers forward when Major Poore was killed. There was no artillery support because of the many men out in no man's land while the German barrage had turned the three tanks sent to hold the line into 'a blazing mass of twisted metal'. Captains Coster and Williams were hit but their men 'swept forward with extreme bitterness and very few prisoners were taken.' They could not reach Cameron House but Captains Lloyd Evans and Radford helped stabilise the line south of Polygon Wood.

The Welsh Fusiliers were being driven back in the late afternoon until the artillery scattered the counter-attack. The 60th Australian Battalion made a raid later on and Lieutenant Stillman's small group took Cameron House where hundreds had failed before. The 31st Australian Battalion then moved up on the left while the Welsh Fusiliers made a 'superb advance' on the right.

39th Division, Tower Hamlets

Major General Edward Feetham's men faced the strong German fortifications south of the Menin road. Brigadier General Hornby's 116 Brigade climbed the steep slope to reach Tower Hamlets and Lieutenant Colonel Robinson's 13th Royal Sussex took forty prisoners. Major Goldsmith had given up his leave to command the 14th Hampshires only to be killed in no man's land but Captain White and Second Lieutenants Howard and Taberer reached Tower Hamlets.

Brigadier General Bellingham's 118 Brigade lost the barrage as it waded across the Bassevillebeek while two tanks were unable to cross the muddy valley. Even so, the 1/1st Cambridge and 4/5th Black Watch cleared the Quadrilateral. Machine-gun fire from the Wilhelm Line killed Captain Plimpton, forcing Captain Peterson to withdraw some of the Black Watch. The Germans then drove the Cambridge men and the rest of Lieutenant Colonel Sceales' Black Watch out of the Quadrilateral.

The Counter-Attack

Both Fifth and Second Armies had put a lot of thought into how they would defend in depth. The same arrangements for holding back a quarter of the troops at each level were kept the same while the machine-gun teams were divided into three groups:

> One in four would defend the new front line along the final objective
> One in four would be deployed in strongpoints behind the line
> One in two would deployed further back to fire creeping and protective barrages

The weather was clear in the afternoon and the aerial observers spotted infantry marching along all the roads and tracks, which the artillery had already registered.

The 4th and 5th Australian Divisions fired the first SOS flares around Polygon Wood and no one got anywhere near their front line. Another pushed 33rd Division's left back to its support line near Black Watch Corner when the forward companies ran short of ammunition. The troops returned to Cameron House as soon as the barrages had dispersed the German infantry. The next attack failed to dislodge 33rd Division's right, north of the Menin road. Three attempts to retake Tower Hamlets late in the afternoon were also dispersed by artillery fire.

An evening attack reached Hill 40, north-west of Zonnebeke, just as 3rd Division was trying to retake it. There was a stalemate and the hill remained in German hands. The final attack of the day against 33rd Division was dispersed barrages and was stopped by machine-gun fire.

The Germans had found the British and Australian troops to be *eingenistete* which meant 'settled down'. Ludendorff was concerned how easily they had stopped his *Eingrief* divisions. They had taken '1½ to 2 hours to advance 1 kilometre, their formation broken and their attack power lamed'. They arrived too late and too disorganised to break the British and Australians.

Ludendorff decided they had to change tactics. They would deploy as many machine guns as possible in the outpost zone to break up the attack while local reserves would strike back before the enemy dug in. Raiding parties would then spend the afternoon determining the enemy positions and finding targets for the artillery in preparation for a formal attack the following day.

Summary

Both Fifth and Second Army had taken most of their objectives for the second time in a week, proving the step-by-step approach was working. British and Australian casualties had topped over 15,000 but optimistic estimates put the number of Germans killed, injured or captured at more than double that. The Germans did not seem to have an answer to the huge barrage. Over 1.7 million shells had been fired on 26 September, on an area only 1,350 yards deep. However, the British and Australian gunners had not had it all their own way. Their batteries had to be deployed where they could be seen by the German observers and casualties had been double what they were for 20 September; nearly 350 gunners were being hit every day.

As the battle of Polygon Wood drew to a close, Prime Minister Lloyd George was speaking to Haig and his staff at GHQ. The situation in Russia was deteriorating and he wanted to know what the BEF's course of action would be if it dropped out of the war? He received his answer on 8 October. Germany would be able to concentrate its divisions on the Western Front but that would take time. Meanwhile, the Allies were expecting American divisions to even up the balance.

Haig still believed Germany could only be beaten on the Western Front and would only accept an offer of peace when their armies were finished. He did not expect the French to contribute much for some time and did not want to take control of more of their front because he wanted a large reserve. Haig wanted the War Cabinet to send enough men to keep the divisions up to strength but above all 'he wanted their firm faith in the possibility of success.' Whether he would get it was a different matter.

Chapter 15

A Great Keenness and Determination

Planning for 4 October

Haig met Gough and Plumer on 28 September to discuss the next step. He wanted Fifth Army to capture Poelcappelle and the Abraham Heights, around 's Gravenstafel, while Second Army reached the top of Broodseinde ridge and cleared the rest of the Gheluvelt plateau. Haig again reminded the two generals how close the BEF had been to collapse in the same area in the autumn of 1914 and believed the Germans could be in the same desperate state.

Gough thought the short advances were doing nothing to reduce the effectiveness of the German artillery. They fired every time they attacked and then withdrew across good ground to a safe distance. Meanwhile, his own gunners were dragging their guns across the flooded streams and muddy wastes.

Haig was hoping to get onto the Passchendaele ridge, where the ground was better drained, and he was moving another ten divisions to Flanders to make sure it happened. Exploitation brigades were being organised and each corps was given a reserve division while each army had a cavalry division. Five tank battalions were also in reserve and their crews were looking forward to operating across good terrain.

Haig wanted to attack on 4 October but there was so much to do in five days. For a third time the tracks and railways had to be extended and dozens of artillery batteries had to relocate. But this time there was insufficient time to carry all the ammunition forward so the artillery made fewer practice barrages while the machine guns did not take part in any of them. A seven day barrage had preceded the attack on 20 September and a twenty-four hour bombardment had been fired before the 26 September offensive. This time there would be no preparatory barrage but the guns would fire the successful 1,000-yard-deep creeping barrage.

The creeping barrage landed only 150 yards beyond the tapes and it remained stationary for three minutes while the assault troops formed up. They advanced at 25 yards a minute across no man's land and then slowed to 17 yards a minute en route to the first objective. The barrage moved slower still during the advance to the final objective.

German Counter-Attacks

Just before dawn on 30 September, bombers attacked 23rd Division north of the Menin road. The 11th Sherwoods and 8th KOYLIs could see the fire-belching flamethrowers but the artillery spotters could not see the SOS flares in the mist. Two attacks had been driven off before a runner reached Brigadier General Gordon with a request for help.

The Germans wanted to recapture the short section of the Flanders I Line at the north-east corner of Polygon Wood from 7th Division. Shells showered the 1st Welsh Fusiliers with plumes of liquid mud early on 1 October and Lieutenant Colonel Holmes's men shot down the first wave in front of Jubilee and Jetty Trenches before delivering a charge which drove the rest back through the British barrage. Brigadier General Steele sent two companies of the 2nd Warwicks carrying ammunition forward and Holmes used them to bolster his line.

Another attack hit the 23rd Division, driving the 9th Leicesters out from the south-east corner of Polygon Wood and the 9th Green Howards out of Cameron Covert. Lieutenant Colonel Philip Bent led the Leicesters' reserve company forward shouting 'Come on the Tigers' and they restored the line. Bent was killed as his men consolidated their position and he was posthumously awarded the Victoria Cross.

Assault groups from an elite *Sturmbataillon* tried all day long to retake Polygon Wood and Cameron Covert but the Leicesters, the Green Howards and the 10th Duke's held on. They gave up at dusk and the German high command decided to reschedule their next attack against Polygon Wood at dawn on 4 October. As luck would have it, they timed it for a few minutes after Second Army's zero hour.

Preparations for 4 October

All the divisions were relieved before zero hour and the spearhead of the attack was going to be an all-Anzac affair. The II Anzac Corps took over V Corps sector facing 's Gravenstafel as I Anzac Corps shifted north to face Zonnebeke. General Birdwood had decided to use the 1st and 2nd Australian Divisions for a second time, because there had been relatively light casualties on 20 September. It meant four Anzac divisions would be fighting side-by-side and there was fierce competition, particularly between the Australians.

Each brigade intelligence officer prepared the jumping off position using string lines and then used tapes held down with clods of earth or sticks. He started by determining the centre and then used a compass to guide his scout as he rolled out the tape; one pull meant step right; two pulls mean step left and one long pull signified stop. The process was repeated with fifty reels of tape on each brigade front.

Drizzle and a cold breeze chilled the troops to the bone as they marched up to the front. An evening shower made the mud sticky but the mist hid the deployment in no man's land. Those on higher ground found it easy to get into position and one brigadier reported that 'the going was not too bad… the infantry had no difficulty and in fact they were elated. Shells ricocheted too, showing the ground was hard in places.' But those on lower ground said, 'the rain soused the troops, swelled the beeks [streams] and put shell holes into good drowning condition.' The night was dry but the rain returned before zero hour.

Flares appeared above the German line at 5.20 am and the guns brought down a heavy barrage a few minutes later; 'crump, crump, crump, crump, crump – like empty biscuit tins banging down into the valley ahead'. There were heavy losses and the Australians thought their attack had been betrayed. But the Germans had planned to move at 6.10 am following a forty-minute barrage, whereas Gough and Plumer had chosen to advance at 6 am with no preparatory barrage. The British and Australian infantry were assembling under the enemy barrage.

One New Zealand gunner described the thrill of loading and firing a field gun for the creeping barrage:

'I heard nothing but the vicious whanging of our own guns, nothing but the jerk of the breach as it opened and the snap as it closed again, nothing but the clang of falling empties and the rattle of the live shells as the No.4 jammed them on, nothing but the ticking of the watch covering the interval between the rounds and the No.1's voice: "Thirty more left! Elevate five minutes! Drop one hundred!" then the watch's ticking again till he opened his mouth once more, and before the "Fire!" had hardly left it, the spiteful tonguing of the gun, her rattle and quiver as she settled down, and the hiss of the buffer coming home.'

Some observers thought the columns of smoke created by the howitzer barrage 'looked like a crowd of steaming plates', while others thought it looked 'like a wall of flame'. Either way the wall of exploding shells disorganised the Germans waiting to advance in no man's land. All along the line the British and Australians were moving forward and there were a few moments of disbelief before everyone 'blazed at once' in a bloody encounter.

The German gunners were gathered around their guns when high explosive and gas shells began hammering their battery positions. The disruption to their barrage happened just as the BEF's attack began. Flares reported progress and success all along the front but it was some time before the corps and army headquarters became aware of the tough struggle in no man's land.

Each battalion commander had deployed three companies and held one in reserve. Each company pushed one platoon forward with the barrage while two others mopped up and the fourth was in reserve. The support companies formed an outpost line along the objective, so the assault companies could deploy without fear of being attacked. The supports then fell back, ready to follow the advance before the artillery moved forward again.

Fifth Army, 4 October
XIV Corps
29th Division, Staden Railway

Corporals M'Knight and Chitterden captured one pillbox, forcing another group to abandon their bunker as the 1st KOSBs advanced north of the Staden railway. Sergeant James Ockenden bayoneted the machine-gun team pinning down an adjacent platoon of the 1st Dublin Fusiliers as his men cheered him on. He then stormed Goed ter Vesten Farm, killing four and capturing another sixteen; he would be awarded the Victoria Cross. The Irishmen waded across the Lauterbeek and then went through the German defences 'the way the devil went through Athlone – in standing jumps' (a saying from the Rudyard Kipling sketch 'Captain Hayes and the Horse'). They dug in on a spur overlooking the Broembeek valley, having taken around 500 prisoners.

4th Division, 19 Metre Hill

Major General Torqhil Matheson's men had to cross the Lauterbeek stream and cross 19 Metre Hill. He recognised it was going to be difficult to supply the forward troops, so the Lewis gunners were told to save their ammunition to stop the counter-attack rather than fire at low-flying planes. The barrage was weak and ragged but the assault troops kept close to it in the face of a sporadic resistance.

In 10 Brigade's sector, the 2nd Seaforths were hit by machine-gun fire from across the Broembeek stream as they advanced north of 19 Metre Hill.

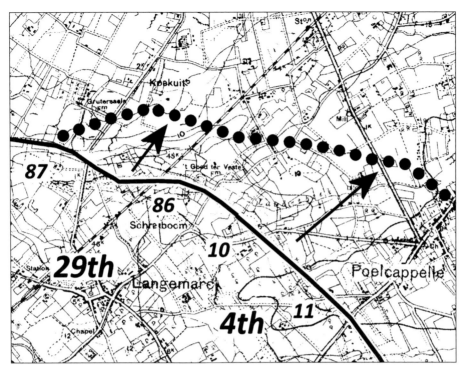

XIV Corps' advance astride the Staden railway on 4 October.

Captain De Gaury and Lieutenant Gullick led the 1st Hampshires beyond Kangaroo Trench and took Beek Villa in 11 Brigade's area. Captain German and Lieutenant Harding then waded across the Lauterbeek and took Imbros House. Captains Walker and Hawker led the 1st Somersets as they suffered many casualties clearing Lemnos House and Ferdan House. A wounded Lance Corporal Watkins captured one pillbox single-handedly but few men reached the objective around Tragique Farm. An afternoon counter-attack drove the Seaforths off 19 Metre Hill and Lieutenant Stannard rallied the Hampshires until the 1st Rifle Brigade reinforced him, but the hill remained in German hands.

XVIII Corps
11th Division, Poelcappelle
Ten tanks of D Battalion crawled up the St Julien road towards Poelcappelle, stacked high with timber and fascines, which were thrown into the craters. The drivers carefully angled their lumbering machines, so they could shove tree trucks off the road, rolling them into the gutter. They then rumbled down the main street as the infantry spread out to clear the ruins.

The 7th South Staffords moved along the south side of the Lauterbeek but the 9th Sherwoods came under fire from the west side of the village.

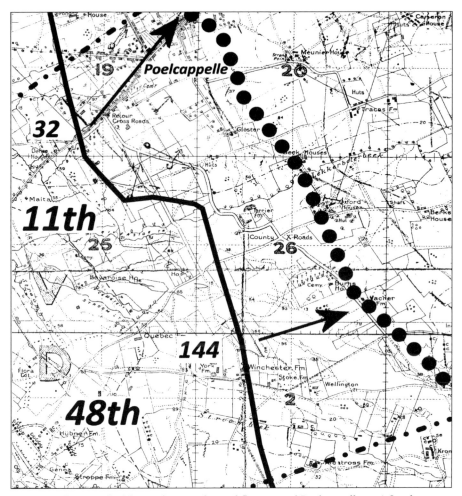

XVIII Corps pushed forward across the mud flats around Poelcappelle on 4 October.

Corporal Fred Greaves and Sergeant Terry rushed forward after Second Lieutenant Adamson was hit and they threw bombs into a pillbox, injuring many and forcing the rest of the garrison to run.

The 11th Manchesters came under fire as they moved past the south side of the village but Sergeant Harry Coverdale silenced many of the snipers and machine-gun teams. He then cleared Meunier House, south-east of the village, and would be awarded the Victoria Cross. The 9th Lancashire Fusiliers suffered many officer casualties even though they had dressed like their men. Snipers watched carefully for those issuing orders and Major Milne was hit as he questioned an injured Captain Parke on his company's progress. A trench mortar helped the Lancashire men capture nine machine guns around Gloucester Farm.

Plans to advance towards Tancras Farm, north of the Lekkerboterbeek, were cancelled when an afternoon counter-attack drove the Manchesters back through Poelcappelle. Corporal Greaves would be awarded the Victoria Cross for playing a leading role in halting it.

The tanks had tracked down machine-gun posts and pillboxes on the east side of the village, being careful not to get stuck in the mud. All but one returned as the infantry consolidated their position and General Maxse suggested that the 'success of the operation was due to a very large part played by the tanks'.

48th Division, Wallemolen Spur

Major General Robert Fanshawe's men deployed between the Lekkerboterbeek and Stroombeek while the Germans waited in their pillboxes, little islands standing above the muddy wasteland. Brigadier General Sladen's 143 Brigade faced the Wallemolen spur and the 1/7th Warwicks suffered many casualties clearing Tweed House, Terrier House and Winchester Farm. Private Arthur Hutt led his company forward after all his officers had been hit and he shot the first four men near the door of a strongpoint, forcing the fifty inside to surrender. Hutt would later rescue four wounded men under fire when there were no stretcher bearers available; he would be awarded the Victoria Cross.

The 1/6th Warwick cleared Winzig dugouts and Albatross Farm before wading across the Stroombeek stream to tackle Winchester Farm. But neither battalion could reach the objective because the Wallemolen pillboxes had it covered, so they established a line lower down the slope. A late afternoon attempt by the 1/5th Gloucesters to capture Vacher Farm, Inch Houses and Adler Farm failed.

Summary

General Gough was pleased with the progress made across the mud flats around Poelcappelle. In most cases the troops had established the best possible line of defence and it was usually very close to the final objective. It had been noted that the drafts, many of them only 19 years old, had acted with 'great keenness and determination' under fire. Sadly for many it was their first and last time in battle because the four divisions had suffered over 4,250 casualties.

Chapter 16

Like Beaters on a Pheasant Shoot

Second Army, 4 October
II Anzac Corps
Lieutenant General Sir Alexander Godley's troops had to take Abraham Heights, around 's Gravenstafel. It had a 2-mile-wide front and had to advance around 1,800 yards, far more than I Anzac Corps, so General Plumer had given it far more artillery batteries.

<u>New Zealand Division, 's Gravenstafel</u>
Major General Sir Andrew Russell was concerned that German machine-gun teams could be hiding in shell holes close to the New Zealanders' line, a term known as 'cuddling up'. So the jumping off tapes were placed 200 yards behind his outposts, so they would not see the battalions deploying. Many Germans were caught out in the open in no man's land, waiting to advance, when the barrage started.

Scouts led the way, 'like beaters on a pheasant shoot', while the rest followed in small columns, deploying when they came under fire. The New Zealanders found dead men in every shell hole as they moved forward and the 1st Auckland Regiment alone counted 500 bodies. Meanwhile, the German gunners missed the assault battalions but they did hit the support battalions as they moved forward.

Brigadier General Melvill's 1 New Zealand Brigade advanced up the 's Gravenstafel spur but the 1st Auckland Regiment veered left until Second Lieutenant Seaward cleared Dear Farm and Aviatik Farm. It left Captain Keir and Lieutenants Malone and Dixon of the Wellington Regiment to capture Boetleer's Farm. But the Auckland men then waded across the Stroombeek and veered north towards Winzig, losing a lot of men clearing Yetta Houses. It left Major Holderness's Wellingtons having to fan out, so they could cover the whole brigade objective.

Brigadier General Hart's 4 New Zealand Brigade was in action for the

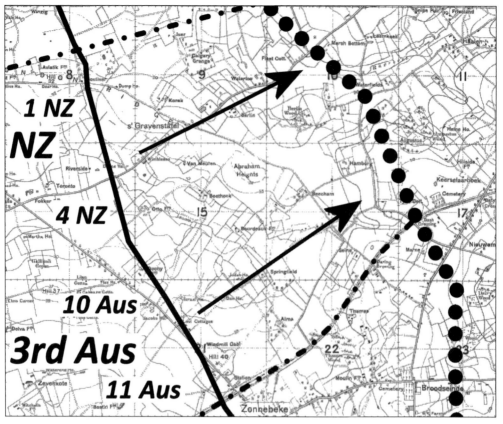

II Anzac Corps' capture of Abraham Heights on 4 October.

first time and his men were anxious to prove themselves. The 3rd Otago and 3rd Auckland Regiments quickly cleared Dochy Farm, Wimbledon and Riverside but the men inside Otto Farm kept firing until the 3rd Auckland got close. They surrendered to Private Mackenzie and he rounded up thirty-five prisoners hiding in the shell holes nearby. The Hanebeek stream was not as difficult to cross as anticipated and the Otagos took fifty prisoners around Van Meulen while the 3rd Auckland Regiment cleared several pillboxes.

Fighting was often brutal and Sergeant Chappell threw bomb after bomb into one large pillbox until the garrison stopped firing at the 3rd Otago Regiment. Corporal Paterson found a pile of mangled bodies inside but the survivors had retreated into an inner room and refused to come out. The officer burned his papers, setting fire to the room, and they chose to burn to death rather than surrender.

The left-hand gun of each battery fired a smoke shell and the line of exploding white puffs would let the infantry know they had reached the Red Line. During the hour-long wait, the Otagos cleared 's Gravenstafel while the Aucklanders silenced the pillboxes overlooking their line, bringing the number of prisoners to 400.

The artillery fired smoke shells to cover the New Zealanders advance across Abraham Heights. Sergeant Foot led the 2nd Wellington Regiment across the Stroombeek, taking seven machine guns in Kronprinz Farm; they also brought the battalion's total of prisoners to over 200. Second Lieutenant Cornwall then captured two pillboxes positioned behind the crest, next to Adler Farm. The mortar teams carried their weapons forward slung over their shoulders and used them to help the 2nd Auckland Regiment round up eighty prisoners at Korek; they took one hundred more around Calgary Grange and Peter Pan. The 3rd Wellington Regiment cleared Berlin and captured 150 prisoners, including a battalion headquarters at Waterloo, while the 3rd Canterbury Regiment took another eighty in Berlin Wood.

Altogether the division had taken over 1,150 prisoners, sixty machine guns and a lot of useful documents. It stopped midday counter-attacks against Kronprinz Farm and Peter Pan and spent the rest of the day digging in close to the Ravebeek stream. Across the valley they could see the pillboxes of the Flanders I Line on the Bellevue spur.

3rd Australian Division, Abraham Heights

The 37th Australian Battalion led 10 Australian Brigade's advance shouting 'we're in it boys'. Lance Corporal Peeler, a Lewis gunner of the 3rd Australian Pioneer Battalion, was at the forefront of the advance, shooting snipers by firing his Lewis gun from the hip. He then silenced a machine-gun post near Levi Cottages before shooting others with his pistol. The rest ran into a concrete shelter where a well-aimed bomb convinced them to surrender. Peeler accounted for over thirty Germans and was awarded the Victoria Cross. One company outflanked Israel House before closing in on Judah, bringing 37th Battalion's total to eight blockhouses and 420 prisoners. The 38th Australian Battalion were pinned down until they crossed the Hannebeek and outflanked the Beacham pillboxes. They had lost the barrage but Brigadier General McNicoll was pleased to report his men had cleared Abraham Heights.

Both 39th and 40th Australian Battalion were pinned down in front of the wire and the barrage had moved on by the time the Stokes mortars had silenced the machine guns covering the gaps. Captain McVilly and Lieutenants Gatenby and McMillan were hit around Dab Trench, leaving Lieutenant Boyes facing ten machine guns. Captain Ruddock was trying to outflank the position when Sergeant Lewis McGee broke the deadlock. He ran forward and shot a machine-gun team firing from the roof of a pillbox with his revolver. Ruddock then silenced a nearby machine-gun post, inspiring the rest of the company to advance again; he would be awarded the Victoria Cross. Lieutenant Meagher was killed trying to take Hamburg Redoubt but Lieutenant Grant captured it along with twenty-five prisoners. It allowed Captains Dumaresq and Redmond to clear several Flanders I Line pillboxes.

The 43rd Australian Battalion led Brigadier General Cannan's 11 Australian Brigade across Hill 40, clearing the pillboxes around Alma. Then 42nd Australian Battalion continued the advance and Captain Skinner's men captured thirty prisoners at the Thames pillboxes. The battalion found itself under fire from the direction of Zonnebeke, so Lieutenant Dunbar formed a flank before clearing nearby pillboxes. The Australians had lost the barrage by now but they continued to advance astride the Roulers railway to Daring Crossing.

Both 44th and 41st Australian Battalion then dug in to act as supports. Lieutenant Bremner captured Seine pillbox for 44th Australian Battalion, allowing it to reach Tyne Cot (now home to the largest Commonwealth War Graves Cemetery in the world). Lieutenant Fraser took another pillbox so 41st Australian Battalion could reach Dash Crossing on the right.

I Anzac Corps

The barrage supporting Lieutenant General Birdwood's attack was weaker because many batteries had been transferred to II Anzac Corps. The 1st and 2nd Australian Divisions were going into action for the second time in two weeks and they faced a long slog across the Zonnebeke stream and through the Flanders I Line to reach the summit of the Broodseinde ridge. The Australians encountered German infantry, some advancing towards them through the mist while others were crouching in shell holes. They fought hand-to-hand in 'quite the heaviest battle to date' until all the Germans had either been killed or had fled.

2nd Australian Division, Zonnebeke

Major General Nevill Smyth's front line ran through the middle of Zonnebeke village and his two brigades were deployed either side of the Château lake. Captain Smith led 25th Australian Battalion through the ruins astride the main street on 7 Australian Brigade's front. The Germans made a controlled withdrawal, with some men giving covering fire as their comrades fell back to the next position. A few machine-gun teams remained hidden, emerging from the cellars to hit many, including Captain Gray, as 26th Australian Battalion mopped up. Lieutenant Ryan cleared the gas works east of the village but his men came under fire as they crossed the summit north of Broodseinde crossroads. Brigadier General Wisdom was

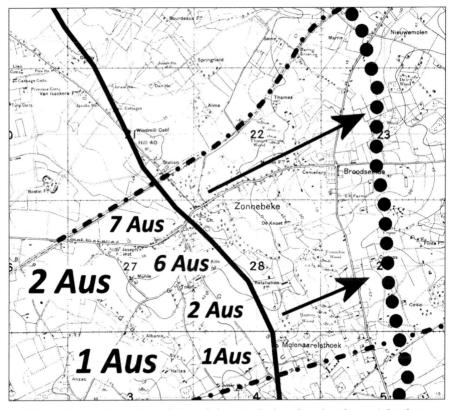

I Anzac Corps' advance through Zonnebeke onto the Broodseinde ridge on 4 October.

still able to report that the objective had been taken and some men had even silenced the pillboxes beyond it.

The 22nd Australian Battalion advanced along the south side of Zonnebeke Château's lake, on 6 Australian Brigade's front, clearing De Knoet Farm as well as Romulus and Remus Woods. The 21st and 24th Australian Battalions advanced across the summit of the Broodseinde ridge, silencing four field guns which had been deployed to stop tanks using the Zonnebeke road. Brigadier General Paton was pleased to hear they had reached Broodseinde crossroads where, again, men went ahead to silence troublesome pillboxes overlooking the objective.

The Australians were amazed to see the green fields beyond the ridge. They could see grass, hedges, trees and the occasional church spire; a complete contrast to the muddy wasteland behind them. Exploding smoke shells marked the end of the advance but some lamented, 'it would have been easy to go further had the barrage allowed it.' Captains Smith and Herbert decided against sending 26th Australian Battalion into Daisy Wood and Captain Gould made 27th Australian Battalion stay in an abandoned trench, rather than attack the wood. His men were surprised to find it full of rotting bits of British kit dating from the autumn of 1914.

1st Australian Division, Broodseinde Ridge

Major General Harold Walker's men had to climb the slope where the Flanders I Line pillboxes 'lay so thickly they resembled a village'. In 2 Australian Brigade's sector, the men of 8th Australian Battalion suffered heavy casualties clearing Retaliation Farm and picking their way through the rest of Romulus and Remus Woods. Major Taylor and Captain Annear were both mortally wounded capturing one large pillbox half buried in a huge crater. Captain Traill then charged a battery of field guns and cleared a nearby bunker which served as an artillery headquarters. The loss of the guns sparked a general retreat over the crest of the ridge.

The 1st Australian Battalion came under so much fire from around Molenaarelsthoek that it veered into the path of 2 Australian Brigade. No one saw the exploding smoke shells indicating they had reached the objective and they chased the Germans over the ridge. They then set about clearing the many observation posts and command bunkers in the area, capturing the staff of two battalion headquarters.

Despite the chaotic beginning to 1st Australian Division's attack, both Brigadier Generals Hearne and Lesslie reported an organised advance to the final objective. Both 7th and 6th Australian Battalions dug in along the grassy slope around Cyclops while 1st and 4th Australian Battalions did the same facing Celtic Wood.

General Walker's men started building strongpoints but it was difficult to evacuate wounded and carry ammunition over the crest under fire from Celtic Wood. But they continued mopping up, finding men either waiting to surrender or hoping to escape. One group of Australians found a carrier pigeon so they wrote a note saying 'Deutschland uber Alles Ha, ha! We don't think.' Then they let it fly back to its loft.

X Corps

Lieutenant General Morland was to clear the rest of Polygon Wood and push towards Gheluvelt on Second Army's right.

7th Division, Reutel Ridge

Major General Herbert Shoubridge's first objective had a special significance. It was the line 7th Division had held during the hard-fought battle of October 1914. But few men had survived three years with the division to note the occasion. The barrage was 'accurate, regular and most effective' and smoke shells blinded the machine-gunners. It was also noticed that 'the Germans were in unusual strength but proved strangely ready to surrender.'

On 20 Brigade's front, the 8th Devons advanced from Jubilee Trench but Captain Drake was killed during the capture of Jay Barn. Lieutenant

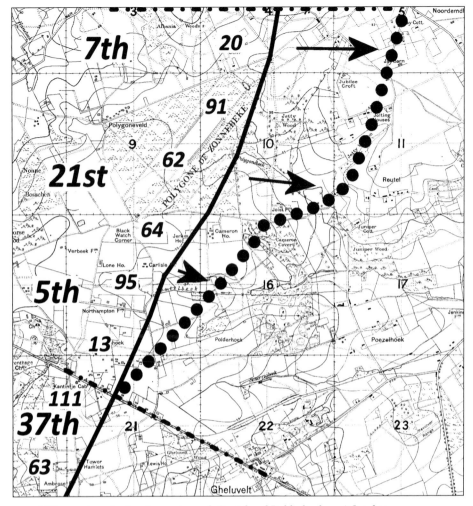

X Corps struggles to advance towards Reutel and Polderhoek on 4 October.

Colonel Worrall's men had taken 200 prisoners, allowing the 2nd Gordons and the 2nd Border Regiment to advance onto the Reutel ridge, north-east of Polygon Wood.

On 91 Brigade's front, Brigadier General Peely's men found many Germans hiding in shell holes and they 'disposed of many with the bayonet'. They took 600 prisoners who said they had been waiting to counter-attack; many of their comrades had run away or were dead. The 22nd Manchesters were pinned down in front of Joiner's Rest until the 21st Manchesters helped them secure the objective, overlooking the German rear area. Captains English-Murphy and Hassell led the 1st South Staffords to Jolting Houses under enfilade fire because 21st Division was lagging behind on the right. The creeping barrage then hit them, disorganising them even more.

The 2nd Queen's were ordered up but Major Driver and his senior company commander were hit, so Lieutenant Colonel Beaumann deployed them in Jetty Trench and along the Jolting Houses road to cover the Staffords exposed flank.

The men of 7th Division were 'almost finished for want of sleep', low on ammunition, and with weapons clogged with mud. Fortunately the Germans were also too exhausted to counter-attack. The biggest danger was from the low-flying planes strafing the shallow trenches.

21st Division, Reutel

Four tanks had been given to Major General David Campbell's division and Captain Clement Robertson led them on foot along the roads. Second Lieutenant Hunniken's tank was damaged by shellfire early on but the other three crossed the stream and headed for Reutel. Robertson was killed near the objective but the tanks silenced targets around Judge Cottage and Juniper Cottages. Lieutenants Ehrhardt and Foxwell had to abandon their ditched tanks but Sergeant Davies returned; Robertson was posthumously awarded the Victoria Cross.

Captains Edwards and Young led the 1st Lincolns east of Polygon Wood, on 62 Brigade's left. Captain Neilson's company kept going but a pillbox near Juniper Trench pinned down Captain Newbury's men. Lieutenant Colonel Lewis Evans fired through the aperture and the 'Germans came out with their hands up but were not taken back as prisoners. Men showed a decided preference to use their rifle rather than the bayonet.' An injured Evans led the Lincolns until he collapsed and then staggered back to the aid station; he would be awarded the Victoria Cross.

One of the tanks helped the 3/4th Queen's secure the pillboxes on the far side of the Polygonbeek. The 12/13th Northumberland Fusiliers and the 10th Green Howards then advanced to the far edge of the plateau but they were out of contact with each other. The 9th KOYLIs advanced from the south-east side of Polygon Wood on 64 Brigade's front and Brigadier General Headlam reported they could see across the boggy Reutelbeek.

5th Division, Polderhoek

Major General Reginald Stephens' men had stopped the counter-attacks the previous day, leaving them little time to prepare for the battle. Tapes had to be laid behind the trenches north of the Menin road, so the troops would be moving perpendicular to the objective. The German gunners hit the empty trenches when the advance began while their infantry were found waiting to advance in no man's land. Over 250 prisoners were taken but most were hit by the German barrage as they headed to the rear.

On 95 Brigade's left, Captain Hughesdon and Second Lieutenant Clarke led the 1st DCLI towards Cameron Covert under enfilade fire from Polderhoek Château. A tank silenced the pillboxes in the surrounding park and Lieutenant Colonel Norton's men captured 200 prisoners while the fifteen captured machine guns were turned on their former owners. The rest of the tanks accompanied Captain Baines and Second Lieutenant Dench along the Reutel road but they soon had to withdraw from their exposed position.

Lieutenant Colonel Blunt was killed leaving Captain Wells to lead the 1st Devons until Major Anderson Morshead took over. The men lost the barrage moving astride the boggy Ravebeek, an 'impenetrable morass 100 to 200 yards wide which, in better times, may have been a stream'. After navigating around the shell holes in the smoke, they dug in west of Polderhoek woods under fire from the Château pillboxes. A counter-attack drove the DCLI and the Devons back north of the stream so Brigadier General Lord Gordon-Lennox had to send the 1st East Surreys forward to reinforce the line.

The 2nd KOSBs lost the barrage as it moved across the swamp south of the Scherriabeek stream on 13 Brigade's front, but a tank helped Lieutenants Aucott and Cappy capture the pillboxes in Polderhoek park. Second Lieutenant Dunn was killed trying to storm the Château, 'a veritable fortress, packed with machine guns which covered the grounds on all sides.' A counter-attack overran two of Lieutenant Colonel Furber's companies but Captain Machin's company stopped six more with the help of Lance Corporal Vaughan's Lewis gun team. Only ninety KOSBs would answer the morning roll call. Lieutenant Colonel Johnstone's 1st Queen's Own made some progress but Captain Cobb was killed before he reached Gheluvelt. He was just one of nearly 370 men hit astride the Menin road.

IX Corps
37th Division, Tower Hamlets
Major General Hugh Bruce-Williams's men only had to advance a short distance astride the Menin road. Lieutenant Allen's men of the 13th Royal Fusiliers veered to avoid fire from one pillbox only to become pinned down because the 13th KRRC had been unable to capture Lewis House on their right. Brigadier General Compton had to report that 111 Brigade had not advanced but it had cost his men dear; only thirty-eight Fusiliers answered the next roll call.

Machine-gun fire hit 63 Brigade as it advanced over the crest and Brigadier General Challenor's men lost the barrage. Some men reached Tower Hamlets but the 8th Lincolns were forced to withdraw from their exposed position while a counter-attack drove the 8th Somersets back. A wounded Private Thomas Sage found himself sheltering in a shell hole with seven other Somerset men. His sergeant was hit in the act of throwing a grenade and it fell to the ground, so Sage put his greatcoat over it and sat down. He was badly injured but all but one of his comrades survived and they crawled back to safety. Sage would be awarded the Victoria Cross.

Summary
A combination of sound tactics and good luck meant that 'an overwhelming blow had been delivered and both sides knew it'. Fifth Army had advanced around 1,000 yards on a 2-mile front around Poelcappelle, taking around 600 prisoners. Second Army had advanced up to 1 mile deep on a 4-mile-wide front around Zonnebeke, taking an incredible 4,100 prisoners. The Germans did not try to dislodge Fifth Army from its positions around Poelcappelle but there were signs of a counter-attack towards Broodseinde on Second Army's front. The artillery were instructed to limit all SOS barrages to fifteen minutes, to conserve ammunition, but the observers had kept a look out for signals calling for more.

Ludendorff's decision to hold the front line with a stronger force had failed. The decision to increase the strength at the front line had ended in disaster because the artillery barrage had stunned the defenders before the assault troops overran them. The result was there were no men left to break up the later stages of the advance. Luck over the timing of the two attacks had added to the Germans' woes. Only their artillery had escaped relatively unscathed, because the guns were spread out in camouflaged positions.

Ludendorff said the battle had been 'extraordinarily severe and again we only came through it with enormous losses.' The German official history would go further, describing it as the 'black day of October 4th'. General Plumer called it the 'greatest victory since the Marne', the battle which had turned the tide of the German advance in September 1914. Commanders on both sides thought a decisive success was close. The only thing that could change it was the weather.

Chapter 17

An Incredible Degree of Mismanagement

Battle of Poelcappelle, 9 October

The battle of Broodseinde was the third German setback in just two weeks but the success created problems. The bombardments had torn up the ground, leaving men and animals to drag the guns across the marsh, a journey which was becoming longer with each advance. Yet the British and Australian soldiers on the Broodseinde ridge were looking out over green fields.

The state of the battlefield meant hundreds of men were falling ill with dysentery, flu and trench foot and units 'simply faded away'. A war correspondent watched horrified as 'a couple of men passed, going very slow. They were white and drawn and detached and put one foot in front of the other, as I had not seen men do since the Somme winter... but these men looked whiter...' They were 'always looking the worst and sometimes looking like a dead man looks and scarcely able to walk.' He asked a New Zealand officer if the mud was 'nearly as bad as Flers [on the Somme]' and he replied 'oh no – we've never had anything like that!'

Lieutenant General Birdwood was shocked when the stories reached I Anzac Corps' headquarters and he passed them on to Second Army. Whether they went any higher or not is immaterial; Haig and Plumer were determined to keep pushing. The ground and weather were against the British and Anzac troops but their spirits were high because of the three recent successes. One wounded Digger called out to the war correspondent from his stretcher, 'we got the bastards good on the second ridge.'

General Gough wanted to advance further but the loss of 19 Metre Hill, near the Staden railway, endangered his flank, so he called it off. On Second Army's front, Lieutenant General Godley wanted II Anzac Corps to keep pushing onto the Passchendaele ridge but Lieutenant General Birdwood wanted to move I Anzac Corps' field artillery forward first. Lieutenant General Morland reported X Corps was too weak to advance towards

Becelaere and instead lost Reutel and Cameron Covert during the afternoon.

The arrangements for the attack copied what had been successful during the three previous ones. Each division would hold a brigade ready to take advantage of a German withdrawal. Each corps had a division ready to exploit any breakthrough. Each army had a cavalry division ready to join in, while another three divisions would follow.

Fifth Army had to reach the Flanders I Line half way to Westroosebeke but Gough only dared send two companies forward because of the bad ground. The rest of his men would exploit any breakthrough on firm ground. Second Army had to get beyond Passchendaele but the ground was too soft for the two tank battalions Plumer had available.

On 7 October both Gough and Plumer said they wanted to end the campaign, because of the bad conditions, but Haig wanted to keep pressing before more German reserves arrived. Although Haig's view is now hard to understand, we have to look at the situation without the benefit of hindsight. The Australian official history sums up what GHQ had to consider in the following words: 'In view of the results of three step-by-step blows, what will be the result of three more in the next fortnight?'

Fifth and Second Armies had developed good tactics in all the combat arms: infantry, artillery, engineers and air. They had the guns, the ammunition and the men and more attacks could destabilise the German position. Haig also had to consider that Pétain wanted the British to continue attacking, to assist the French army. He wanted 'no postponement unless absolutely necessary' so the army commanders agreed the date of the next attack would be 9 October with a follow up on 12 October.

The problem was, the drizzle which had started on 3 October had turned to heavy rain, turning the battlefield into 'a porridge of mud'. Senior officers were finding it increasingly difficult to justify another attack and while Second Army's Chief of Staff, Major General Harington, tried to convince the war correspondents that attacking was the right thing to do, they thought it was 'a great, bloody experiment – a huge gamble'. More and more people were feeling 'terribly anxious' that the ridge had to be taken at all costs and whatever the weather.

That was the view from the top but some at the bottom believed they had the upper hand over the Germans. Lieutenant Sharland, 40th Australian Battalion, wrote, 'if the weather had only held over another two or three weeks, we would have had Fritz well on the run in Flanders... Now I fear that it must be a wash out for the year – tough luck. But we have got to take these things as they are and keep plugging away.'

The rains continued and while life was bearable on the higher ground, the infantry squelched forward through the slime only to stand in mud and water at the front line. A lucky few found shelter in a pillbox or beneath corrugated iron shelters. The combination of rain, mud and lack of cover exhausted the toughest of men and made the rest sick.

The roads were disappearing beneath the mud and the horse-drawn wagons sometimes slithered off the planks or broke through them. Mules and pack horses sometimes crowded around looking for firmer ground but they had to be shooed away because they blocked the roads and churned up the tracks.

The gun platforms had to be built close to the roads, creating dense targets. It took two days to build a platform of fascines and stone covered by beech planks but they began sinking as soon as the gun opened fire. The crew struggled to keep their weapon and the shells clean as they disappeared into the mud.

Medics did what they could to help the wounded but there were never enough stretcher bearers. It took eight men and sometimes sixteen to make the long slog through the mud. The pillboxes used as aid posts were overflowing with wounded and while the fortunate sheltered inside, the rest lay in the mud outside. Infantry were called upon to help but they did not have the training, while prisoners were being held back for interrogation.

The rain ceased during the early hours of 8 October but the weather forecast was for more of the same. The troops spent a miserable night either shuffling along the slippery duckboards or wading through the mire. They followed lines of dim lamps hanging from stakes or white tapes through the maze of 'innumerable shell holes full of mud and water'. But it took hours to cover the shortest of distances, resulting in zero hour being postponed by two hours.

Heavy rain turned the sky black, making the conditions 'almost indescribable' as they trudged forward. The postponement was not enough; some companies were late and it was little short of a miracle that any found the jumping off tapes. The artillery began firing at 5.15 am but the barrage was weak due to the lack of guns and many were firing inaccurately because they had not had time to register their position. The creeping barrage moved forward five minutes later at only 12 yards a minute. But it was still too fast because the mud was just too deep.

Fifth Army, 9 October
XIV Corps

The low-lying ground north of Poelcappelle was boggy but the streams were still running and getting rid of the rainwater. They were waist deep in places but the engineers had made trestle bridges for the infantry to carry forward. The artillery had also managed to get most of their guns into position on time and they were well supplied with ammunition. Lieutenant General Rudolph Lambart, the Earl of Cavan, wanted to push north towards the Houthulst Forest, alongside the French, but he also wanted to advance east of Poelcappelle, towards the Flanders I Line.

The Guards Division, Houthulst Forest

Major General Feilding had made sure patrols had worked out where the troops could cross the Broembeek stream, west of the Staden railway. They plotted the boggy parts and the flooded areas where it was dangerous to venture but they also located flooded culverts and bridges where the men could cross. The Guardsmen had 200 bridges and mats ready but in most cases they were able to wade across, even if the muddy water came up to their armpits at times.

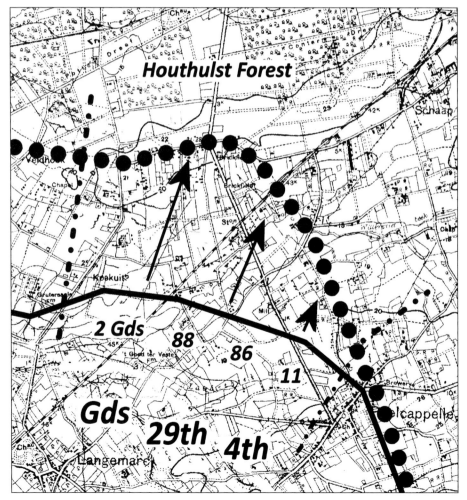

XIV Corps had the only success on 9 October astride the Staden railway.

On 2 Guards Brigade's front, the 2nd Irish Guards and 1st Scots Guards waded across the mud flats, scrambled over fallen trees and followed abandoned duckboards. Fortunately, the Germans had only just taken over the line and had not had time to settle in, so many surrendered. The 3rd Coldstream Guards used rifle grenades to silence the blockhouses around Les Cinq Chemins and Lance Sergeant John Rhodes then entered Suez Farm alone and forced the artillery observer, who was on the telephone to a battery, to surrender; he would be awarded the Victoria Cross. The 3rd Coldstream Guards stopped a counter-attack from Houthulst Forest, aimed at driving a wedge between them and the French. Another attack against the 1st Coldstream Guards' around Panama House was halted and Brigadier General Sergison-Brooke was able to report Fifth Army's flank was safe.

The 2nd Grenadier Guards and 2nd Scots Guards encountered little opposition on the south side of Houthulst Forest but it was a dangerous place, filled with pillboxes and machine-gun posts. The Irish Guards were hit by fire from 29th Division's sector as they cleared Egypt House and then were 'worst-sniped from the shell holes' as they advanced to their objective.

29th Division, Staden Railway

On 88 Brigade's front, Brigadier General Nelson's men crossed the Broembeek using bridges left by the Germans. The Newfoundland Regiment advanced slowly north of the Staden railway while Lieutenant Colonel Linton's 4th Worcesters cleared Namur Crossing. They were then pinned down by a pillbox until the firing stopped; 'a minute later every man in sight was on his feet, cheering and laughing, for stumbling through the mud came a little crowd of the enemy with hands raised in surrender. Behind them came a solitary British soldier labouring along under the weight of the machine gun.' Private Fred Dancox had outflanked the pillbox and entered, threatening those inside with a grenade. He took forty men prisoner and there were shouts of 'good old Dancox' as he escorted them to the rear. He would be awarded the Victoria Cross.

The 1st Essex advanced to Pascal Farm on the right and while the 2nd Hampshires reached Cairo Farm, they could not reach Egypt House. Lieutenant Colonel Spring's Hampshires reinforced the Newfoundland men when they were driven back and Captain Cudden then cleared the area around Cairo Farm.

The 1st Lancashire Fusiliers were astride the Staden railway on 86 Brigade's front and Lieutenant Colonel Hart Synnot proudly noted the 1st and 2nd Battalions would advance side-by-side for the first time. Some platoons became lost moving across the mud flats and they only reached the jumping off line a few minutes before zero. Lieutenant Rougier and

Captain Downes led the advance but Lieutenant Winterbottom had to take over when Downes was hit. Sergeant Joseph Lister approached Olga House alone, silenced a nearby machine-gun team and made the men in the bunker give themselves up after shooting one of their number. He then rounded up around another one hundred prisoners in the nearby shell holes, so his men could resume their advance. Lister would be awarded the Victoria Cross.

But casualties were high and Second Lieutenant Addison led the survivors to Tranquille Farm after Second Lieutenant Garnet was killed by a British shell. Second Lieutenant Le Mesurier organised the stragglers around Senegal Farm but Sergeant Driver had to take over when the battalion's last officer was wounded. Captain Hood and Second Lieutenant Saul led the 2nd Royal Fusiliers beyond the Lancashire Fusiliers in 'a filthy advance; it was costly; it was unsatisfactory.' Sergeant John Molyneux's bombing team cleared Conde House taking around twenty-five prisoners; he would be awarded the Victoria Cross.

4th Division, North-West of Poelcappelle

In 12 Brigade's sector the 1st King's Own and the 1st Lancashire Fusiliers advanced to the north of Poelcappelle. Major Watkins noted that they were advancing 'like a practice parade' but Captain Judd and Second Lieutenant Lloyd soon came under sniper fire from Landing Farm, Compromis Farm and Millers Houses as well as enfilade fire from Poelcappelle, where 11th Division was struggling. Lieutenant Macdonald and Captain Elkington led the rest of the Lancashire men forward as they dodged between the shell holes.

Lieutenant Colonel Horsfall was leading the 2nd Dukes forward to reinforce the line at Landing Farm when he too was shot by a sniper. Captains Watkins and Clarke reorganised the brigade line while a few men pushed forward but Brigadier General Carton de Wiart had to report his men could not go any further until Poelcappelle was cleared.

XVIII Corps

Lieutenant General Sir Ivor Maxse was hoping for more progress after the success on 4 October but there were many factors against him. His two divisions had to walk for nearly fifteen hours in the pouring rain on the night of 7/8 October. They found a shambles waiting for them around Poelcappelle. They were wet, hungry and exhausted before zero hour and in no state to make a vigorous advance beyond the village.

The infantry advanced behind a weak barrage towards a fresh German division which had deployed its machine guns well forward. The lack of artillery fire meant they could shoot down the advancing infantry with ease.

11th Division, Poelcappelle

Brigadier General Price's men found that the barrage 'was very ill-defined and the heavy batteries fired very short'. The 6th Green Howards captured around 175 prisoners in Poelcappelle but it took them too long to clear the ruins. Corporal William Clamp took twenty prisoners in the largest pillbox but he was later killed by a sniper while hunting down a machine-gun team; he was posthumously awarded the Victoria Cross. But the Green Howards were unable to capture the brewery because the tanks were unable to get through the village. Heavy casualties meant that the Germans could infiltrate back into the ruins, forcing the Howards to withdraw.

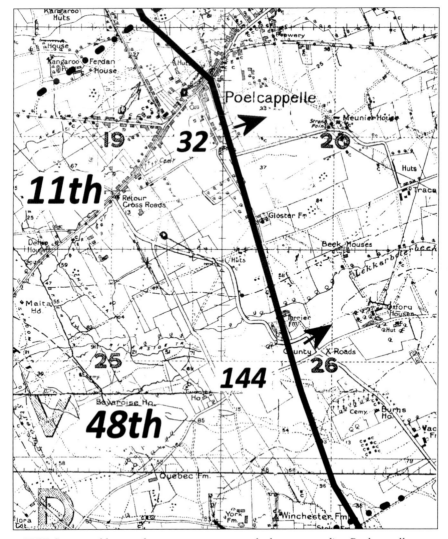

XVIII Corps could not make any progress across the bog surrounding Poelcappelle.

48th Division, Wallemolen Spur

Major General Robert Fanshawe's men were to attack south of Poelcappelle for the second time in five days. They had been successful on 9 October but the rain and the fighting had flooded the Lekkerboterbeek and Stroombeek streams. It left Brigadier General Done's 144 Brigade facing an advance 'through mud and water and across soft, spongy ground'.

The 1/4th Gloucesters got lost en route to the front line and they only just deployed in time. But Lieutenant Colonel Crosskey's men were stopped by machine-gun fire from Oxford Houses. They were also under enfilade fire from the cemetery until Lieutenant Colonel Schomberg's 1/6th Gloucesters cleared it. Captains Fletcher and Titley led the 1/6th Gloucesters but Titley's company went too far and they were never seen again. During the afternoon the 1/8th Worcesters could not capture Oxford Houses while the 1/7th Worcesters could not reach Vacher Farm.

Second Army
II Anzac Corps

II Anzac Corps' gunners had been unable to get all their field guns across the Steenbeek stream in time. It meant they would be firing the creeping barrage at their extreme range of 6,000 yards. It was also too dangerous to cross the 's Gravenstafel ridge in daylight, so the men had to move into line when it was dark. The staff officers guided the men along two tracks called Jack and Jill but part of the journey was across mud and some of the guides got lost. The relief was then 'marked by an incredible degree of mismanagement'. It had taken eleven hours instead of five, while some companies arrived after zero hour. Officers spread out their men to fill the gaps in their line the best they could, but they could barely see the weak barrage in the rain, let alone follow it. Some rounds landed short and many shells sent showers of mud into the air when they exploded.

49th Division, Bellevue Spur

Major General Edward Perceval's men faced the Ravebeek stream which Second Army intelligence reported as 'saturated ground. Quite impassable. Should be avoided by all troops at all times.' But still the Yorkshire men waded across it. The barrage crept forward slowly but the men were slower wading through the clinging mud. They dared not take cover in the water-filled shell holes but many Germans had also been beaten by the weather and they surrendered rather than fight.

The 1/4th and 1/5th York and Lancasters of 148 Brigade complained that 'no single German was found killed by the shell fire. There was no curtain of fire at all and it was impossible to see where the edge of the

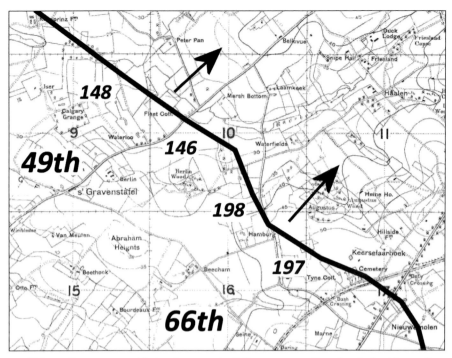

II Anzac Corps was unable to advance onto Bellevue spur or Passchendaele ridge on 9 October.

barrage was intended to be.' They reached Wolf Farm but the pillboxes on Wallemolen spur had hit many of Brigadier General Aldercorn's men. On the right, the West Yorkshire men of 146 Brigade followed the 's Gravenstafel road across the stream but they were shot to pieces as they clawed at the barbed wire around Marsh Bottom.

It was obvious that the attack was a failure and while some commanders refused to send their battalions forward others sent theirs forward to suffer the same fate as the assault battalions. Communication with the front proved impossible and the lack of information was ominous. Some questioned a message from an aerial observer, reporting flares on Bellevue spur after midday, but Major General Perceval still ordered 147 Brigade forward.

It was dark by the time Brigadier General Lewes's men crossed the front line and they were shot down by waiting German troops. It later turned out the observer had misread the map and the flares had been fired around Peter Pan, very close to the start line. The division had suffered 2,500 casualties and the Ravebeek still had to be crossed. Major General Perceval was replaced a few days later.

66th Division, Augustus Wood
Major General the Hon. Herbert Lawrence's division was going into battle for the first time and everything was stacked against the East Lancashire

men. The 198 Brigade advanced on time but Brigadier General Hunter's men struggled through the mud and had to jump across water-filled trenches. The 2/9th Manchesters and the 2/4th East Lancashires moved towards Waterfields under enfilade fire from the Bellevue spur while the 2/5th East Lancashires cleared Hamburg Redoubt on the right. They were pinned down 300 yards short of the objective and it was some time before 197 Brigade appeared behind their right flank. They withdrew to a safer position and had to stop a counter-attack at dusk.

Brigadier General Borrett's men had a real problem reaching 197 Brigade's front around Tyne Cot. Lieutenant Colonel Bates's 3/5th Lancashire Fusiliers arrived just before zero hour and immediately advanced towards Hillside Farm. But Lieutenant Colonel Anderton's 2/6th Lancashire Fusiliers were forty minutes late and 'the men were so done they could hardly stand up and hold a rifle.' Even so, they advanced beyond Augustus Wood where they were soon joined by 2/8th Lancashire Fusiliers, which had been led by Captain Macpherson since Lieutenant Colonel Gordon Roberts had been wounded.

Captain Bentley of the 3/5th Lancashire Fusiliers and Captain Miller of the 2/8th Lancashire Fusiliers went exploring and returned to report that Passchendaele village was deserted. However, the rain had stopped and the German machine-gun teams could now see the East Lancashire men while they could see no one on their flanks. There was a lot of fire from Bellevue spur, where 49th Division should have been, so Captain Chesnutt-Chesney pulled the 2/6th Lancashire Fusiliers back towards Augustus Wood around midday. This attempt to form a flank was mistaken for a general withdrawal and the rest of 198 Brigade fell back. An afternoon counter-attack was stopped but Major General Lawrence was still concerned about the enfilade fire from Bellevue, so the East Lancashire men had to give up 500 yards of hard-won ground.

I Anzac Corps
The Australians were in a better situation on the Broodseinde ridge until the main track to Zonnebeke gave way under the weight of traffic. It meant most of the field guns had to deploy in the Hanebeek valley where they too would be firing at their extreme range. The gunners' problem was increased because the light railways could not carry enough ammunition forward in time.

2nd Australian Division, Keiberg Spur
Casualties and illness had reduced many of the companies in Brigadier General Smith's 5 Australian Brigade to only fifty men. They deployed in

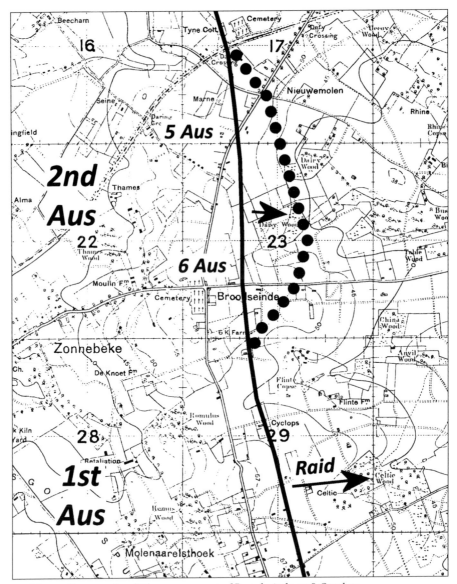

I Anzac Corps made a little progress east of Broodseinde on 9 October.

single lines, ready to advance along the Keiberg spur, only for the barrage to land on the 20th Australian Battalion. Both they and the 17th Australian Battalion were then pinned down by enfilade fire from 66th Division's sector. The Australians were too weak to stop the Germans infiltrating their lines and reoccupying the pillboxes. Brigadier General Smith sent reserves forward but they were too late to restore the situation. As the Australians fell back they saw the Lancastrians advancing onto the Passchendaele ridge across the railway; the bad conditions had made them late.

The weak barrage meant the machine-gun teams in Daisy and Dairy Woods could keep firing at 6 Australian Brigade as they crossed the Broodseinde ridge. The 23rd Australian Battalion swerved north into 5 Australian Brigade's sector, avoiding Dairy Wood, while 21st Australian Battalion could not make progress in the centre, but Captain Smythe led 24th Australian Battalion into Daisy Wood after Captain Williams was killed. It was a long time before Brigadier General Paton heard any news and Brigadier General Smith had to lend him two companies of the 19th Battalion to hold the line. Captain Taylor and Lieutenant Blake had cleared the two woods before dusk.

<u>1st Australian Division, Celtic Wood</u>
A raid against Celtic Wood, east of Molenaarelsthoek, was a disaster. Only fourteen men out of eighty-five returned.

X Corps
<u>7th Division, Reutel</u>
Brigadier General Steele had instructions to clear the high ground north of the Reutelbeek stream and 22 Brigade advanced at 5.20 am. Lieutenant Colonel Holmes thought the 1st Welsh Fusiliers had fired green flares to

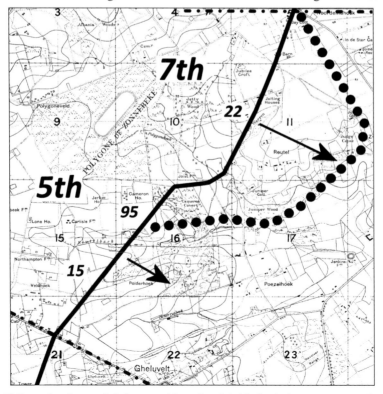

X Corps faced a tough fight around Reutel and Polderhoek chateau on 9 October.

indicate they had captured Reutel but they were German SOS flares. Second Lieutenant Noel of the 9th Devons later captured Judge Copse, east of the hamlet. Sixteen officers were hit as the 2/1st Honourable Artillery Company advanced towards Juniper Cottage. Meanwhile, the 2nd Warwicks struggled to reach Juniper Copse until Captain Raffin's company of the 9th Devons filled the gap. Casualties had been so severe that General Steele had to deploy the rest of the 9th Devons to reinforce the line.

5th Division, Polderhoek Château

The men of Brigadier General Gordon-Lennox's 95 Brigade were exhausted before the attack started and they could make no progress along the muddy Reutelbeek, east of Cameron Covert. Meanwhile, the 16th Warwicks could not reach Polderhoek Château and the survivors fell back to 15 Brigade's start line.

Captains Clements and Dickinson were hit by heavy fire from Gheluvelt and the 1st Norfolks veered north towards the Château. Brigadier General Turner complained the village had not been shelled and 'the intensity of the bullets and the appalling mud rendered further progress impossible.' Stragglers found their way back to the jumping off line where the single surviving officer reorganised them into a defensive line.

Chapter 18

Rain is Our Most Effective Ally

The First Battle of Passchendaele, 12 October

Haig immediately issued orders for another attack because he was anxious to clear the rest of the Passchendaele ridge. The plan was to advance another 2,500 yards but there were three problems. Firstly, Fifth and Second Armies only had two days to prepare; secondly, he had had no feedback from the 9 October attack and finally, the bad weather was about to get worse. Opinions were mixed and while Gough wanted to stop attacking across the mud flats south of Houthulst Forest, Plumer was confident he could make progress on the higher ground around Passchendaele.

Haig had instructed Lieutenant General Arthur Currie to move the Canadian Corps to Flanders, ready to exploit the situation after Passchendaele had been taken. Plumer had reported that II Anzac Corps had established a position on the Wallemolen spur but he had been given incorrect information. He soon learnt that Second Army's front was not as far forward as initially reported. He also thought the mud had interfered with the advance on 9 October; it had but not in the way he thought. The mud had stopped the artillery cutting the thick belts of wire on Bellevue spur and they had stopped the infantry.

The battlefield was a disaster area and the logistics chain was breaking down. Men often went hungry or ran out of ammunition and it was virtually impossible to evacuate the wounded. It took men over four hours to walk a mile through the mud while wheeled traffic was backed up along the congested plank roads. These few words sum up their gun teams' dilemma: 'Heavy rain during night. Ground a sea of mud. Guns were ordered to advance. With superhuman efforts some were got forward to new positions. A few were bogged. Almost hopeless task to get them out. Our boys are determined to do so and [they] will.'

The gunners were forced to work on tiny gun platforms, which stood out above the sea of mud. They were easy to see and became targets as they aimed at what remained of Passchendaele church on the horizon: 'The guns sank even lower into the mud with each shot. Planks, timber and sandbags were secured from all around the district but eventually fairly good platforms were out of sight.' The gunners had to re-lay their guns after every shot, sometimes resulting in poorly aimed shots, making it a struggle to fire fast enough.

Supplying the guns was nigh on impossible and the horses suffered as much, if not more than their drivers: 'many horses, on the short stretch of road from the main road to the battery sank down out of sight, the driver just keeping the [horse's] head up until assistance arrived.'

The artillery batteries faced another serious problem. The infantry were being relieved every couple of days but the gunners had to work for prolonged periods in the bad weather and many were falling ill. There was no one to take their place, leaving those left behind with all the work to do.

Again the infantry struggled to find their way across the muddy wastelands. To make matters worse, II Anzac Corps learnt its line was not as far advanced as it thought. The gunners had to start firing at a revised line and make it creep forward at double the speed to the first objective to catch up with the programme. There was no way the infantry would be able to keep up.

Neither Lieutenant General Alexander Godley (II Anzac Corps) nor Major General John Monash (3rd Australian Division) had served on the Somme the previous autumn, so it is possible they did not appreciate the impact of the weather and ground conditions. Others had, but their concerns took time to reach Second Army headquarters and even longer to reach GHQ.

Brigadier General Charteris visited the battlefield on 9 October and it is reported that he said, 'my God, did we send men to fight in this?' He returned to GHQ believing 'there is now no chance of complete success here this year.' While Haig was 'still trying to find some grounds for hope that we might still win through this year', Charteris thought they had none. If Haig heard the bleak assessments, he chose to ignore them when he spoke to war correspondents on 11 October. He said 'we are almost through the enemy defences, the enemy only has flesh and blood against us, not blockhouses and they take a month to make.' He thought German morale was close to breaking point and a couple more attacks could break them. The problem was, could the Fifth and Second Armies defeat the mud?

The optimism did not take into account that divisions were being sent to the front for the second time, even though they only had half the drafts they needed. Many had been taken from the RAMC and the Labour Corps because they had been 'reclassified owing to the adoption of a less rigorous physical standard: their military training was therefore less than perfect.'

While Haig was optimistic, the men at the front line were anything but.

The experience of Lieutenant Fisher of 42nd Australian Battalion is typical of the chaos on Passchendaele ridge. His patrol found wounded British and Australian soldiers sheltering in some pillboxes. Others were huddled outside, trying to shelter from the snipers who were picking them off one by one. Some had been there for four days, living off rainwater and rations taken from the dead. Many were unable to walk and Fisher returned to his battalion reporting that he had 'never seen men so broken or demoralised'.

The rain continued on 10 and 11 October, delaying the work on the plank roads. It stopped some of the field batteries moving forward while some of the heavy guns were late getting into position. It meant the German guns were still operating, the wire was intact and the pillboxes were still active.

The men walked through the crater fields in the dark in single file, each holding onto the man in front of him. They shuffled across the duckboards and balanced on the coconut mattresses laid across the streams. Mustard gas shells rained down but the Anzacs could not put on their masks because they could not see through the visors in the rain. All they could do was grip the mask tube between their teeth and soldier on. Fortunately, the shells often detonated beneath the slime and the wind dispersed what little gas escaped.

Zero hour was set for 5.25 am but the wind just got stronger and the rain became heavier. Gough asked Plumer if they should postpone the attack but both Generals Birdwood and Godley wanted to go ahead with it. Crown Prince Rupprecht summed up the situation with the following words: 'a sudden change of weather. Most gratifying; rain is our most effective ally.'

The German high command had been concerned about their recent setbacks and it again had to reconsider its defensive tactics. Conferences on 27 and 29 September resulted in a return to holding the forward area with more men, in an attempt to break up the attacks before they had any momentum. Small counter-attacks could be launched within hours while a larger, deliberate affair could be made a couple of days later.

General Ludendorff had suggested the *Kraftfeld* or 'Force Field' method of defence in June and it was now about to be tried even though it had failed on the Somme. There the artillery had hit the front-line divisions so hard that the counter-attack divisions had to shore up the line.

Snipers, outposts and machine-gun teams covered a strip some 500 to 1,000 metres deep. The lucky ones sheltered in pillboxes but the rest huddled in slit trenches, deploying to shell holes when the attack began. Some of the German artillery was registered to fire at this outpost zone and they had to watch for SOS flares indicating the front-line troops were withdrawing. But it was going to be challenging to coordinate the infantry and the artillery in the middle of a battle, especially in bad weather.

Fifth Army

General Gough was expecting better results after the problems on 9 October because most of the artillery had not had to relocate. Zero hour was set at 5.35 am and the drizzle turned to heavy rain, bringing down a thick mist which blinded that German observers on the Passchendaele ridge.

XIV Corps

Lieutenant General Rudolph Lambart, the Earl of Cavan, had to push north-east astride the Staden railway on Fifth Army's left. He also had an important captain on his staff, the 23-year-old His Royal Highness, Edward the Prince of Wales.

Guards Division, Houthulst Forest

Major General Feilding had only deployed the 3 Guards Brigade south of Houthulst Forest. Both the 1st Welsh Guards and 4th Grenadier Guards advanced the short distance to the edge of the tangle of broken branches and smashed stumps. The only problem came from Angle Point, which 17th Division had missed on their right flank, and its enfilade fire hit many of the Scots Guards. Brigadier General Lord Seymour moved the 1st Grenadier Guards forward to help clear Angle Point and Aden House.

This was the third time the Guards had been in action in the campaign and it had always taken its objectives. The Earl of Cavan congratulated Feilding's men with the following words: 'Well done everybody – wonderful performance in awful conditions – hearty congratulations and thanks to you and all your troops.'

17th Division, Staden Railway

Major General Philip Robertson had deployed 51 Brigade either side of the Staden railway. Brigadier General Bond's three battalions huddled together in shell holes next to the jumping off tape, ready to fan out into waves. The Germans did not spot them during the stormy night while the single patrol out in no man's land was stalked and every man bayonetted, so they did not raise the alarm.

Machine-gun fire made the 8th South Staffords veer towards the railway and they missed Angle Point, so the Guards had to capture it. Captains Tredinnick and McCarroll made sure the 7th Lincolns cleared the strongpoints either side of the railway. Brigadier General Bond's men then watched as the British barrage hit the German reinforcements as they waded through the mud.

Over 200 prisoners had been taken from thirteen different battalions and nearly half were taken by Major Peddie of the Lincolns. His men had missed

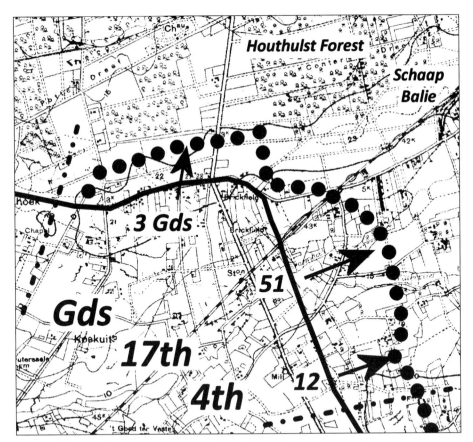

XIV Corps made some progress towards Houthulst Forest on 12 October.

Taube Farm because the garrison had initially been too stunned to fight. They emerged as Major Peddie and his signalling officer Captain King were taking a basket of pigeons forward. King was unarmed, their orderly had dropped his rifle into a water-filled shell hole, and all Peddie had was a pistol with no bullets, leaving 'nothing to shoot at them with but a basket of blinking pigeons'. The unarmed orderly escorted no less than ninety prisoners to the rear while Peddie and King continued on their way to their new battalion headquarters.

Meanwhile, the 10th Sherwoods could not advance far because 4th Division was lagging behind, north of Poelcappelle. The 7th Border Regiment helped it form a defensive flank, running back from Memling Farm.

4th Division, North of Poelcappelle
A composite battalion of the 1st Warwicks and the Household Battalion advanced across 'a vast sea of malignant mud and water'. They suffered heavy casualties advancing towards Water House and Landing Farm,

because 18th Division was unable to clear Poelcappelle on their right. A company of the 1st King's Own was sent to cover 12 Brigade's flank around Requette Farm while Private Albert Halton went deep into German territory to silence a machine gun. He returned with twelve prisoners and would be awarded the Victoria Cross. But casualties had been heavy and a counter-attack forced Brigadier General Carton de Wiart's men back.

XVIII Corps

Lieutenant General Sir Ivor Maxse's artillery batteries were still struggling to find battery positions around the Lekkerboterbeek and Stroombeek. Many had still not reached their positions, while the horse-drawn wagons were struggling to carry ammunition across the Steenbeek. Maxse remained positive and told his men during training, 'I have arranged a nice battle for you gentlemen, with lots of Huns to kill.' But come zero hour, the assault troops were soaked to the skin, covered in mud and exhausted.

18th Division, Poelcappelle

Major General Richard Lee had deployed 55 Brigade but late amendments to the orders did not reach everyone in time because the men were scattered across many shell holes. The creeping barrage started thirty seconds late, landing amongst the advancing troops. One company commander had chosen to wait until it started and his men were hit by the German artillery instead.

The 8th East Surreys were pinned down in front of Requette Farm and a counter-attack drove Captain Place and Lieutenant Dawson back until Lieutenant Jordan brought two abandoned Lewis guns into action. Machine-gun fire from Helles House hit many of the 7th Queen's Own as they cleared Poelcappelle while the 7th Buffs were hit by crossfire from the Brewery, Meunier House and Gloucester Farm, south of the village. Captain Nicholson reported that his men 'could not swim nor fight, only drown or stay where they were,' while Knight's company was overrun when the Germans counter-attacked from the Brewery. Less than one hundred Buffs escaped and the 7th Queen's Own were driven back through the village until they were reinforced by the 8th Surreys.

Brigadier General Higginson's men had struggled to get into position on time, north of the Lekkerboterbeek stream. One company of the 6th Berkshires was five minutes late by which time the rest of the battalion was advancing towards Meunier House. Captain Wacher was killed leading the 8th Suffolks towards Beek House, across ground which was 'torn up by shells, greasy and sodden'. Lieutenant Colonel Longhurst was killed and Captain Rochfort was wounded when he went forward to find out what had happened. In a word, 53 Brigade's attack had failed.

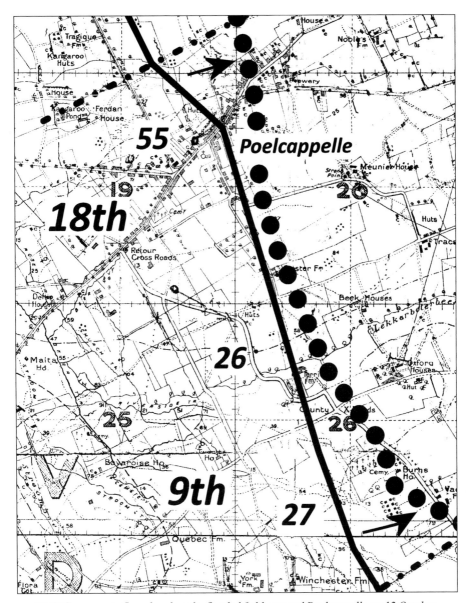

XVIII Corps again floundered on the flooded fields around Poelcappelle on 12 October.

9th Division, Wallemolen Spur

The Germans suspected an attack was imminent so their artillery shelled Major General Lukin's assembly area with shrapnel and gas shells. Brigadier General Kennedy's 26 Brigade advanced through the deep mud on the south side of the Lekkerboterbeek stream. Lieutenants Dickson and Harper were killed as enfilade fire from Oxford Houses forced half the 8th Black Watch to veer north while Captain Shepherd struggled to clear Adler

Farm. The 5th Camerons only advanced a short distance towards Wallemolen while the 10th Argylls were pinned down in boggy ground after trying to avoid a German barrage. Some even waded across the Lekkerboterbeek only to be stopped by Beek and Meunier Houses. Lieutenant Colonel Crichton had to move the 7th Seaforths forward into the gap between the brigades.

On 27 Brigade's front, the 6th KOSBs could do little and Lieutenant Colonel Campbell reported 'only men with webbed feet could fight with comfort' on Wallemolen Spur. Captains Grant and Stuart were killed when a pillbox flying the white flag opened fire on the 11th Royal Scots. Major Scott's 12th Royal Scots made the final advance towards Wallemolen, but Captain McMurray was killed at the head of a mixed group of Scots. They had to fall back to Inch House and the nearby cemetery to avoid the worst of the fire from the pillboxes higher up the spur. The failures left the Black Watch isolated on Wallemolen spur, so Lieutenant Colonel Hadow's men withdrew as soon as they could.

The attack was a disaster made worse by the willingness of battalion commanders to push forward more men when they 'were so exhausted that they were unable to carry on the amphibious warfare'. Only Lieutenant Colonel Lumsden had held the 9th Scottish Rifles back; the rest had been cut to pieces in the 'foul quagmire'.

Second Army, 12 October
II Anzac Corps

The German infantry around Bellevue Spur were nervous and the artillery responded to the SOS flares, shelling the New Zealanders while they assembled.

New Zealand Division, Wallemolen and Bellevue

Major General Russell's men were supposed to clear the Wallemolen and Bellevue spurs before advancing to Goudberg. The two brigades each deployed one battalion for each of the three objectives but the men were exhausted after six weeks in the salient. The artillery had been unable to cut the two wire entanglements and the creeping barrage was no better.

The 3rd New Zealand Brigade had to advance past Wolf Copse to reach Woodlands Copse. Sergeant Coley captured the cemetery on the 4th New Zealand Rifles' left while Company Sergeant Major Voyles cleared the first strongpoint on the 2nd New Zealand Rifles' front. The New Zealanders were disorganised by the first belt of wire and no one got through the second belt, so Lieutenant Puttick's men dug in around Wolf Farm and cleaned their weapons. Brigadier General Stewart decided against sending the 1st New

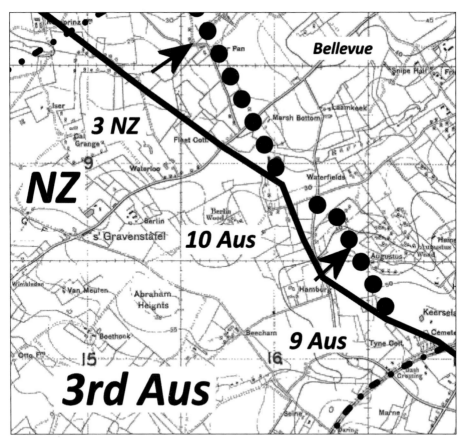

II Anzac Corps failed to take any ground on Bellevue spur or Passchendaele ridge on 12 October.

Zealand Rifles forward and they formed a support line instead. The Germans took the opportunity to return to their abandoned positions and placed their machine guns on top of the pillboxes to get a better view of their targets.

The flooded upper reaches of the Stroombeek meant there was a gap on the 2nd Otagos' left as they struggled across Marsh Bottom under fire from the Bellevue pillboxes. The Germans had their machine guns trained on the only gaps in the wire on the 's Gravenstafel road. Major Turner was killed at the first belt while Captains Fawcett and Rawlings were wounded trying to outflank the pillboxes beyond. The 1st Otagos cut or crawled through the wire but Lieutenants Bishop and Watson were killed crossing Marsh Bottom. Second Lieutenant Cockerell was the only man standing from his platoon but he still captured the pillbox, taking eighty prisoners.

A large shell explosion killed Lieutenant Colonel King and hit the rest of his staff as the 1st Canterburys moved forward to support the advance.

Snipers targeted Lieutenant Hunter and his platoon officers as machine-gun teams cut down their men as they struggled towards Snipe Hall. Brigadier General Braithwaite came to the conclusion that no further progress could be made towards Bellevue. The men at the front would have agreed; the division had just suffered over 2,700 casualties.

3rd Australian Division, Ravebeek

Major General John Monash's men had to advance onto the ridge and beyond Passchendaele. One unit even planned to plant an Australian flag in the village and Monash wanted to make sure the news was cabled to Australia. But the Diggers faced a nightmare march across the crater field through a barrage of gas and high explosive shells.

There were rumours that the 66th Division was not holding the line it was supposed to be, so the officers went forward to find out they were true. There was nothing they could do so the exhausted men were told to lay on the mud in no man's land and wait for zero hour. Many an exhausted Digger pulled a groundsheet over his head and slept, ignoring the shells exploding around them. Officers and NCOs had to go along the line waking them up, so they would be ready for zero hour. The German artillery was accurate but the Australian barrage was weak and ragged, so the infantry 'made no attempt to conform to it. There was really nothing to conform to.'

On 10 Australian Brigade's front, the 37th Australian Battalion was pinned down by fire coming from the Waterfields and Augustus Wood. The 38th and 40th Australian Battalions took over the advance, but they could not keep up with the barrage and were pinned down by the Bellevue pillboxes, where the New Zealanders were in difficulties across the Ravebeek valley. Brigadier General McNichol learnt that Major Giblin had organised the majority of the survivors around Haalen but a few men kept going. One patrol even entered a deserted Passchendaele but it did not have the coveted Australian flag.

There was a 'terrible mix-up' and 'great confusion' on 9 Australian Brigade's front as men tried to find firm ground on the north side of the Roulers railway. Some men got lost, some got stuck in the mud and others bunched together, making them easy targets for the German machine-gunners.

Captains Carr and Dixon could not work out whether the creeping barrage was too far in front or way behind their men but 35th Australian Battalion kept going. Both Major Buchanan and Captain Jeffries were killed clearing Augustus Wood and Hillside Farm. Captain Clarence Jeffries captured thirty-five men in a pillbox covering the Passchendaele road; he would be awarded the Victoria Cross. But the men of 34th Australian

Battalion were horrified to find wounded men of the 66th Division who had been left in the open for three days.

Brigadier General Rosenthal's men became disorientated when they came under fire at the crest of the ridge and they could not see the barrage to guide them to the objective. The few Germans covering the road into Passchendaele were withdrawing but the Bellevue pillboxes, away to the left, were firing into their flank. The men inside the bunkers did not see Sergeant Charlesworth moving up the Ravebeek gully with twenty men of the 38th Australian Battalion. He captured Crest Farm and then found Passchendaele to be deserted, but wisely chose to withdraw.

Major General Monash asked Major General Russell if the New Zealanders' guns could bombard Bellevue ridge, to reduce the volume of enfilade fire aimed across the Ravebeek valley at his men. He was told to wait because the New Zealanders were going to attack again soon so a bombardment was about to begin. Captain Giblin saw the New Zealanders fail to make any progress for a second time, so he decided to withdraw his men from the exposed Passchendaele ridge.

News of the deteriorating situation reached brigade headquarters when Lieutenant Jackson of 40th Australian Battalion started flashing lamp signals from a pillbox in the Ravebeek valley. Brigadier General McNichol reported the bad news to Monash and he gave the order to withdraw to the start line. Captain Carr made sure 10 Australian Brigade kept up a covering fire as men ran back in small groups. Captain Gadd did the same with 9 Australian Brigade and the survivors were met by the 39th and 33rd Australian Battalions at their start line. They had been sent forward to capture Passchendaele but the moment had passed.

I Anzac Corps
Lieutenant General Birdwood's position was fairly safe on the Broodseinde ridge but his men had to make a short advance beyond Defy crossing to cover II Anzac Corps' flank.

<u>4th Australian Division, Nieuwmolen</u>
Major General Ewen Sinclair-Maclagan deployed the 12 Australian Brigade to clear the Keiberg spur. Lieutenant Colonel Leane's 48th Australian Battalion captured Nieuwmolen while Lieutenant Colonel Imlay's 47th Australian Battalion advanced towards Assyria. The position became untenable when 3rd Australian Division fell back and they had to withdraw south of the railway line. The two battalion commanders were injured by shellfire after leaving their pillbox to watch the withdrawal.

Chapter 19

No Troops Have Had to Face Worse Conditions

The Preparations, 22 October

On 13 October there was a lot of discussion over when to launch the next three attacks. Haig informed his commanders that the Canadian Corps was heading to Flanders but he had assumed the Passchendaele ridge would have fallen by the time it had arrived. The commander-in-chief, at long last, conceded that the strategic plan for the Ypres offensive was no longer possible. The troops which had been training all summer for the landing on the Flanders coast were stood down and let out of their camp on 20 October as Operation Hush was cancelled.

Haig was instead considering another operation near Cambrai, where General Sir Julian Byng's Third Army was planning to attack late in November. Brigadier General Elles had been granted his wish to plan an attack in which the Tank Corps could demonstrate its full potential and his staff were planning to use 300 tanks to lead an advance across dry ground. Byng was anxious that Second Army kept pushing, to keep the Germans' attention on Flanders.

Haig, Gough and Plumer agreed the destructive bombardment would start on 21 October and that Fifth Army would attack the following day, to draw the Germans attention away from the Canadian preparations around Passchendaele. Their engineers would need time to complete the roads, so the artillery had time to prepare the ground for the attack.

The Canadians would soon encounter the appalling sights and smells of the Salient. The odour from the mud increased when it stopped raining; the stench 'told of desolation and decay, of gas shells and dead men'.

Fighting in the Houthulst Forest, 22 October
XIV Corps

Lieutenant General Lambart, Earl of Cavan, wanted to improve his position in front of Houthulst Forest, to create a solid flank for Fifth Army. But he had no desire to send his troops into what was described as a 'flat, low-lying area of six hundred acres of broken stumps and wreckage, a swamp with many a deep and treacherous hole to trap the unwary walker and let him sink up to his neck'. Fifth Army's zero hour was timed for 5.35 am and Second Army artillery would fire at the same time, to give the impression the attack would extend as far south as Broodseinde.

35th Division, South of Houthulst Forest

The 16th Cheshires and 14th Gloucesters reached Panama House, The Farm and Marechal Farm, on 105 Brigade's front only to be stopped by machine-gun coming fire from a row of pillboxes which they thought others had captured. Artillery fire stopped the reinforcements crossing the flooded Broembeek while a counter-attack forced part of the brigade back to the start line.

Brigadier General Sandilands had a problem because 104 Brigade's objective was much wider than the jumping off line. So Lieutenant Colonel

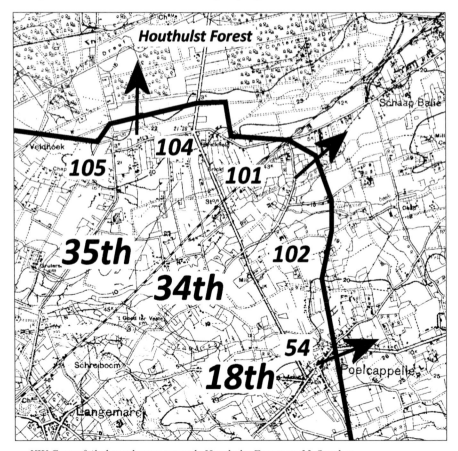

XIV Corps failed to advance towards Houthulst Forest on 22 October.

Irvine had placed 18th Lancashire Fusiliers close in support ready to fill the increasing gap astride the Dixmude road. Captains Heape and Kitchin led the 17th Lancashire Fusiliers, reporting it was the 'best sport going – right in our barrage' as they reached Colombo House ahead of time. The 23rd Manchesters were also going well until the 34th Division were delayed astride the Staden railway. They then fell back after failing to cut through the wire entanglement protecting Six Roads pillboxes. A counter-attack drove the Lancashire Fusiliers from their exposed salient and Major General George Franks' men were soon all back on their start line.

34th Division, Turenne Crossing and Watervlietbeek Stream

An oversight meant that the barrage line cut across 101 Brigade's salient astride the Staden railway. British shells landed behind Brigadier General Gore's men and then crept over the two battalions of Royal Scots, adding to the misery caused by the German bombardment.

Captain Russell led the 16th Royal Scots towards Six Roads Crossroads and they gave covering fire while the Manchesters cleared pillboxes to their left. But the right was pinned down east of Turenne Crossing: 'the men were forced to embed themselves in the mud, without stirring a limb above the surface.' Captain Sutherland's company crawled back when there was a counter-attack but Second Lieutenant Hope's company fought on until they were overrun.

Major Shelby's 15th Royal Scots waded through the mud astride the Broembeek but the left company was pinned down by the same concrete shelters and hardly any men returned. The right did not advance the line beyond Gravel Farm. The 20th Northumberland Fusiliers were unable to advance either side of the flooded Watervlietbeek but the 24/27th Northumberland Fusiliers made progress south-east of Bower House. They soon had to pull back, under enfilade fire from Poelcappelle.

18th Division, Poelcappelle

Brigadier General Higginson had wanted his men to shelter in shallow ditches but the 8th Norfolks were in the middle of a bog while the 10th Essex encountered a high water table. The men were forced to lie down and wait while a burning farm lit up the horizon. One company of the Essex used dummies as they performed a fake attack (called a Chinese attack) south to Poelcappelle. Lieutenant Symonds was killed leading the Norfolks towards Requette Farm and Helles and then the British howitzers began shelling their new position after they captured the brewery. Captain Skeat's company captured Noble's Farm at the east end of Poelcappelle while the rest of the Essex took Meunier's Farm to the south. Major Banks also cleared Tracas Farm beyond the objective because it overlooked the Essex line.

Fifth Army, 26 October

Although GHQ's emphasis was on taking Passchendaele, General Gough still had to push forward across the sodden landscape towards the Flanders I Line. Conditions were already dreadful but the artillery bombardment made them worse; 'every shell that burst threw up ghastly relics and raised stenches too abominable to describe.' For once it did not rain but German snipers took advantage of the moonlit night to target officers as they moved between their men before zero hour at 5.45 am.

XIV Corps

Lieutenant General Lambart, the Earl of Cavan, had to advance astride the marsh around the Stadendrevebeek and Watervlietbeek streams. Zero was set for 5.40 am and while the creeping barrage was moving as slowly as possible, at only 100 yards in eight minutes, the infantry could still not keep up.

50th Division, Staden Railway

Major General Percival Wilkinson had to advance astride the Staden railway towards the Schaap Balie railway sidings, south of the Houthulst Forest. The Northumberland men of 149 Brigade had to bunch together to get around the shell holes, making easy targets for the double line of pillboxes near the objective. Casualties drowned in the mud if their comrades could not drag them out of the slime in time.

Most of the Germans ran into Houthulst Forest but a few snipers stayed behind and killed ten officers, leaving the 1/7th Northumberland Fusiliers pinned down and disorganised in front of a line of shelters. Many of the 1/5th Northumberland Fusiliers were hit as they cut through the wire blocking the railway, the only piece of dry land in the area. Few men reached Hill 23 and no one made it to Colbert Crossroads, north of the tracks. Meanwhile the commanding officer of the 1/4th Northumberland Fusiliers reported that 'the right of my battalion is in a swamp. Even if it is possible to assemble the right company, I do not consider it would be able to advance; it would have to be dug out.' Snipers again targeted the officers as they moved about their men and the leaderless 1/5th and 1/4th Northumberland Fusiliers soon fell back, forcing the 1/7th Northumberland Fusiliers to withdraw.

The report said 'all wounded as far as possible were brought in.' Brigadier General Riddell's brigade had suffered over 1,000 casualties and

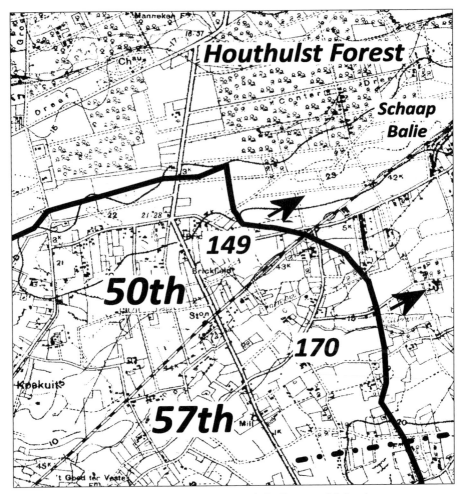

XIV Corps gained a little ground south of Houthulst Forest on 26 October.

it had gained nothing. The attack had pushed the Northumberland men beyond their limits and one battalion commander said 'this has fairly done me', while tears trickled down his face. The 50th Division had suffered another 2,000 casualties by the time XIX Corps took over from XIV Corps on 29 October.

57th Division, North of Poelcappelle

The task given to Major General Reginald Barnes's men was equally daunting. Even more so because it was the first attack by the 2nd West Lancashire territorials. They 'went over with rifles and Lewis guns bound up with flannel, so as to keep the mud out. We had special cleaning apparatus in our pockets but you cannot clean a rifle when your hands are covered an inch thick [in mud].'

The 170 Brigade slogged through a sea of liquid mud and slimy water astride the Stadendrevebeek and Watervlietbeek streams. The 2/4th Loyals were soon pinned down on the left but the 2/5th and 4/5th Loyals kept going. One man pushed a Lewis gun through a bunker's firing slit, pulled the trigger and shot everyone inside. But firearms were rarely fired in the brutal battle and one man killed thirteen with his bayonet.

German planes seemed to be the only ones in the sky and while some strafed and bombed the British lines, others were busy observing for the artillery until the heavy rain started at midday. The German infantry found how difficult it was to achieve anything when they tried to advance from Devoust Farm. The Loyals stopped them but they were outnumbered, had exposed flanks and their ammunition was low. Brigadier General Guggisberg had no option but to recall the survivors at dusk.

XVIII Corps

Lieutenant General Sir Ivor Maxse again had to push astride the Lekkerboterbeek valley towards the Flanders I Line.

58th Division, Lekkerboterbeek Stream

Major General Albemarle Cator's men struggled through the mud, moving no more than a yard a minute, and they soon lost the barrage. Captain Harper cleared three pillboxes around Cameron House, as the 2/2nd London Regiment advanced south of the Poelcappelle–Spruit road. Meanwhile, Second Lieutenant Howie had to fall back along the north side of the Lekkerboterbeek after failing to capture Moray House. The 2/3rd London Regiment were easy targets as they waded through waist-deep slimy water and a counter-attack overran Lieutenant Colonel Beresford's men; only nineteen made it back. Captain Clarke's company of the 2/4th London Regiment made some progress on the right, next to the Naval Division.

The Lekkerboterbeek stream was a death trap of mud and water-filled shell holes overlooked by the pillboxes of the Flanders I Line. The Londoners stood no chance and many of the injured had sunk into the slime and drowned, never to be seen again; others were cut off and surrendered. Over 670 men were reported missing when the roll calls were made; their bodies were lost in the mud.

63rd Division, Wallemolen Spur

Major General Laurie chose Brigadier General Prentice's 188 Brigade to cross the Stroombeek. Two lines of skirmishers led the 1st Marines and Anson Battalion while section columns closed in on pillboxes. Lieutenant Careless cleared Banff Farm for the Marines but Captain Pipe was killed

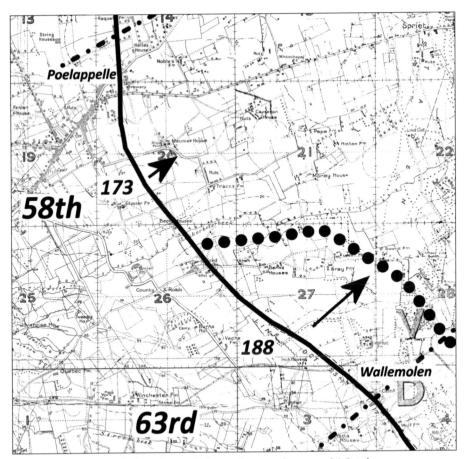

XVIII Corps struggled to advance in horrendous conditions on 26 October.

while Sub-Lieutenant Stevenson incorrectly reported that he had taken Varlet Farm. Machine-gun fire from Tournant Farm and Source Farm pinned down the centre of the attack but the Howe Battalion and 2nd Marines pushed their flanks forward. Captain Ligertwood was hit three times but he still kept leading his men; he succumbed to a fourth wound after standing up one last time to cheer his men on.

The Hood Battalion could not push the centre any further forward so Commander Asquith took his artillery officer, Lieutenant Garnham, for a long walk and they discovered that Lieutenant Arblaster had just stopped the Germans breaking through the Hood Battalion. The reconnaissance allowed the artillery to shoot an accurate SOS barrage but the left flank still had to withdraw across the Stroombeek after it had run out of ammunition. Ground had been taken but it had cost each battalion around 500 casualties. General Gough summed up the battle for Wallemolen spur with the words, 'no troops have had to face worse conditions.'

Second Army, 26 October

Second Army was given control of the Canadian Corps 'because the Canadians do not work kindly' with General Gough. Problems during the battle of Courcelette ridge on the Somme, in the autumn of October 1916, had led to bad feeling between Fifth Army and the Canadian Corps. Ironically the Canadians were returning to the area they had held back in April 1915, before chlorine gas had swept over their trenches. But the few men who had survived two and a half years of warfare would not have recognised the muddy Bellevue and Broodseinde spurs either side of the Ravebeek bog. One observer noted, the 'battlefield looks bad, no salvaging has been done and very few of the dead are buried.'

Second Army's artillery commander, Major General Buckle, summarised the sorry state of the heavy artillery to the Canadian Corps' artillery commander, Brigadier General Morrison. Only 100 of the 250 heavy howitzers available could fire because the rest were out of action or stuck in the mud. Around half of the three hundred 18-pounders were out of action and those in action were 'dotted about in the mud wherever they happened to get bogged'.

The Canadian Corps had a large number of experienced engineer and pioneer units and they started work on 17 October. The weather improved but the Germans' guns shelled the Salient around the clock and there were a lot of night bombing raids. Gas was used in large quantities and while there were few deaths, hundreds of men were affected. A huge amount of labour was required to repair the existing roads and an equally large number of men were needed to extend them across the 's Gravenstafel ridge. But they laid one mile of double-plank road and over 2,000 yards of light railways over the next two weeks.

Currie favoured set piece actions supported by well organised logistics and preceded by a well-planned artillery bombardment. He saw to it that every officer and NCO was trained to know what was expected of them. He said, 'I am convinced that this reconnaissance and close liaison between the artillery, the infantry units, and the staff is vital to the success of any operation.' But the Canadians were going to find it very difficult to achieve.

Currie's troops would make their first 'bite and hold' attack on 26 October, providing the rains did not return. The same divisions would make a second attack three days later. A relief would follow and the fresh divisions would make two more attacks.

Despite the efforts of the engineers and gunners, nearly half of the Canadian Corps' heavy and medium howitzers remained out of action at any one time. They were either sinking in the mud, waiting for ammunition, or short of crew due to enemy action or sickness.

The Germans had reverted to holding an outpost zone around Passchendaele with just a few men. Patrols kept the Canadians at bay while snipers and teams armed with light machine guns waited in shell holes for the attack to begin. They would disrupt the attack, giving the men in the main line of resistance time to deploy while the artillery and heavy machine guns put down a defensive barrage.

The Canadian Corps

The 50th Canadian Battalion pushed forward outposts along the Passchendaele ridge, to harass their German counterparts around Augustus Wood, Hillside Farm and Defy Crossing. They could see the smashed wire on Wallemolen ridge, across the Ravebeek stream, but the Bellevue pillboxes were still firing at them.

The German positions were bombarded every morning and afternoon for four days. The Canadian infantry found it tough going picking their way along the tracks between 's Gravenstafel and Zonnebeke on a dark and rainy night. But at 5.40 am they surged forward through the thick mist and the German plan to break up the advance failed at the first step. A captured officer summarised the situation with the following words: 'your men attacked so closely upon the barrage that they seemed mixed up with their own shell fire.'

3rd Canadian Division, Bellevue Spur

On 8 Canadian Brigade's front, Captain Galt's 4th Canadian Mounted Rifles had to stop north of Wolf Copse because their flanks were exposed. Nineteen-year-old Private Tommy Holmes single-handedly silenced two machine-gun teams with bombs and then returned for more. He then ran up to a bunker and threw a bomb into the entrance, encouraging nineteen men to surrender; he would be awarded the Victoria Cross. Galt's men had cleared part of Flanders I Line but they were cut off. Brigadier General Elmsley wanted him to make contact with 63rd Division, which was pinned down around Wallemolen, but he had to wait until it was dark before he could try.

Brigadier General Hill's 9 Canadian Brigade advanced along the Bellevue spur towards Meetcheele. Lieutenant Bob Shankland reached the Bellevue pillboxes on the horizon but only fifty men of the 43rd Canadian Battalion were still standing. Meanwhile, 58th Canadian Battalion reported his men had reached their objective but they were actually stuck in the marshy ground around Snipe Hall. Artillery and machine-gun fire stopped a counter-attack but more men were needed, so Shankland returned to his battalion headquarters to report the situation. Only twenty of his men were

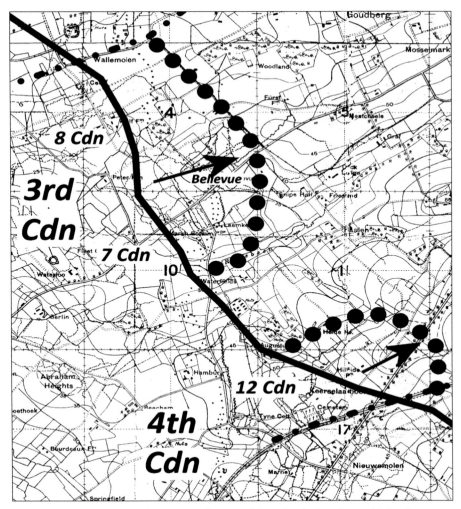

The Canadian Corps' advance on Bellevue and Passchendaele ridge on 26 October.

still standing by the time he returned but he urged them to fight on with a promise that reinforcements were on the way.

Captain Christopher O'Kelly led two companies of the 52nd Canadian Battalion forward and he captured nine pillboxes around Bellevue and Laambeek with the help of Lieutenant Grant. They also stopped counter-attacks, increasing the battalion's total to 200 prisoners and 21 machine guns. O'Kelly and Shankland were both awarded the Victoria Cross for securing the Flanders I Line between Wolf Copse and the Ravebeek.

4th Canadian Division, Main Road into Passchendaele
The 46th Canadian Battalion advanced between Augustus Wood and the Passchendaele road. Over 400 men reached the first objective but their left

flank was under fire from Bellevue spur and their right from Decline Copse. One company went beyond Tiber and Vienna cottages on the right but counter-attacks pushed them all back towards the start line.

Brigadier General Hilliam deployed the 44th and 47th Canadian Battalions during the night and they retook the lost ground the following morning. A company from the 85th Canadian Battalion helped the 44th Canadian Battalion clear Decline Copse on the evening of 28 October. The 4th Canadian Division had taken 370 prisoners and had reached drier ground but it had cost nearly 2,500 casualties.

X Corps

Lieutenant General Morland's plan was for 7th and 5th Divisions to clear the area around Polderhoek and Gheluvelt.

5th Division, Gheluvelt Château

Major General Reginald Stephens instructed 13 Brigade to withdraw a short distance, so the artillery could fire a straight barrage, in line with 7th Division. A German patrol reported the British had abandoned their front trench and it was occupied before the attack began. It mean that Brigadier General Jones's men had to fight for the trench they had just left before they could advance any further. Then they plodded through the 'almost impassable morass' which the Scherriabeek stream had become.

The 14th Warwicks could not cross the Reutelbeek but the 15th Warwicks took 100 prisoners, including a battalion commander, around Gheluvelt Château. The 1st Queen's Own were advancing towards Gheluvelt when 7th Division withdrew on their right, leaving Captain Price and Second Lieutenant Fry cut off. They fought on until they ran out of ammunition and nearly 350 men were reported missing; the second time the battalion had lost as many in just two weeks.

It left the 15th Warwicks isolated, so the senior surviving officer withdrew them to Jackson Trench. A counter-attack drove the last of 5th Division's troops all the way back to the start line. The colonel of 1st Queen's Own collected every man he could find to form a line along the division's front. He also decided everyone in front was either dead or German so he called for an SOS barrage. The attack had gained nothing and 5th Division had suffered over 3,300 casualties.

7th Division, Gheluvelt Village

Captain Pridham and Second Lieutenant Austin led the 9th Devons through Gheluvelt on 20 Brigade's front, while Lieutenant Evans mopped up the ruins. The slow barrage meant Second Lieutenant Monk's company

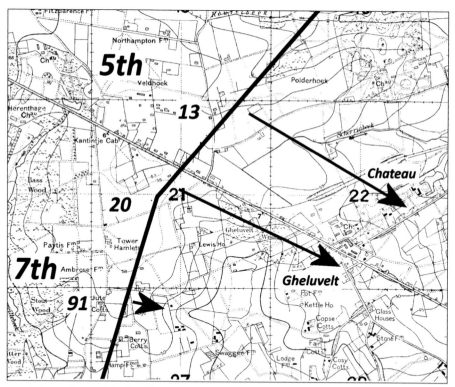

X Corps' bitter fight for Gheluvelt and its château on 26 October.

swerved towards the Château with his company of the 8th Devons while Lieutenant Evans's men became involved with the fight for the village. Both battalions of the Devons were under enfilade fire from pillboxes which had pinned down the 2nd Border Regiment down across the Menin road. Captain Marshall was unable to silence them before counter-attacks drove the Devons out of Gheluvelt. They then had to abandon Johnson Trench because they were running out of ammunition. Captain Jupe and Second Lieutenant Wyatt were killed during the retirement so it was left to Captains Marshall and Pridham to rally the survivors on the start line.

The 2nd Border Regiment advanced from Tower Trench under fire from the pillboxes along the Menin road. Captain Moor and many of his men were hit so the survivors took cover in a big crater. Captain Little led his company into Gheluvelt and waited for the 2nd Gordons but crossfire from Swagger Farm and Lewis House had scattered them. Captain Dempster was killed at the Kroombeek on the right and his men could not cross the waist deep mud. Neither could Captain Streeter and Second Lieutenant Howells who were following with the 2nd Queen's.

The 21st Manchesters were stopped after advancing only a few yards from Tower Hamlets on 91 Brigade's front. The 1st South Staffords' left company was pinned down by fire coming from Berry Cotts while the centre was 'mown down wholesale by a cross-fire of machine guns' from Hamp Farm. Second Lieutenant Pullen was hit as his men reached The Mound but all the runners were killed so no reinforcements came and it had to be evacuated. The attack had been a complete failure and the two divisions had suffered over 3,300 casualties between them.

All along the line, officers rallied the stragglers and got them to clean their weapons and collect ammunition from the casualties. The Lewis guns, which usually formed the backbone of any defence, were of no use in the mud. Some noticed that the Germans carried little equipment and many were armed with revolvers because they were easier to keep clean.

Many of the drafts who had just joined the battalions were often seen doing nothing except wandering around looking for cover. But Major General Shoubridge later wrote 'they went forward under the worst condition of mud and fire and would not give in until they died or stuck in the mud – no soldier could do more.'

Chapter 20

They Touched Bottom in the Way of Misery

30 October

Haig received the instruction he had been dreading from the War Cabinet on 26 October. Austro-Hungarian troops, supported by German troops, had just broken through the Italians' front and there was a real danger Italy could capitulate. GHQ was instructed to send Lieutenant General Lambart, the Earl of Cavan, with XIV Corps headquarters to reinforce the crumbling front. The 7th, 23rd and 41st Divisions would start leaving for Italy on 2 November; another three divisions would follow.

Lieutenant General Currie was determined his men had the ammunition, food and support they needed around Passchendaele. Each infantry brigade was allocated a timber track and 250 pack animals; more carried ammunition to the batteries. But it was dangerous to stray from the tracks, even though they were under artillery fire, as many animals and men were drowning in the mud.

The next attack was planned for 30 October and while fog prevented accurate artillery fire for long periods, a cold wind on the night before the battle meant the troops had to assemble in bright moonlight. Come zero hour, at 5.50 am, many guns started firing two minutes earlier than expected, warning the German gunners so they caught the Canadians crossing no man's land. The barrage moved forward only 100 yards in eight minutes, but it was again too fast for the infantry. There were too few guns to create an effective barrage and some were firing short.

XVIII Corps

<u>58th Division, South of Poelcappelle</u>

A company of the 2/6th London Regiment company occupied Nobles Farm but the 2/8th London Regiment faced nine machine guns in Track Trench. Captain Gunning's and Second Lieutenant Booth's men were stopped by deep mud and only Second Lieutenant Tweddle returned unwounded from the first wave on the right; the second wave gave up after they 'sank up to their knees or thighs'. Many of 174 Brigade's 275 casualties were reported missing.

63rd Division, Lekkerboterbeek

Major General Laurie placed 190 Brigade in line astride the Lekkerboterbeek ready for the next attack. The early firing of the British guns meant the German bombardment disorganised Brigadier General Hutchinson's troops in no man's land. The creeping barrage had moved on by the time they advanced and the 'machine guns merely picked off the infantry one by one' as the 4th Bedfords staggered around in the knee-deep mud. Second Lieutenant Snelling was killed as his men were pinned down in front of Varlet Farm but the 7th Royal Fusiliers' right reached the Paddebeek stream. The 1/28th London Regiment suffered particularly badly wading through mud in front of Source Farm and one company of the Artists' Rifles was 'annihilated'.

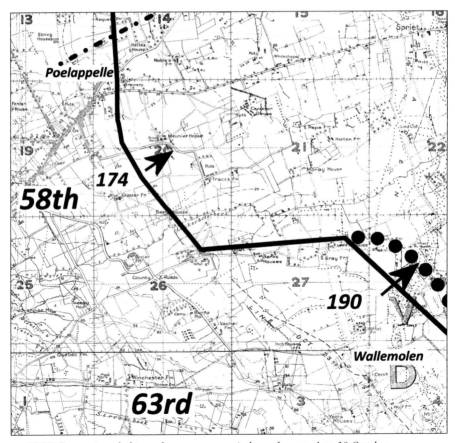

XVIII Corps struggled to make any progress in knee-deep mud on 30 October.

Second Lieutenant Tricker of the Royal Fusiliers closed in on Sourd Farm the following morning but he could not clear the flank. General Hutchinson sent two companies of the 1/4th Shropshires forward and Major Litt led as the 'ncos could be heard checking intervals and dressing despite the fire and the lines moved forward as accurately as he could.' They cleared the gap between Varlet Farm and Source Farm. A small victory in an action which Lieutenant General Sir Ivor Maxse summarised with the following words: 'Nothing but the impossibility of crossing the mud prevented their usual complete success.'

The Naval Division had already suffered over 3,000 casualties on Wallemolen spur and Commander Asquith organised surprise attacks when Major General Lawrie was instructed to make a third attempt. Lieutenant Stear and Sub-Lieutenant Perry cleared the Banff Farm area with just a handful of the Hawke Battalion on the night of 1 November. Five nights later Sub-Lieutenant Brearly's fighting patrol of the Nelson Battalion cleared Source Trench where two battalions had failed. Lieutenant Harris's patrol of the Drake Battalion then took Sourd Farm by surprise, the last post on the west side of the Paddebeek. Asquith's methods had worked; three important positions had been taken for only 150 casualties.

The Canadian Corps
Lieutenant General Currie was looking to the 3rd and 4th Canadian Divisions to repeat their success of 26 October. Again the troops were eager to get forward as quickly as possible along the Bellevue and Passchendaele spurs and they were across no man's land before the German artillery opened fire.

<u>3rd Canadian Division, Meetcheele</u>
Brigadier General Elmsley's 8 Canadian Brigade had to clear Woodland Plantation at the head of the Stroombeek valley. Major George Pearkes was wounded early on but he continued to lead his men through the boggy maze of tree stumps; he would be awarded the Victoria Cross. The 5th Canadian Mounted Rifles advanced towards Vine Cottage and Vapour Farm as the Germans fell back towards Mosselmarkt. One platoon cleared Source Farm while others captured Vapour Farm but they were pinned down by Vine Cottage. They then had to fight off counter-attacks until reinforcements arrived several hours later.

Brigadier General Dyer's 7 Canadian Brigade faced a tough fight for the Bellevue Ridge. Lieutenant Colonel Palmer's 49th Canadian Battalion was pinned down near the jumping off line until Private Cecil Kinross threw his equipment to the floor and ran forward, shooting or clubbing to death

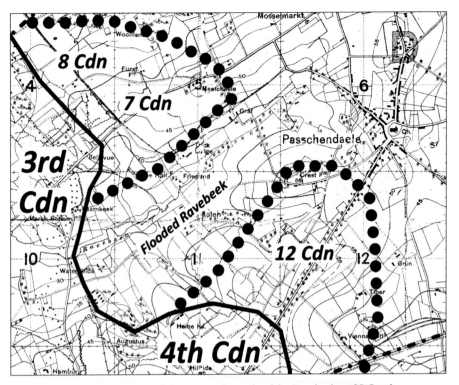

The Canadian Corps cleared the spurs either side of the Ravebeek on 30 October.

the six-man machine-gun team, and returned with their weapon. His one-man crusade meant his company could advance towards Meetcheele but the left company could not capture Furst Farm. Private 'Hoodoo' Kinross was awarded the Victoria Cross.

Lieutenant Colonel Adamson's Princess Patricia's Canadian Light Infantry had taken Snipe Hall, south of the Meetcheele road during the night. They cleared Duck Lodge but were then pinned down in front of Meetcheele and Graf House. Lieutenant Hugh McKenzie was a member of 7th Company, Machine Gun Corps, but he took command of a company of infantry after all its officers and NCOs had been hit. McKenzie was killed as he cleared his second pillbox but he had inspired the Princess Pats to keep going. Sergeant George Mullin took the lead, bombing a machine-gun post before climbing onto a pillbox, so he could shoot the two machine-gunners inside with his revolver. He jumped down to take the rest prisoners, as they filed out with their hands up. Both McKenzie and Mullin were awarded the Victoria Cross. The Germans were desperate to drive the Canadians back, counter-attacking three times.

4th Canadian Division, South of Passchendaele

Brigadier General MacBrien's 12 Canadian Brigade took its turn to deploy astride the main road into Passchendaele. The 72nd Canadian Battalion rushed Crest Farm and then fanned out on the dry ground west of the village. It appeared the Germans were withdrawing, so several patrols investigated the village and they confirmed the Germans were pulling back. It was, however, unsafe to occupy the ruins until the rest of the Canadian Corps had moved up, so they had to withdraw.

Meanwhile, both the 75th and the 85th Canadian Battalions had cleared the ridge south of the village, where they could look east over the green fields towards Moorslede. In both cases the Germans had fled but they were soon back, making four counter-attacks. This time the decision to hold a deep outpost zone had worked; they had inflicted over 2,300 casualties on the Canadian Corps while only a few had been taken prisoner.

Passchendaele, 6 November

Second Army took over the part of Fifth Army's line which XVIII Corps held around Poelcappelle on 31 October. It meant that General Gough was only left with XIV Corps, which faced Houthulst Forest. A couple of days later Lieutenant General Jacob's II Corps replaced Lieutenant General Maxse's XVIII Corps.

GHQ had abandoned plans to cross the flooded marsh west of Poelcappelle on Second Army's left but still wanted to extend the hold on Passchendaele ridge. Plumer wanted the Canadian Corps to take the area in two steps, on 6 and 10 November.

Canadian Corps

The Canadian artillery fired small barrages at random points every evening but every gun took part in the bombardment on 5 November and it triggered a response from the German guns. The plan was for the 1st Canadian Division to advance from the Goudberg spur, west of Passchendaele, while the 2nd Canadian Division attacked from the south.

At 6 am on 6 November, the Canadian troops moved quickly across no man's land and the German barrage missed them as they began storming the pillboxes. Many Germans did not have time to mount their weapons before they were under attack.

1st Canadian Division, Mosselmarkt

Brigadier General Griesbach's 1 Canadian Brigade deployed on Goudberg spur and Bellevue spur, either side of the bog called Woodland Plantation. Lieutenant Colonel Bart's 3rd Canadian Battalion deployed around Vapour

Farm but Captain Crawford and Lieutenant Lord struggled to capture Vine Cottages on the division's left flank. Corporal Colin Barron crawled around the flank and shot two machine-gun teams with his Lewis gun before charging a third. He then turned one of the captured weapons on those who ran from the cottages; he would be awarded the Victoria Cross.

The 2nd and 1st Canadian Battalions encountered many Germans hiding in shell holes around Meetcheele and Graf House on the Bellevue spur. Fifty surrendered when they were surrounded in the pillboxes at Mosselmarkt. The Canadians also captured the two field guns and four machine guns covering Vindictive Crossroads. Two hours after zero hour, Major General Archibald Macdonell was pleased to hear that his men had contacted troops of the 2nd Canadian Division.

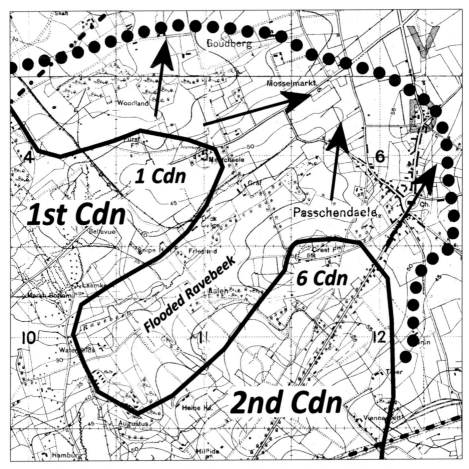

The Canadian Corps' capture of Goudberg and Passchendaele on 6 November.

2nd Canadian Division, Passchendaele

Brigadier General Ketchen's 6 Canadian Brigade had to capture Passchendaele village. To begin with, the 28th Canadian Battalion found themselves 'knee deep and in places waist deep in mud and water' in the Ravebeek valley. It was a relief to advance onto the ridge, where the ground was much drier, and advance to the north side of the village. The 31st Canadian Battalion cleared the north-west side of the ruins under heavy machine-gun fire from Passchendaele Alley but the 27th Canadian Battalion were pinned down astride the road, south of the village. After the third failure, Private Peter Robertson ran forward, jumped over the barbed wire fence and bayoneted the machine-gun team. He then used the captured weapon as he led the Canadians into the ruins behind a 'splendid barrage'. The 26th Canadian Battalion advanced on the right flank, east of the village, at the same time.

The Canadian troops knew how to silence the pillboxes. Most resistance was encountered at the north end of the village where the last strongpoint was cleared after three hours of fighting. There had been over 2,200 Canadian casualties but they had taken over 450 prisoners. German artillery soon hit the ridge from all directions but the Canadians had already dispersed into shell holes. Robertson was killed as he rescued wounded men under fire; he was posthumously awarded the Victoria Cross.

Brigadier Generals Ketchen and Ross had been kept fully informed of progress by continuous wave wireless sets. Everyone had been wary of relying on this new form communication but it would revolutionise how battles were fought once it had been tried and tested.

Passchendaele had been taken and Second Army had the firm hold on the ridge GHQ had expected to reach four months earlier. Two days later, Plumer handed over command of the Salient to Rawlinson and headed for Italy. He had been fighting around Ypres for three long years.

X Corps, Broodseinde and Gheluvelt

There was no large-scale offensive action on Lieutenant General Morland's front. The men tried to dig trenches but the rain turned the semi-solid mud into liquid slime and 'the usual deluge would treat it as the incoming tide treats a child's castle on the sands'. Another said they were 'literally standing up to their knees in water from the time they went into the line till they came out'. Some thought the men 'were simply magnificent and they were so cheery through it all,' but others saw how their comrades 'touched bottom in the way of misery'. Men unfortunate enough to slip into a shell hole, could be stuck for up to 36 hours before enough ropes could be found to haul them out. One man of the 1st Devons was stuck up to his neck for 48 hours before he was freed.

The Menin road was an easy target for the German gunners; it was turned into 'a ghastly nightmare' which was 'at all times blocked by horses' and lined by debris and carcasses. Many wounded drowned in the slime while those fortunate enough to be found faced two hours on a stretcher before they reached the Hooge Crater aid posts. Even carrier pigeons became disorientated above the desolate land, taking many hours to get back to their base.

Passchendaele, 10 November
The final attack on the Passchendaele ridge was designed to secure the Canadian Corps' hold on the village. The Germans appeared to have given up trying to recapture the village and a mixture of units were content with holding a perimeter around it. The plan was for the 1st Canadian Division to push north of the village while the 1st British Division pushed forward on the left and the 2nd Canadian Division covered the right.

II Corps
1st Division, Goudberg Ridge
The artillery had the same problems of trying to find battery positions and then registering their guns. The barrage was ragged and some shells exploded amongst the two battalions as they moved towards the summit of the ridge. The 2nd Munsters advanced from Vapour Farm and Vanity House, heading for Goudberg copse, and the 1st South Wales Borderers moved from Valour Farm towards Vocation Farm. Lieutenant Colonel Taylor was wounded early on and Captain Lochner took over the Borderers but he could not stop them veering to the right. The Germans counter-attacked through the gap in 3 Brigade's line, and nearly 400 Welshmen had been hit by the time the survivors had fallen back to their start line. The Munsters found themselves cut off and they suffered a similar number of casualties, many of them missing.

Canadian Corps
1st Canadian Division, Vindictive Crossroads
Brigadier General Loomis' 2 Canadian Brigade advanced at 6.45 am in heavy rain. The 8th Canadian Battalion captured four 77 mm guns around Venture Farm but it had to form a flank after the Welsh and Irishmen fell back on their left. The 7th Canadian Battalion advanced beyond Vindictive Crossroads on the Westroosebeke road and went far beyond the objective to silence the machine-gun teams overlooking it. The 10th Battalion then cleared the final objective.

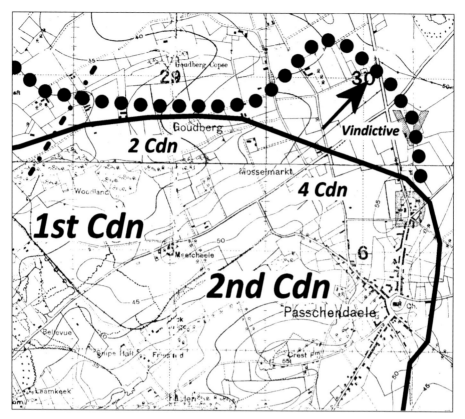

The Canadian Corps' advance north of Passchendaele on 10 November.

2nd Canadian Division, North of Passchendaele
Brigadier General Rennie had placed 20th Canadian Battalion in line on 1st Canadian Division's right and it extended 4 Canadian Brigade's front east of Vindictive Crossroads.

The Campaign Ends
The withdrawal of 1st British Division's troops from the Goudberg spur meant that the German artillery could focus on shelling the Canadians. They had to spread out into shell holes to reduce the number of casualties but many prisoners were hit as they headed to the rear. The Canadians also pushed outposts down the slope to keep the Germans at a safe distance from the summit of the ridge.

The constant rain made the Australians think Passchendaele was 'almost as bad as Pozières', the place where Diggers had fought on the Somme in the summer and autumn of 1916. They had nothing but respect for their fellow colonial troops as they endured rain, mud and shells on the ridge; 'the night had been vile, and the day too. If the Canadians can hold on they are wonderful troops.'

Canadian troops started leaving the Ypres Salient on 14 November. They had suffered over 15,600 casualties; the approximate number Lieutenant General Currie had estimated it would take to clear the ridge. But many others were sick. The ridge was now safe and GHQ had no more reserves for the Ypres campaign because it had extra responsibilities and fewer troops. The four divisions on the coast were heading south to join Fourth Army on the Somme, so it could extend its sector by taking part of the French line. Another five divisions were en route to Italy, to shore up the front following the disaster at Caporetto, and there was talk of sending another three.

After fifteen long weeks of fighting in the Salient, Haig's only choice was to close down the offensive. On 15 November GHQ announced that 'any further offensive on the Flanders front must be at once discontinued, though it is important to keep this fact secret as long as possible.' However, GHQ had other plans for a new offensive. Brigadier General Elles had asked some time ago to stop wasting tanks in the mud of the Salient. The Tank Corps now had a reliable tank to fight with, it had trained crews and it had tried and tested tactics. All they needed was dry ground to fight across and Third Army was planning a huge tank attack at Cambrai to prove the point.

One Final Attack

Although 10 November saw the end of the Passchendaele campaign, it did not see the end of the bloodshed. There was the constant drain of casualties from gas or artillery and sniper fire while many men were sent to the rear suffering from illnesses cause by the appalling conditions. The cold, rain and mud made it a struggle to do anything more than survive but Second Army wanted to improve its line north of Passchendaele.

The plan was to attack during the early hours of 2 December but the sky was clear and the moon was bright, illuminating the snow which covered the battlefield. The men of Brigadier General Coffin's 25 Brigade and Brigadier General Blacklock's 97 Brigade assembled after a long march across the crater field. Zero hour had been timed for 1.55 am and the infantry were supposed to rush the German outpost line before the British artillery hit the main trenches eight minutes later. Only there was no way they could rush across the crater field and the Germans would surely see them coming.

Machine guns opened fire and flares were fired into the sky as the waves of infantry trudged across no man's land. The moonlight silhouetted them against the snow and many were cut down before the British artillery opened fire; the German artillery joined in moments later.

The 15th Lancashire Fusiliers were unable to form a flank around

Tournant Farm on 32nd Division's left while the 17th Highland Light Infantry could not reach Vat and Veal Cottages. The 11th Border Regiment captured Veldt Farm and Mallet Copse but they were left isolated because the 16th Highland Light Infantry had dug in around Void Farm after coming under crossfire. Troops on both flanks moved across the 2nd KOYLIs' front but they still reached Hill 52 on the Westroosebeke road, despite heavy fire from Teall Cottage on their right flank.

There was a complete disaster on 8th Division's front where the 2nd Rifle Brigade failed to reach the Northern Redoubt. The 2nd Lincolns inexplicably stopped short of Venison Trench while the 2nd Berkshires were shot down before Southern Redoubt. The men who did not fall back before dawn were driven back by a morning counter-attack. The tragic attack had cost the two brigades over 1,600 casualties.

Conclusions
on the Campaign

Planning for the Messines ridge has been described as meticulous but Second Army had over twelve months to prepare everything. A few months later, planners would only have two or three days to plan and execute attacks on a similar scale. One of the most intriguing things about the Messines attack is the fact that the Germans did not discover most of the mines and that they did not destroy the few that they did locate.

After many months of worry and consideration over when to blow the mines, they all detonated on time. Their effect was devastating and an important position fell quickly with far fewer losses than anyone anticipated. Ironically the success led to losses later on because so many men crossed the ridge, creating crowding in front of the German observers. Second Army only had two things to decide once the ridge had fallen: *when* to start the final advance and then *where* to stop it. In both cases General Plumer made sensible decisions so the decision to take control of the Salient from him shortly afterwards surprised many.

Looking back at the reasons behind the Passchendaele campaign we can understand why the BEF became the main driving force in the second half of 1917. The Italians were in need of men and guns to help break the deadlock in the Isonzo valley but no one was prepared to support Lloyd George's plan to give them some. Meanwhile, Russia was in the throes of revolution. The French armies were exhausted and mutinous and the likes of Haig and Kiggell thought the German armies could be in a similar condition.

So the Allies were faced with two choices. They could either do nothing until the United States deployed a large army in Europe, handing the initiative to Germany. Or the British could go on the offensive to keep Germany focused on the Western Front at a point of their choosing. Haig wanted to go on the offensive and Foch was anxious for the British to use its growing strength in men and material to take the pressure off his armies.

Flanders had been on the operational books for a long time but the reasons behind it are questionable. Unrestricted submarine warfare was causing losses and one in four ships were being sunk by March 1917. But the Admiralty overplayed the danger from the Ostend and Zeebrugge situation, giving GHQ's plan a strategic aim: the clearing of the Flanders coast. However, the Admiralty's refusal to implement convoying or escort ships contributed to the high numbers of ships being sunk. Convoying started at the end of April 1917 and monthly losses had reduced by the time the Flanders campaign began (down from 860,000 tons in April to below 500,000 tons by July).

Haig overemphasised how successful a new offensive would be when he spoke to the War Cabinet. Prime Minister Lloyd George did not want to become embroiled in another battle of attrition like the Somme in 1916. But Haig convinced him that the BEF could achieve great things and while his estimates seem widely overoptimistic now, they did not have the benefit of hindsight. The plans which said the Passchendaele ridge could be reached in a short space of time used the battle of Arras as a template.

Haig promised a step-by-step battle and specific objectives were set so progress could be monitored, to get the War Cabinet's agreement. Zero hour was timed for 25 July to catch the high tide of 7-8 August, so the overland advance could be coordinated with the amphibious operation. But the promises did not last long.

The attack was postponed by six days because the successful counter-battery work was, ironically, too successful and it forced the Germans to relocate their guns. Poor visibility also played a part as did the inability to stockpile enough shells fast enough. Delaying the offensive meant Fifth Army had to advance faster than the step-by-step advances promised to the War Cabinet. Major General John Davidson, Director of Military Operations at GHQ, questioned the advisability of advancing faster on the first day but Haig, Gough and Plumer all advocated an all-out attack.

The attack on 31 July was the predicted success – well, almost – as troops advanced 2½ miles in places, but the defence against the afternoon counter-attack was a failure. It appears that Fifth Army did not expect the Germans to attack so soon. The assault divisions had used up all their reserves, the corps reserves were too far away and the artillery was unable to help. A mixture of bad planning and poor weather meant the counter-attacks were not seen until it was too late, so the weakened infantry battalions were left without support. Only sheer determination and a flooded stream saved the day. The failure to reach objectives on the first day and the bad weather that followed meant that the offensive became one of mixed aims.

After waiting for the ground to dry and the shells to be delivered, the high hopes for the second half of August were immediately dashed. The BEF's basic platoon tactics were in place but questions were being asked about how to deal with the large numbers of pillboxes the Germans were building. The conclusion was they could 'not try and penetrate too deeply' and the troops allocated to mopping up and consolidating captured positions had to be increased. The number of aerial observers was also doubled, so the artillery would be ready to disperse the counter-attacks.

Again weather and the need to improve logistics resulted in a four-week delay and the Germans began to think the Flanders offensive was over. They were mistaken because it was about to intensify. The BEF planned three weeks to prepare their artillery and logistics but the wet weather returned and further operations were cancelled until the ground dried out.

GHQ's staff decided to set objectives to match the infantry's ability to capture and then hold ground. They also studied how they could make a series of attacks in quick succession to wear down the enemy. Their findings would be applied to the attacks that started on 20 September and there were three rapid advances over the next two weeks. Haig was optimistic that the end was in sight but there were problems because the logistics route was getting longer, resulting in more problems at the front. There were also concerns that the Germans were repeatedly withdrawing their guns back to safe positions while his own had to be dragged across the muddy battlefield.

There had been a seven-day preparatory barrage on 20 September and a twenty-four-hour barrage on 26 September. There was no ammunition to fire one on 4 October but as luck would have it the creeping barrage smashed a German attack timed for a few minutes later. The German official history would go further, describing it as the 'black day of October 4th'.

Everything was looking good as the attack ended on 4 October. The Australian official historian, Charles Bean, poses the question from the general point of view: 'In view of the three step-by-step blows all successful, what will be the result of three more in the next fortnight.' Many German divisions had been engaged and on 11 October Crown Prince Rupprecht reported 'in order to save material and men, it may become necessary to withdraw the front so far from the enemy that he will be compelled to make a fresh deployment of his artillery.' It turned out the persistent rain would be the Germans' 'best ally', turning the battlefield into the BEF's worst enemy.

The bad weather can easily be blamed for the BEF's poor showing in the campaign. Written and photographic evidence prove that the Salient turned into a dangerous and unhealthy marsh which took a long time to dry out. The Official History states that the rainfall in Flanders was 14 inches (350mm) between July and October (inclusive). The modern average is 13.5

inches for the same period. So it was not the rain which was the problem, because the streams and ditches can drain the low-lying areas during wet periods. It was the decision to conduct warfare on an industrial scale on this low-lying area. The combination of impermeable clay, a high water table and a complicated drainage system meant the Salient was an unsuitable area for conducting a prolonged battle. Haig chose the ground but he did not chose a prolonged battle, it was forced on him.

Haig was always confident in the abilities of his own army but he often assumed the German army was in difficulties. Some of his generals and the war correspondents were not always so sure.

The BEF needed replacements but the War Cabinet was wary of sending too many men to a failing campaign. As early as 23 August Lloyd George wanted to stop the Flanders offensive and send divisions to the Italian front. It was another two months before he got his wish.

There was a ban on replacements being sent to Flanders in the meantime but Haig found a way around it by instructing a search of all the support units for fit men. After a brief period of training they found themselves in the front line where their conduct was sometimes less than heroic.

The decision to send troops and guns to reinforce the Italian front definitely ended the Passchendaele campaign on 10 November, although it could be argued the weather had already done so a month earlier. The strategic plan had been abandoned in the middle of October, when Operation Hush was cancelled. After that it was just a case of acquiring the best line possible for the winter.

Haig had two options. He could withdraw his men to a safe distance. That was difficult because of the topography of the salient which would give the Germans their observation posts back. Such a withdrawal would have been a political disaster and a morale disaster. He chose to keep pushing forward onto the Passchendaele ridge, which, when you consider the alternative, was the only option, as bloody as it was. Haig also argued the French wanted him to keep pushing.

The BEF had only advanced 4½ miles by the time the campaign closed and the Germans still held the Belgian ports. Whether the Passchendaele was a successful battle of attrition depends on how the controversial casualty figures are interpreted. It is definite that both sides were struggling by the autumn. The BEF was having to comb the ranks of its support units to keep divisions up to strength. Germany had deployed every able man on the war industry many months before and it was now deploying 18-year-olds to the front. Even so the attrition was hard to stomach.

Conclusions on the Tactics and Weapons

By mid-September the BEF had a bombardment which taught 'the enemy to lie at the bottom of shell holes or dugouts wherever any barrages are going on.' The five 'curtains' of shells took a long time to pass over the German lines. The mixture of high explosive and shrapnel shells exploding in ground and air bursts created a terrifying experience.

It was important to keep the infantry close to the barrage and battalions became adept at deploying in no man's land ready to move quickly, missing the German SOS barrage. Usually the speed of the creep worked but the state of the battlefield towards the end of the campaign caused an unsolvable problem. The infantry moved so slowly in the mud that the enemy machine-gunners always had time to deploy. Several methods had been devised for communicating between the creeping barrage and the infantry. Sometimes sound was used, with the guns increasing or decreasing rate of fire to denote a change in pace. Sometimes smoke shells were fired to give a visual signal.

Plumer's memorandum on infantry tactics on 12 August called for a line of skirmishers who found routes across the mud and located enemy positions. Platoons moving in worms, columns or diamonds followed, heading for specific objectives. The planners designed short, strong attacks through the lightly held outpost zones and then dug in on ground favourable to their own troops and not to enemy trench lines, which were on the German artillery's target list. New arrangements were made for providing enough troops to mop up behind the advancing troops.

The planners also put much thought into how to defend in depth. A quarter of the troops at each level were kept as reserve while the machine guns were deployed to provide direct and indirect fire. The Germans were concerned to keep finding their enemy to be *eingenistete* or 'settled down' by the time they were ready to counter-attack. While his men kept building pillboxes, shelters and wire entanglements, Ludendorff had to keep changing the defensive tactics. Sometime the outpost zone was held with as few troops as possible, but they were too weak to stop any attack. Sometimes many troops were deployed in the outpost zone but the creeping barrage caused too many casualties. Then he tried putting as many machine guns as possible forward ready to break up the attack. The tactics usually failed and in most cases it was the weather which defeated the British and Anzacs.

The Heavy Branch of the Machine Gun Corps had played a useful role during the capture of the Messines ridge but they had not played a decisive role. The new Mark IV tanks were in action for the first time and while they were still too slow to keep up with the infantry they were very good at dealing with strongpoints which had been bypassed by the infantry following the creeping barrage. There are many examples of the male tanks suppressing strongpoints with their 6-pounder guns while the female tanks sprayed the surrounding area with bullets. The infantry were learning to cooperate with the tanks, moving in to occupy a position once it had capitulated.

The tanks had to deploy too far back from the front line before zero hour to keep them hidden. It meant they could not lead the advance to the first objective, only help the mopping-up troops. But the wait on the second and third objectives allowed them to take part in the later attacks. Tanks had proved that they were good at crushing gaps in the wire for the infantry to pass through. The best move was to drive along the parapet side of a trench, so they could fire into enemy territory.

Brigadier General Elles had to watch as his tanks struggled in the mud in the Ypres Salient. The crews learnt to stick to roads but they knew it was difficult to follow them because it was difficult to see from the driver's position. The best plan was to keep the tank's mission simple and, if possible, the crews needed to see the objective from their start point.

Experience showed that the tanks could be refuelled and rearmed but they needed a maintenance check after driving an 8-mile circuit, including the mileage behind the British lines. But the crews also had a limit to their endurance and they could not be expected to stay inside a tank for more than eight hours before the heat, vibration and fumes got the better of them.

Plenty of work had been done to improve coordination between tanks and infantry. Identification numbers were painted on the back of each tank and infantry were told the routes they would follow and their objectives; a green flag indicated it had been successful. They were also told that tank drivers sometimes had to make detours to avoid bad ground.

The crews in turn were taught the infantry's SOS signals, so they could use their weapons to help. A rifle waved over the head indicated the enemy was nearby. A helmet placed on a rifle above the head meant the infantry needed help. The infantry were told not to gather behind tanks, looking for cover, because they drew fire. They were also instructed not to wait if one ditched or had engine trouble. The tank commanders carried a red flag to indicate they were stuck or broken down while a white square on the roof reported the fact to the RFC's observers.

Calling for SOS artillery bombardments had sometimes been a problem. The infantry sometimes needed immediate support but the flares were occasionally missed. By late September a new flare which floated in the air for several minutes displayed three lights (red, green and yellow) so would always be seen and they would never be mistaken.

Wireless communication was starting to make an impression on the battlefield. The problem was the equipment was bulky and unreliable. It was first used in the air, so spotter planes could instantly report enemy troop movements to the artillery. Planes worked in pairs, with one checking the front line and the other watching the rear.

Ground communications had always been a problem because it was difficult to get cables deep enough and power buzzers were unreliable during a battle. Visual signalling was only useful in clear visibility and it was often left to the runners to carry messages. Tanks were used to carry wirelesses and by the end of October the Canadian infantry were using continuous wave wireless sets. This new form of communication would revolutionise how battles were fought as soon as it became accepted.

Index